Sjaak Laan

IT Infrastructure Architecture

Infrastructure Building Blocks and Concepts

Third Edition

Title:	IT Infrastructure Architecture –
	Infrastructure Building Blocks and Concepts
	Third Edition
Author:	**Sjaak Laan**
Publisher:	**Lulu Press Inc.**
ISBN:	**978-1-326-91297-0**
Edition:	**Third edition, 2017**
Copyright:	**© Sjaak Laan, 2017**

Trademarks

All trademarks used in this book are the property of their respective owners.

- IBM, AIX, IBM MQ, DB2, and ibm.com® are trademarks or registered trademarks of International Business Machines Corporation in the United States, and/or other countries.

- Linux is a registered trademark of Linus Torvalds.

- Microsoft®, Hyper-V, Windows, Windows NT®, Microsoft Azure Cloud Service, Windows .Net, Microsoft Internet Information Services, BizTalk, Microsoft SQL Server, and the Windows logo are trademarks of Microsoft Corporation in the United States and other countries.

- Java and all Java-based trademarks are trademarks of Oracle, Inc. in the United States, other countries, or both.

- UNIX is a registered trademark of The Open Group in the United States and other countries.

- Apple, Mac, iOS, and Mac OS are trademarks of Apple Inc., registered in the U.S. and other countries.

- AIX is a trademark of IBM Corp., registered in the U.S. and other countries.

- DEC™, DECnet™, VMS™, and VAX™ are trademarks of Digital Equipment Corporation.

- Intel, Intel Core, Xeon, and Thunderbolt are trademarks of Intel Corp. in the U.S. and other countries.

- Google, Android, Google App Engine, and Kubernetes are registered trademarks of Google Inc

- IOS is a trademark or registered trademark of Cisco in the U.S. and other countries.

- Apache®, Apache Tomcat, and Apache Mesos are either registered trademarks or trademarks of the Apache Software Foundation in the

While every precaution was made in the preparation of this book, the author can assume no responsibility for errors or omissions. If you feel the author has not given you proper credit or feel your rights were violated, please notify the author so corrective actions can be taken.

Pictures used in this book are created by the author of this book or are freely distributable pictures, retrieved from the internet. Most of the used pictures are from the public domain. When a picture is used that contained copyrights, a link to the source of the picture and its copyright notice is provided. If you feel a picture used in this book is not freely distributable, or any other copyright is violated, please inform the author, so it can be corrected in the next version of the book.

Table of Contents

List of figures

I think there is a world market for maybe five computers.

Thomas Watson, IBM Chairman, 1943

There is no reason for any individual to have a computer in his home

Ken Olsen, founder of legendary minicomputer company DEC, 1977

We live in a society exquisitely dependent on science and technology, in which hardly anyone knows anything about science and technology.

Carl Sagan, American astronomer, 1990

It's hardware that makes a machine fast. It's software that makes a fast machine slow.

Craig Bruce

Introduction

In the summer of 2011, Sjaak showed me the first ever printed version of the book he had been working on for quite some time. It was also the first time we discussed in detail the reasons for writing it, and the target audience that he was aiming for. After some hours of discussing the contents of the book Sjaak asked me if I was willing to write the introduction for it. Needless to say, I was flattered and proud he suggested this.

At first I was puzzled about his decision to have the introduction written by someone who is not directly involved in core IT infrastructures, but much more into software development. For 17 years, my company has been developing back and front office applications for large multinationals, and is currently involved in SaaS solutions in the field of Social Media Intelligence, Online Health Applications, Event Management, and Storage Management. As I am much more into the "soft-side" of automation, it was like if a car designer asked a road designer to write an introduction on engine mechanics.

But from a different point of view, it seemed very obvious. Where would software application developers be when the infrastructures their applications run on were not working flawlessly? How many times have we been in meetings with customers trying to figure out why software applications were not performing as they were supposed to? How many times did it occur that after implementation of a new software system we were confronted with unforeseen costs because the underlying computer systems had difficulties running the developed software? How many times did we accuse the infrastructure guys of not understanding the requirements and vice versa?

I strongly believe that most of these problems originate from a lack of knowledge software engineers have about the problems and challenges infrastructure specialists face when setting up a system for running the software we develop. We as software engineers are primarily concerned with functionality required by the customer. Customer assume that when they talk about an application handling 100,000 visitors a day, or running large reports on millions of records, software engineers fully understands their needs. And indeed, software engineers understand everything regarding select statements, thread handling, and database calls, but they will also assume that the hardware and operating systems they build upon are capable of supporting this.

I think there is a great need for software engineers to understand more about IT infrastructures to allow them to communicate with the infrastructure architects on a more professional level.

What was really appealing to me in this book was that it was written out of experience, rather than presenting just theoretical knowledge. Far too often we see that decisions made on IT infrastructures have little sense of reality. For security and availability sake, systems are often made far too complex, hence far too expensive, resulting in a system even less secure and less reliable than intended. Sjaak has hit the nail right on the head with his chapters on availability and security. What this book really shows is that the biggest risks for failures and security breaches are not in the infrastructure itself, "but it sits between the chair and the keyboard".

A good example, from my own experience, was the case where we needed to implement a contingency plan, including an emergency response team. In order to minimize downtime in case of a failure, we found it was much more effective to see who of the systems management team was living closest to the datacenter, than to focus on "putting the best man on the job". We were better off training the guy living next door, then to have the chief infrastructure manager drive 1.5 hours to the datacenter!

The entire book is an excellent piece of work to be read by each software developer, it is an outstanding educational tool for system engineers and it is great reference material for IT consultants, regardless of the specific area they expertise on.

If you take IT seriously, you have to read this book!

Herman Vissia PhD, M.Sc.

Herman Vissia is the CEO and owner of Byelex Multimedia Products B.V. Together with his colleagues from Minsk he has written more than 10 scientific articles on software related technologies, more specifically on Artificial intelligence and sentiment analysis on the World Wide Web. In 2012 he earned his PhD from the State University in Minsk, Belarus.

Foreword by the author

When I started writing this book I tried to remember the first time I came in contact with technical infrastructures. And then I realized I have been in the infrastructure business almost all my life.

When I was six years old, I spent an entire afternoon figuring out how to connect a D-type battery to a bicycle light bulb using a small wire in order to get it to lighten up. For some reason, I could not get it to work. While I tried endlessly my mother (not very technical herself) told me to wait for my father to return from his work, so he could explain to me how to do it. When my father finally arrived, and explained what I did wrong, and when the light bulb finally lightened, I was very excited. My first electrical circuit worked! It made quite an impression as I still remember it after all these years.

From that moment on I explored all types of technical equipment. I disassembled my new toys and my alarm clock, just to see how they worked. After disassembling, sometimes I managed to get the pieces back together again to get a working device, but most of the time the toys, radios and other equipment were not working anymore after my exploration. It drove my parents crazy. Sorry for that, mum and dad!

When I was around 14 years old, I was building electronics hardware in my spare time. Starting from rebuilding electronic circuits from Elektor magazine, I quickly started to design my own hardware. While most of those hardware projects were just for fun, when I was about 18 years old, I designed and built electronic devices for the photo lab company a friend of mine worked for.

For my 18th birthday I got a very special (and for my parents very expensive) present – a Sinclair ZX-81 home computer, including a 16 kB memory expansion module. After writing my very first program in BASIC (tic-tac-toe, which I lost from the computer all the time) I could not resist opening up the computer to examine its inner workings. After breaking down the computer and fixing it, I eventually expanded the system to connect to an external keyboard.

Picture 1: ZX-81 with 16kB expansion module[1]

The ZX-81 was quite limited, because of its highly integrated electronics. Coincidentally, I got hold of a Datapoint 2200 programmable terminal. It turned out to be a full-blown computer with an integrated monitor and keyboard, 8kB of RAM, two cassette tape recorders, capable of storing 130 kB of data each, and a bunch of software programs including a basic interpreter, a Cobol-like compiler and an assembler.

Picture 2: Datapoint 2200 computer[2]

The computer came with the full schematics of the system. Its processor was not a single chip, but was built from approximately 100 standard TTL chips on a circuit board. And because I had the schematics, I studied how the CPU worked in detail. I found out how numbers were added using discrete flip-flops and how memory addressing worked. This helped me a lot in understanding how computer infrastructures worked. And programming the Datapoint system in assembler helped me understand how the assembler statements were handled in the CPU circuit.

Later, from my earnings delivering newspapers, I bought an Acorn Atom home computer running on an 8-bit 6502 CPU. This was not only an affordable machine for me, and much more modern than the Datapoint, but it also was delivered with a schematic diagram of the circuitry. It had a built-in assembler and a standard BASIC interpreter. The availability of the circuit diagram enabled me to expand the memory of the system using an Elektor 16 kB RAM circuit board I built. And when my father gave me a left-over large and heavy 8-inch floppy drive from his work, I built my own disk drive circuit board to connect it to the Acorn Atom. I programmed a small disk operating system for it in assembler to enable me to store my programs and data on floppy disk instead of on a tape recorder. Writing my own disk operating system took up all of my spare time for about a year, but finally it worked and I could write, read and catalog multiple files on one 8-inch floppy disk.

My first full-time job at the age of 24 was working as a PC repair technician for a company called Checksum Computer Repair. About 25 technicians repaired PCs and their system boards by replacing defective components like ICs (Integrated Circuit), capacitors, and oscillators. And apart from system boards we repaired power supplies, monitors, hard disks, keyboards (!) and floppy drives (!!). Believe it or not, but we could actually make money repairing floppy drives and keyboards in those days. During this job, I fixed a large number of IBM PS/2 system boards and other components. This helped to gain much knowledge about how these system boards were designed and how they worked.

After two years, I became head of the R&D department, responsible for creating new repair techniques. My team and I designed and built specialized testing hardware and software (like a multisync video board to test multisync monitors and a RAM chip diagnostic tool that could test RAM chips without removing them from the circuit board).

Coincidentally, we could get our hands on a retired Philips minicomputer from 1972. We could get it for free from a school, where it was not used for many years, under the condition that we managed to get it working again. The machine comprised a central processing unit (fully wire wrapped) with core memory, reel tapes, disk packs, and a line printer. All documentation, software, schematics, and compilers were available as well. The system had the size of half a room.

During evening hours, with a group of colleagues we managed to refurbish the machine by adjusting the mechanics of the tape units, disk packs, and line printer, fixing the core memory and fixing numerous faults in the wire wrapped system. After about half a year the job was done: the machine worked and we played minesweeper on it. It was a great experience and we learned a lot from it!

My next job was more serious: IT manager for a small but quickly expanding company. Here I not only managed the internal IT systems for five international subsidiaries, but also worked on redesigning the internal logistic software and processes for handling orders and purchases (the "business side" of IT). I "invented" a rudimentary application transaction system that we would now call an application server.

As an infrastructure architect at a computer retailer I rationalized a Lotus Notes environment of approximately 25 servers to a smaller set more reliable servers based on Windows NT 4.0. I also redesigned the Token Ring network based on a core networking consisting of three ATM (Asynchronous Transfer Mode) switches. ATM was the fastest technology around these days running at a stunning 155 Mbit/s!

In 2000 I joined CMG, later rebranded to Logica and CGI, where I still work. In my role as Principal IT architect and Security consultant I work for many customers in the energy, public, and financial sector, designing and implementing IT infrastructures and solutions, usually in a lead architect or consultant role.

More than 45 years of loving electronics and IT infrastructures. A good reason for writing a book about it I think.

Sjaak Laan

January 2017

Preface

What this book is about

This book is about Information Technology (IT) Infrastructure Architecture. With *infrastructure,* I mean all hardware and system software components needed to run IT applications. And infrastructure *architecture* describes the overall design and evolution of that infrastructure.

This book explains how infrastructure components work on an architectural level. With architectural level is meant that the components are described in building blocks, bound to specific technologies. Choices made on this level are architecturally relevant, meaning that once choices on building block level are made, it is relatively hard to change these choices afterwards. For instance, the choice to use a certain network cable infrastructure in a datacenter cannot be changed easily when the datacenter is in operation.

This book does not provide in-depth details needed by technicians, but instead describes the main architectural building blocks and concepts.

IT infrastructures are complex by nature and provide non-functional attributes, like performance, availability, and security, to applications. This book describes each infrastructure building block and their specific performance, availability, and security concepts.

Until now there were no publications describing the complete field of IT infrastructure. Books and papers are available about every part of IT infrastructures, like networking, installation, and management of operating systems, storage systems, and virtualization, but no publications existed yet describing IT infrastructure as a whole. This book intends to fill this gap.

Intended audience

This book is meant for infrastructure architects and designers, software architects, systems managers, and IT managers. It can also be used in education, for instance in a computer science class. This book is very suitable for beginners, since almost every term is explained, while for experts and professionals this book is more of a review and overview.

Infrastructure architects and designers can use this book to learn more about infrastructure designs that are not their core competence. This means that for instance network designers will probably not learn anything new on networking, but they will most likely learn quite a lot about all other parts of the infrastructure, like datacenters, storage, and servers. The same goes for other designers.

Software architects create software that runs on infrastructures. Good software architects need knowledge of infrastructures and their properties. They need to know what challenges an infrastructure architect faces and what they can do in their software solution to optimize for the non-functional characteristics of the infrastructure. Understanding infrastructures helps software architects build more reliable, faster applications that are better manageable and more secure.

Systems managers learn to recognize crucial architectural decisions and principles in an infrastructure and ways to update and change a running infrastructure without jeopardizing the architecture as a whole.

IT managers are provided with a complete overview of IT infrastructures and IT architecture. This will help them work with systems managers and infrastructure architects by having a better understanding of their concerns.

Computer science students will find a wealth of information about IT infrastructures, which is a solid base for computer science studies. This book is used by a number of universities around the world, as part of their IT architecture curricula. It is especially suited for courses based on the IS 2010.4 curriculum. A reference matrix of the IS 2010.4 curriculum topics and the relevant sections in this book is provided in appendix *IS 2010.4 Curriculum reference matrix*.

For more information on using this book in a university course, please contact the author. Some course material is available from the website www.sjaaklaan.com.

Some basic IT knowledge is needed to read this book, but the reader is introduced to each topic in small steps.

Acknowledgements

I would like to thank my wife, Angelina, for the patience she showed when I was working again on this book for a whole evening or weekend, without giving her the attention she deserves, and my three children Laura, Maarten, and Andreas, who I love.

Jan van Til inspired me to think more thoroughly about the definition of infrastructure. His (Dutch) work on information management can be found at www.emovere.nl.

I want to thank Robert Elsinga, Olav Meijer, Esther Barthel, Raymond Groenewoud, Emile Zweep, Cathy Ellis, Jacob Mulder, Robbert Springer, and Marc Eilander for their criticism, useful suggestions, and hard work when reviewing this book

Especially I want to thank Lodewijk Bogaards, who reviewed the book's first edition and provided literally hundreds of useful tips on the described topics. He also made many corrections on my English grammar.

Note to the third edition

In the third edition of this book, a number of corrections were made, some terminology is explained in more detail, and several typos and syntax errors were fixed. In addition, the following changes were made:

- The infrastructure model was updated to reflect the Networking-Storage-Compute terminology used by most vendors today, and to emphasize the position of systems management.

- The chapter on infrastructure trends was removed. The text was blended with the text in the other chapters.

- The amount of text on the historic context for each building block was reduced.

- The Virtualization chapter and Server chapter were combined and renamed to Compute.

- The storage chapter was reorganized to reflect the new storage building block model.

- The chapter on Security was rearranged and updated.

- Part IV on infrastructure management was added, with chapters on the infrastructure lifecycle, deployment options, assembling and testing, running the infrastructure, systems management processes, and decommissioning.

- In various parts of the book, new cloud technology concepts were added, like Software Defined Networking (SDN), Software Defined Storage (SDS), Software Defined Datacenters (SDDC), Infrastructure as a Service (IaaS), infrastructure as code, and container technology.

- A chapter was added explaining the infrastructure purchase process, as this is part of the IS 2010.4 curriculum.

- All footnotes were converted to endnotes.

- The index was renewed.

- Finally, as technology advanced in the past years, the book was updated to contain the most recent information.

PART I

-

INTRODUCTION TO IT INFRASTRUCTURE

1

THE DEFINITION OF IT INFRASTRUCTURE

1.1 Introduction

During the first decades of IT development, most infrastructures were relatively simple. While applications advanced in functionality and complexity, hardware basically only got faster. In recent years, IT infrastructures started to become more complicated as a result of the rapid development and deployment of new types of applications, such as e-commerce, Enterprise Resource Planning (ERP), data warehousing, big data, the Internet of Things, and cloud computing. These applications required new and more sophisticated infrastructure services, secure, highly scalable, and available 24/7.

Most current infrastructure landscapes are the result of a history of application implementation projects that introduced their own specialized hardware and infrastructure components. Mergers and acquisitions made things even worse, leaving many organizations with multiple sets of the same infrastructure services that are hard to interconnect, let alone integrate and consolidate.

Organizations benefit from infrastructure architecture when they want to be more flexible and agile, because a solid, scalable, and modular infrastructure provides a firm foundation for agile adaptations. The market demands a degree of flexibility that can no longer be supported by infrastructures that are inconsistent and hard to expand. We need infrastructures that are constructed with standardized, modular components. And to make infrastructures consistent and in line with business needs, architecture is crucial.

Architecture is the philosophy that underlies a system and defines the purpose, intent, and structure of the system. Various kinds of architecture can be defined, including business architecture, enterprise architecture, data architecture, application architecture, and infrastructure architecture. Each of these disciplines has certain unique characteristics, but at their most basic level, they all aim at mapping IT solutions to business value. Architecture is needed to control the infrastructure when it is designed, in use, and when it is changed.

1.2   What is IT infrastructure?

IT infrastructures have been around for quite a while. But surprisingly enough no generally accepted definition of IT infrastructure seems to exist. I found that many people are confused by the term IT infrastructure, and a clear definition would help them understand what IT infrastructure is, and what it is not.

In literature, many definitions of IT infrastructure are described. Some of them are:

- IT infrastructure consists of the equipment, systems, software, and services used in common across an organization, regardless of mission/program/project. IT Infrastructure also serves as the foundation upon which mission/program/project-specific systems and capabilities are built. *(cio.gov - the website for the United States Chief Information Officers Council).*

- All of the components (Configuration Items) that are necessary to deliver IT Services to customers. The IT Infrastructure consists of more than just hardware and software. *(ITILv2).*

- All of the hardware, software, networks, facilities, etc., that are required to develop, test, deliver, monitor, control, or support IT services. The term IT Infrastructure includes all of the Information Technology but not the associated people, Processes and documentation. *(ITILv3).*

- Information technology infrastructure underpins the distributed operational and administrative computing environment. Hidden from the application-based world of end users, technology infrastructure encompasses the unseen realm of protocols, networks, and middleware that bind the computing enterprise together and facilitate efficient data flows. Yet information technology infrastructure involves more than just the mechanics of data systems; it also includes people providing support and services. *(Technology Governance Board Definition of Information Technology Infrastructure).*

- Infrastructure is the shared and reliable services that provide the foundation for the enterprise IT portfolio. The implementation of an architecture includes the processors, software, databases, electronic links, and datacenters as well as the standards that ensure the components work together, the skills for managing the operation, etc. *(Goethe University of Frankfurt, www.is-frankfurt.de).*

Based on these definitions the term infrastructure seems a bit vague. Let's try to lighten things up a bit.

The word infrastructure originates from the words infra (Latin for "beneath") and structure. It encompasses all components that are "beneath the structure", were the structure can be for instance a city, a house, or an information system. In the physical world, the term infrastructure often refers to public utilities, such as water pipes, electricity wires, gas pipes, sewage, and telephone lines – components literally beneath a city's structure.

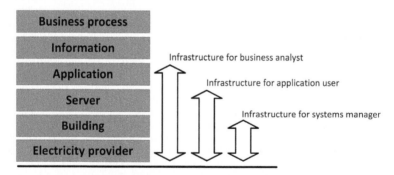

Figure 1: Views on IT infrastructure

For most people, infrastructure is invisible and taken for granted. When business processes are described by a business analyst, the information used in the process is very important. How this information is managed using IT systems is "below the surface" for the business analyst. They consider IT systems to be infrastructure.

For users of IT systems, applications are important, as they use them every day, but the way they are implemented or where they are physically deployed is invisible (below the surface) to them and hence considered infrastructure.

For systems managers, the building in which their servers are hosted and the utility company that delivers the required electricity are considered infrastructure.

So, what infrastructure comprises dependents on who you ask, and what their point of view is.

The scope of infrastructure as used in this book is explained in chapter 2.

2

THE
INFRASTRUCTURE
MODEL

2.1 IT building blocks

The definition of infrastructure as used in this book is based on the building blocks in the model as shown in Figure 2. In this model processes use information, and this information is stored and managed using applications. Applications need application platforms and infrastructure to run. All of this is managed by various categories of systems management.

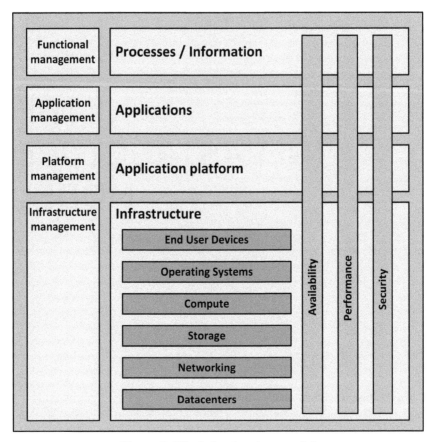

Figure 2: The infrastructure model

A model is always a simplified version of reality, useful to explain a certain point; not covering all details. Therefore, the infrastructure model is not perfect. Remember, as George E. P. Box stated: "Essentially, all models are wrong, but some are useful."[3]

The following sections provide a high-level description of the building blocks in the infrastructure model.

2.2   Processes / Information building block

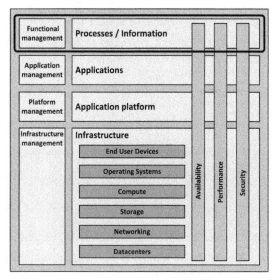

Figure 3: Processes / Information building block

Organizations implement business processes to fulfil their mission and vision. These processes are organization specific – they are the main differentiators between organizations. As an example, some business processes in an insurance company could be: claim registration, claim payment, and create invoice.

Business processes create and use information. In our example, information could be the claim's date or the number of dollars on an invoice. Information is typically entered, stored and processed using applications.

Functional management is the category of systems management that ensures the system is configured to perform the needed business functions.

2.3 Applications building block

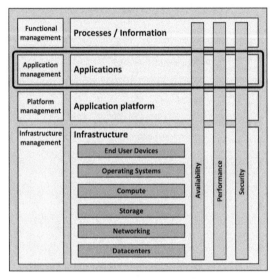

Figure 4: Applications building block

The applications building block includes three types of applications:

- **Client applications** typically run on end user devices like PCs and laptops. Examples of client applications are web browsers, word processors, and email clients.

- **Office applications** provide standard server based applications most organizations use. Examples are mail servers, portals, collaboration tools, and instant messaging servers. Most organizations run these office applications more or less out of the box.

- **Business specific applications** are applications that are typically highly customized or custom built. Some examples are Customer Relationship Management (CRM), Enterprise Resource Planning (ERP), Supervisory Control And Data Acquisition (SCADA) systems, and applications that are created for a specific business process (like an insurance management system).

Applications management is responsible for the configuration and technical operations of the applications.

2.4 Application Platform building block

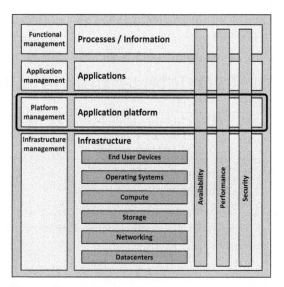

Figure 5: Application Platform building block

Most applications need some additional services, known as application platforms, that enable them to work. We can identify the following services as part of the application platform building block:

- **Front-end servers** are typically web servers (like Apache HTTP Server and Microsoft Internet Information Services – IIS) that provide end users with interactions to applications by presenting application screens in web browsers.

- **Application servers** act as containers running the actual application. Examples are Java or .Net application servers and frameworks (like IBM WebSphere, Apache Tomcat, Red Hat JBoss, and Windows .Net).

- **Connectivity** entails FTP servers, Extraction, Transformation and Load (ETL) servers, and Enterprise Service Buses (ESBs) like Microsoft BizTalk, the TIBCO Service Bus, IBM MQ, and SAP NetWeaver PI.

- **Databases,** also known as database management systems (DBMSs), provide a way to store and retrieve structured data. Examples are Oracle RDBMS, IBM DB2, Microsoft SQL Server, PostgreSQL, and MySQL.

Application platforms are typically managed by systems managers specialized in the specific technology.

2.5 Infrastructure building blocks

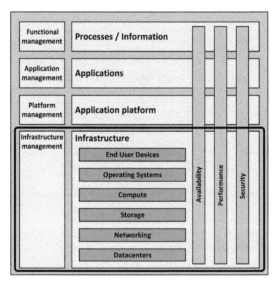

Figure 6: Infrastructure building block

This book uses the selection of building blocks as depicted in Figure 6 to describe the infrastructure building blocks and concepts – the scope of this book.

The following infrastructure building blocks are in scope:

- **End User Devices** are the devices used by end users to work with applications, like PCs, laptops, thin clients, mobile devices, and printers.
- **Operating Systems** are collections of programs that manage a computer's internal workings: its memory, processors, devices, and file system.

- **Compute** are the physical and virtual computers in the datacenter, also known as servers.

- **Storage** are systems that store data. They include hard disks, tapes, Direct Attached Storage (DAS), Network Attached Storage (NAS), and Storage Area Networks (SANs).

- **Networking** connects all components. This building block includes routers, switches, firewalls, WANs (wide area networks), LAN, dial-in, internet access, and VPNs (Virtual Private Network), and (on the network application level) relatively simple services like DNS, DHCP, and time services, necessary for the infrastructure to work properly.

- **Datacenters** are locations that host most IT infrastructure hardware. They include facilities like uninterruptible power supplies (UPSs), Heating, Ventilation, and Air Conditioning (HVAC), computer racks, and physical security measures.

Please note that these building blocks are not per definition hierarchically related. For instance, servers need both networking and storage, and both are equally important.

Infrastructure management includes processes like ITIL and DevOps, and tools like monitoring, backup, and logging.

2.6   Non-Functional attributes

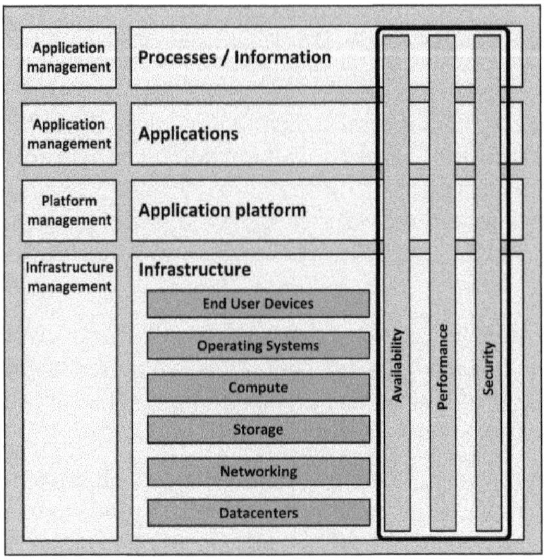

Figure 7: Non-Functional attributes

An IT system does not only provide functionality to users; functionality is supported by non-functional attributes. Non-functional attributes are the effect of the configuration of each IT system component, both on the infrastructure level and above.

Although many other non-functional attributes are defined, as described in chapter 3, availability, performance, and security are almost always the essential ones in IT infrastructure architectures (Figure 7).

PART II
−
NON FUNCTONAL
ATTRIBUTES

3

INTRODUCTION TO NON-FUNCTIONAL ATTRIBUTES

3.1 Introduction

IT infrastructures provide services to applications. Some of these infrastructure services can be well defined as a function, like providing disk space, or routing network messages. Non-functional attributes, on the other hand, describe the qualitative behavior of a system, rather than specific functionalities. Some examples of non-functional attributes are:

- Availability

- Scalability

- Reliability

- Stability

- Testability

- Recoverability

In my experience, the most important non-functional attributes for most IT infrastructures are **security**, **performance**, and **availability**.

Non-functional attributes are very important for the successful implementation and use of an IT infrastructure, but in projects, they rarely get the same attention as the functional services.

There is much confusion about the value of pursuing non-functional attributes. The name suggests they have no function. But of course, these attributes do have a function in the business process, and usually a fairly large one. For instance, when the infrastructure of a corporate website is not performing well, the visitors of the website will leave, which has a direct financial impact on the business. When credit card transactions are not stored in a secure way in the infrastructure, and as a result leak to hackers, the organization that stored the credit card data will have a lot of explaining to do to their customers.

So, non-functional attributes are very functional indeed, but they are not directly related to the primary functionalities of a system. Instead of using the term non-functional attribute, it would be much better to use the term quality attributes. While this term much better represents the nature and importance of for instance performance, security, and availability, the term non-functional attribute (as expressed in non-functional requirements or NFRs) is more frequently used and widely known. Therefore, in this book I keep on using the term non-functional attribute, although I do realize that the term could be misleading.

While architects and certainly infrastructure specialists are typically very aware of the importance of non-functional attributes of their infrastructure, many other stakeholders may not have the same feelings about them. Users normally think of functionalities, while non-functional attributes are considered a hygiene factor and taken for granted ("*of course, the system must perform well*"). Users of systems most of the time don't state non-functional attributes explicitly, but they do have expectations about them.

An example is the functionality of a car.

A car has to bring you from A to B, but many quality attributes are taken for granted.

For instance, the car has to be safe to drive in (leading to the implementation of anti-lock brakes, air bags, and safety belts) and reliable (the car should not break down every day), and the car must adhere to certain industry standards (the gas pedal must be the right-most pedal).

All of these extras cost money and might complicate the design, construction, and maintenance of the car. While all clients have these non-functional requirements, they are almost never expressed as such when people are ordering a new car.

3.2   Non-functional Requirements

It is the IT architect or requirements engineer's job to find implicit requirements on non-functional attributes (the non-functional requirements - NFRs). This can be very hard, since what is obvious or taken for granted by the customers or end users of a system is not always obvious to the designers and builders of the system. And not to forget the non-functional requirements that other stakeholders have, like the existence of service windows or monitoring capabilities, which are important requirements for systems managers.

It is important to remember that the acceptance of a system is largely dependent on the implemented non-functional requirements. A website can be very beautiful and functional, but if loading the site (performance, a non-functional requirement) takes 30 seconds, most customers are gone!

A large part of the budget for building an infrastructure is usually spent in fulfilling non-functional requirements that are not always clearly defined ("*The system obviously must work seamlessly with the existing systems*" or "*The website should always be available*").

Most stakeholders have no clue how hard it can be to realize a certain non-functional requirement. It sometimes helps to quantify these requirements; to make them explicit: "How bad would it be if the website was not available for 5 minutes per day?" or "What if it will take $500,000 to implement this requirement? Is it still important then?"

Many of the non-functional attributes of an application are delivered by the infrastructure. An application using an IT infrastructure built with several single points of failure will probably not reach very high availability figures, no matter how well the application is built. And when the IT infrastructure is not designed to be scalable, the applications built upon it cannot introduce scalability as an afterthought.

The other way around is also true. When an IT infrastructure is setup to be highly available, a badly designed application can make the end result highly unreliable. Similarly, security flaws on the processes level can undo all security measures taken in the infrastructure.

This makes it very important to consider the all design decisions when it comes to non-functional attributes.

It is not unusual to have conflicting non-functional requirements in a system. A classic example is security versus user friendliness. Users expect highly secured systems, but really don't want to be bothered by password changes, smart card authentication, and other annoying security measures. The same goes for performance and cost. Getting a high-performance system usually means getting more and faster hardware, and using strict implementation rules. This leads to higher cost, which is usually not in line with some requirement about the cost of the infrastructure.

It is the infrastructure architect's responsibility to balance these conflicting non-functional requirements. The architect must present the stakeholders with these conflicting requirements and their consequences, so they can make well informed decisions.

In the following chapters the three most important infrastructural non-functional attributes are discussed in more detail: availability, performance, and security. Each of these topics are too complex to fully explain in this book. Many good books and articles are written about them, some of which are recommended in the appendix. In this book, I only describe those aspects of availability, performance and security that are strongly related to IT infrastructures.

4

AVAILABILITY CONCEPTS

4.1   Introduction

Everyone expects their infrastructure to be available all the time. In this age of global, always-on, always connected systems, disturbances in availability are noticed immediately. A 100% guaranteed availability of an infrastructure, however, is impossible. No matter how much effort is spent on creating high available infrastructures, there is always a chance of downtime. It's just a fact of life.

According to a survey from the 2014 Uptime Symposium[4], 46% of companies using their own datacenter had at least one "business-impacting" datacenter outage over 12 months.

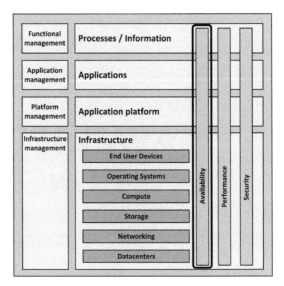

Figure 8: Availability in the infrastructure model

This chapter discusses the concepts and technologies used to create high available systems. It includes calculating availability, managing human factors, the reliability of infrastructure components, how to design for resilience, and – if everything else fails – business continuity management and disaster recovery.

4.2   Calculating availability

In general, availability can neither be calculated, nor guaranteed upfront. It can only be reported on afterwards, when a system has run for some years. This makes designing for high availability a complicated task. Fortunately, over the years, much knowledge and experience is gained on how to design high available systems, using design patterns like failover, redundancy, structured programming, avoiding Single Points of Failures (SPOFs), and implementing sound systems management. But first, let's discuss how availability is expressed in numbers.

4.2.1 Availability percentages and intervals

The availability of a system is usually expressed as a percentage of uptime in a given time period (usually one year or one month). The following table shows the maximum downtime for a particular percentage of availability.

Availability %	Downtime per year	Downtime per month	Downtime per week
99.8%	17.5 hours	86.2 minutes	20.2 minutes
99.9% ("three nines")	8.8 hours	43.2 minutes	10.1 minutes
99.99% ("four nines")	52.6 minutes	4.3 minutes	1.0 minutes
99.999% ("five nines")	5.3 minutes	25.9 seconds	6.1 seconds

Table 1: Availability levels

Typical requirements used in service level agreements today are 99.8% or 99.9% availability per month for a full IT system. To meet this requirement, the availability of the underlying infrastructure must be much higher, typically in the range of 99.99% or higher.

99.999% uptime is also known as carrier grade availability; this level of availability originates from telecommunication system components (not full systems!) that need an extremely high availability. Higher availability levels for a complete system are very uncommon, as they are almost impossible to reach.

As a comparison: the electricity supply in my home country, The Netherlands, is very reliable. Over the last years[5], the average downtime per household was 23 minutes per year. This is equivalent to an availability of 99.9956%. Some other European countries:

Germany: 21 minutes = 99.9960%

United Kingdom: 75 minutes = 99.9857%

France: 71 minutes = 99.9865%

Poland: 260 minutes = 99.9506%

The average downtime in the USA[6] is 127 minutes, leading to an availability of 99.9759%.

While 99.9% uptime means 525 minutes of downtime per year, this downtime should not occur in one event, nor should one-minute downtimes occur 525 times a year. It is therefore good practice to agree on the maximum frequency of unavailability. An example is shown in Table 2.

Unavailability (minutes)	Number of events (per year)
0 – 5	<= 35
5 – 10	<= 10
10 – 20	<= 5
20 – 30	<=2
> 30	<= 1

Table 2: Unavailability frequency

In this example, it means that the system can be unavailable for 25 minutes no more than twice a year. It is also allowed, however, to be unavailable for 3 minutes three times each month. For each availability requirement, a frequency table should be provided, in addition to each given availability percentage.

4.2.2   MTBF and MTTR

The factors involved in calculating availability are Mean Time Between Failures (MTBF), which is the average time that passes between failures, and Mean Time To Repair (MTTR), which is the time it takes to recover from a failure.

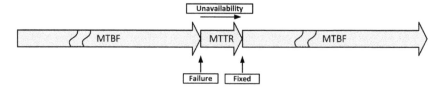

Figure 9: MTBF and MTTR

The term "mean" means that the numbers expressed by MTBF and MTTR are statistically calculated values.

4.2.2.1   Mean Time Between Failures (MTBF)

The MTBF is expressed in hours (how many hours will the component or service work without failure). Some typical MTBF figures are shown in Table 3.

Component	MTBF (hours)
Hard disk	750,000
Power supply	100,000
Fan	100,000
Ethernet Network Switch	350,000
RAM	1,000,000

Table 3: MTBF levels

It is important to understand how these numbers are calculated. No manufacturer can test if a hard disk will continue to work without failing for 750,000 hours (= 85 years). Instead, manufacturers run tests on large batches of components. In case of for instance hard disks, 1000 disks could have been tested for 3 months. If in that period of time five disks fail, the MTBF is calculated as follows:

The test time is 3 months. One year has four of those periods. So, if the test would have lasted one year, $4 \times 5 = 20$ disks would have failed.

In one year, the disks would have run:

1000 disks $\times$ 365 $\times$ 24 = 8,760,000 running hours.

This means that the MTBF = $\frac{8,760,000\ hours}{20\ failed\ drives}$ = 438,000 hours/failure.

So, actually MTBF only says something about the chance of failure in the first months of use. It is an extrapolated value for the probable downtime of a disk. It would be better to specify the annual failure rate instead (in our example, 2% of all disks will fail in the first year), but that is not very good advertising.

4.2.2.2   Mean Time To Repair (MTTR)

When a component breaks, it needs to be repaired. Usually the repair time (expressed as Mean Time To Repair – MTTR) is kept low by having a service contract with the supplier of the component. Sometimes spare parts are kept on-site to lower the MTTR (making MTTR more like Mean Time To

Replace). Typically, a faulty component is not repaired immediately. Some examples of what might be needed for to complete repairs are:

- Notification of the fault (time before seeing an alarm message)
- Processing the alarm
- Finding the root cause of the error
- Looking up repair information
- Getting spare components from storage
- Having technician come to the datacenter with the spare component
- Physically repairing the fault
- Restarting and testing the component

Instead of these manual actions, the best way to keep the MTTR low is to introduce automated redundancy and failover, as discussed in sections 4.4.1 and 4.4.2.

4.2.3   Some calculation examples

Decreasing MTTR and increasing MTBF both increase availability. Dividing MTBF by the sum of MTBF and MTTR results in the availability expressed as a percentage: Availability $= \frac{\text{MTBF}}{(\text{MTBF}+\text{MTTR})} \times 100\%$.

For example:

A power supply's MTBF is 150,000 hours. This means that on average this power supply fails once every 150,000 hours (= once per 17 years). If the time to repair the power supply is 8 hours, the availability can be calculated as follows: Availability $= \frac{150,000 \text{ hours}}{(150,000 \text{ hours}+8 \text{ hours})} \times 100\% = 99.99466\%$

This means that because of the repair time alone this component can never reach an average availability of 99.999%! To reach five nines of availability the repair time should be as low as 90 minutes for this component. Note that if a downtime of 99.999% is acceptable per year (and not over the total lifetime of the component), the repair time must be even lower than 6 minutes!

As system complexity increases, usually availability decreases. When a failure of any one part in a system causes a failure of the system as a whole, the availability is called serial availability. To calculate the availability of such a complex system or device, multiply the availability of all its parts.

For example, a server consists of the following components and the MTTR of any part of the server is 8 hours.

Figure 10: System with serial components

Component	MTBF (h)	MTTR (h)	Availability	in %
Power supply	100,000	8	0.9999200	99.99200
Fan	100,000	8	0.9999200	99.99200
System board	300,000	8	0.9999733	99.99733
Memory	1,000,000	8	0,9999920	99.99920
CPU	500,000	8	0.9999840	99.99840
Network Interface Controller (NIC)	250,000	8	0.9999680	99.99680

Table 4: Availability in percentages

The availability of the total server is: $0.9999200 \times 0.9999200 \times 0.9999733 \times 0,9999920 \times 0.9999840 \times 0.9999680 = 0.9997733 = 99.97733\%$. This is lower than the availability of any single component in the system. Therefore, the more components a system includes (and each component is critical for the total system), the lower the total availability becomes.

To increase the availability, systems (composed of a various components) can be deployed in parallel. This considerably increases the availability, since the combined system no longer contains a Single Point Of Failure. If one component becomes unavailable, the affected system goes down, but the other system can take over. Consider the example below. Two systems run in parallel, each complete system having an availability of 99%.

99% availability

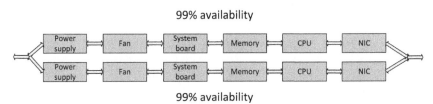

99% availability

Figure 11: Two systems in parallel

The chance of both systems being unavailable at the same time is very small and can be calculated as follows:

$A = 1 - (1 - A_1)^n$

where

A = Availability

n = Number of systems in parallel

A_1 = The availability of one system

When A_1 (the availability of one system) is estimated to be 99% (which is very pessimistic as explained above), the combined availability in a parallel setup is:

Situation	Availability	Yearly downtime
1 system	99%	87h 36m
2 systems	99.99%	52m
3 systems	99.9999%	32s
4 systems	99.999999%	almost 0

Table 5: Availability with multiple components

In this situation, it is important to have no single point of failure that combines the set of systems (for instance, all systems run on the same power supply). In that case, the availability of the system is fully dependent on that one component.

4.3 Sources of unavailability

4.3.1 Human errors

Usually only 20% of the failures leading to unavailability are technology failures. According to Gartner[7], through 2015, 80% of outages impacting mission-critical services will be caused by people and process issues and more than 50% of those outages will be caused by change/configuration/release integration and hand-off issues.

Of course, it helps to have highly qualified and trained staff, with a healthy sense of responsibility. Errors are human, however, and there is no cure for it. End users can introduce downtime by misuse of the system. When a user for instance starts the generation of ten very large reports at the same time, the performance of the system could suffer in such a degree that the system becomes unavailable to other users. Also, when a user forgets a password (and maybe tries an incorrect password for more than five times) he or she is locked out and the system is unavailable for that user. If that user has a very responsible job, like approving some steps in a business process, being locked out could mean that a business process is unavailable to other users as well.

Most unavailability issues, however, are the result of actions from systems managers. Some typical actions (or the lack thereof) are:

- Performing a test in the production environment (not recommended at all).

- Switching off the wrong component (not the defective server that needs repair, but the one still operating).

- Swapping a good working disk in a RAID set instead of the defective one.

- Restoring the wrong backup tape to production.

- Accidentally removing files (mail folders, configuration files) or database entries: *drop table x* instead of *drop table y*.

- Making incorrect changes to configurations (for instance, the routing table of a network router, or a change in the Windows registry).

- Incorrect labeling of cables, later leading to errors when changes are made to the cabling.

- Performing maintenance on an incorrect virtual machine (the one in production instead of the one in the test environment).

- Making a typo in a system command environment (for instance in UNIX:
  `sudo rm -rf / *.back` instead of
  `sudo rm -rf /*.back` where one space too many leads to a complete erasure of a hard disk – did you notice the difference?).

- Insufficient testing, for instance, the fallback procedure to move operations from the primary datacenter to the secondary was never tested, and failed when it was really needed.

Many of these mistakes can be avoided by using proper systems management procedures, like have having a standard template for creating new servers, using formal deployment strategies with the appropriate tools, using administrative accounts only when absolutely needed, etc.

As an example, when in some UNIX environments users log in with an administrative account (root), they automatically get the following message:

```
We assume you have received the usual lecture from the
local systems manager. It usually boils down to these
three things:
#1) Respect the privacy of others.
#2) Think before you type.
#3) With great power comes great responsibility.
```

Simple measures like this make people aware of the impact of their actions, leading to fewer mistakes.

Of course, there are also bad people out there. Hackers can create downtime by for instance executing a Denial of Service attack. More on this subject can be found the chapter 6 on security.

4.3.2   Software bugs

After human errors, software bugs are the number two reason for unavailability. Because of the complexity of most software it is nearly impossible (and very costly) to create bug-free software. Software bugs in applications or system drivers can stop an entire system (like the infamous Blue Screen of Death on Windows systems), or create downtime in other ways. Since operating systems are software too, operating systems contain bugs that can lead to corrupted file systems, network failures, or other sources of unavailability.

4.3.3   Planned maintenance

Planned maintenance is sometimes needed to perform systems management tasks like upgrading hardware or software, implementing software changes, migrating data, or the creation of backups.

Since most systems today must be available 24/7, planned maintenance should only be performed on parts of the infrastructure while other parts keep serving clients. When the infrastructure has no single point of failure (SPOF), downtime of a single component does not lead to downtime of the entire system. This way it is possible to, for instance, upgrade an operating system to the latest software, while the infrastructure as a whole remains available.

During planned maintenance, however, the system is more vulnerable to downtime than under normal circumstances. When the systems manager makes a mistake during planned maintenance, the risk of downtime is higher than normal. When planned maintenance is performed on a component, a SPOF could be introduced, being the component not under maintenance. When that component breaks during the planned maintenance, the whole system can become unavailable.

Another example is the upgrade of systems in a high available cluster. When one component is upgraded and the other is not upgraded yet, it could be that the high available cluster is not working as such. In that period of time the system is vulnerable to downtime.

4.3.4 Physical defects

Of course, everything breaks down eventually, but mechanical parts are most likely to break first. Some examples of mechanical parts are:

- **Fans for cooling the equipment**. Fans usually have a limited lifespan. They usually break because of dust in the bearings, causing the motor to work harder until it breaks.

- **Disk drives**. Disk drives contain two main moving parts: the motor spinning the platters and the linear motor that moves the read/write heads.

- **Tapes and tape drives**. Tapes are very vulnerable to defects as the tape is spun on and off the reels all the time. Tape drives and especially tape robots contain very sensitive pieces of mechanics that can break easily.

Apart from mechanical failures because of normal usage, parts also break because of external factors like ambient temperature, moist, vibrations, and aging.

Most parts favor stable temperatures. When the temperature fluctuates, parts expand and shrink, leading to for instance contact problems in connectors or solder joints. This effect also occurs when parts are exposed to vibrations and when parts are switched on and off frequently.

Some parts also age over time. Not only mechanical parts wear out, but also some electronic parts like large capacitors, that contain fluids, and transformers, that vibrate due to the AC current creating fluctuating magnetic fields. Solder joints also age over time, just like on/off switches that are used frequently.

When used heavily or over an extended period of time, a power supply will wear out; it slowly loses some of its initial power capacity. It is recommended to calculate a surplus of at least 25% of continuously available power for 24/7 running equipment.

Network cables, especially when they are moved around much, tend to fail over time. Another type of cable that is highly sensitive to mechanical stress is fiber optics cable.

Some components, like PC system boards and external disk caches, are equipped with batteries. Batteries, including rechargeable batteries, are known to fail often. Other typical components to fail are oscillators used on system boards. These oscillators are also in effect mechanical parts and prone to failure.

In most cases the availability of a component follows a so-called bathtub curve.

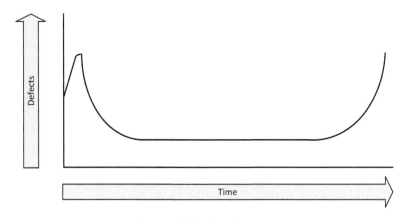

Figure 12: Bathtub curve

A component failure is most likely when the component is new. In the first month of use the chance of a components failure is relatively high. Sometimes a component doesn't even work at all when unpacked for the first time. This is called a DOA component – Dead On Arrival.

When a component still works after the first month, it is likely that it will continue working without failure until the end of its technical life cycle. This is the other end of the bathtub – the chance of failure rises suddenly at the end of the life cycle of a component.

4.3.5   Environmental issues

Environmental issues can cause downtime as well. Issues with power and cooling, and external factors like fire, earthquakes and flooding can cause entire datacenters to fail.

Power can fail for a short or long period of time, and can have voltage drops or spikes. Power outages can cause downtime, and power spikes can cause power supplies to fail. The effect of these power issues can be eliminated by using an Uninterruptable Power Supply (UPS). More information on UPSs can be found in section 7.2.4.2.

Failure of the air conditioning system can lead to high temperatures in the datacenter. When the temperature rises too much, systems must (or will automatically) be shut down to avoid damage.

4.3.6   Complexity of the infrastructure

Adding more components to an overall system design can undermine high availability, even if the extra components are implemented to achieve high availability. This sounds like a paradox, but in practice I have seen such situations.

Complex systems inherently have more potential points of failure and are more difficult to implement correctly. Also, a complex system is harder to manage; more knowledge is needed to maintain the system and errors are made more easily.

Sometimes it is better to just have an extra spare system in the closet than to use complex redundant systems. When a workstation fails, most people can work on another machine, and the defective machine can be swapped in 15 minutes. This is probably a better choice than implementing high availability measures in the workstation, like dual network cards, dual connections to dual network switches that can failover, failover drivers for the network card in the workstation, dual power supplies in the workstation fed via two separate cables and power outlets on two fuse boxes, etc. You get the point.

The same goes for high availability measures on other levels.

I once had a very instable set of redundant ATM (Asynchronous Transfer Mode) network switches in the core of a network. I could not get the systems to failover reliably, leading to multiple instances of downtime of a few minutes each.

When I removed the redundancy in the network, the network never failed again for a least a year. The leftover switches were loaded with a working configuration and put in the closet.

If the core switch would fail, we could swap it in 10 minutes (which, given that this would not happen more than once a year – probably even less, led to an availability of at least 99.995%).

4.4 Availability patterns

A single point of failure (SPOF) is a component in the infrastructure that, if it fails, causes downtime to the entire system. SPOFs should be avoided in IT infrastructures as they pose a large risk to the availability of a system.

For example, in most storage systems, the failure of one disk does not affect the availability of the storage system. Technologies like RAID (Redundant Arrays of Independent Disks) can be used to handle the failure of a single disk (more on RAID systems in section 9.2.3.1), eliminating disks as a SPOF. Server clusters, double network connections, and dual datacenters – they all are meant to eliminate SPOFs. The trick is to find SPOFs that are not that obvious.

While it sounds easy to eliminate singe points of failure, in practice it is not always feasible or cost effective. Take for instance the internet connection your organization uses to send e-mail. Do you have multiple internet connections from your e-mail server? Are these connections running over separate cables in the building? What about outside of the building? Do you use multiple internet providers? Do they share their backbones?

> *While users should not notice a failure, the systems managers should! I have seen in practice that a failing disk was not stopping the system, because of RAID technology, but the systems managers – lacking proper monitoring tools – did not notice it.*
>
> *But when the second disk failed, both the users and the system managers noticed the downtime!*

While eliminating SPOFs is very important, it is good to realize that there is always *something* shared in an infrastructure (like the building, the electricity provider, the metropolitan area, or the country). We just need to know what is shared and if the risk of sharing is acceptable.

To eliminate SPOFs, a combination of redundancy, failover, and fallback can be used.

4.4.1 Redundancy

Redundancy is the duplication of critical components in a single system, to avoid a SPOF. In IT infrastructure components, redundancy is usually implemented in power supplies (a single component having two power supplies; if one fails, the other takes over), network interfaces, and SAN HBAs (Host Bus Adapters) for connecting storage.

4.4.2   Failover

Failover is the (semi)automatic switch-over to a standby system (component), either in the same or in another datacenter, upon the failure or abnormal termination of the previously active system (component).

Examples are Windows Server failover clustering, VMware High Availability and (on the database level) Oracle Real Application Cluster (RAC). Failover is discussed in the chapters on the corresponding building blocks.

4.4.3   Fallback

Fallback is the manual switchover to an identical standby computer system in a different location, typically used for disaster recovery. There are three basic forms of fallback solutions:

- Hot site
- Warm site
- Cold site

4.4.3.1   Hot site

A hot site is a fully configured fallback datacenter, fully equipped with power and cooling. The applications are installed on the servers, and data is kept up-to-date to fully mirror the production system.

Staff and operators should be able to walk in and begin full operations in a very short time (typically one or two hours).

This type of site requires constant maintenance of the hardware, software, data, and applications to be sure the site accurately mirrors the state of the production site at all times.

4.4.3.2   Warm site

A warm site could best be described as a mix between a hot site and cold site. Like a hot site, the warm site is a computer facility readily available with power, cooling, and computers, but the applications may not be installed or configured. But external communication links and other data elements, that commonly take a long time to order and install, will be present.

To start working in a warm site, applications and all their data will need to be restored from backup media and tested. This typically takes a day.

The benefit of a warm site compared to a hot site is that it needs less attention when not in use and is much cheaper.

4.4.3.3 Cold site

A cold site differs from the other two in that it is ready for equipment to be brought in during an emergency, but no computer hardware is available at the site. The cold site is a room with power and cooling facilities, but computers must be brought on-site if needed, and communications links may not be ready. Applications will need to be installed and current data fully restored from backups.

Although a cold site provides minimal fallback protection, if an organization has very little budget for a fallback site, a cold site may be better than nothing.

4.4.4 Business Continuity

Although many measures can be taken to provide high availability, the availability of the IT infrastructure can never be guaranteed in all situations. In case of a disaster, the infrastructure could become unavailable, in some cases for a longer period of time.

Business continuity is about identifying threats an organization faces and providing an effective response. Business Continuity Management (BCM) and Disaster Recovery Planning (DRP) are processes to handle the effect of disasters.

4.4.4.1 Business Continuity Management

BCM is not about IT alone. It includes managing business processes, and the availability of people and work places in disaster situations. It includes disaster recovery, business recovery, crisis management, incident management, emergency management, product recall, and contingency planning.

A Business Continuity Plan (BCP) describes the measures to be taken when a critical incident occurs in order to continue running critical operations, and to halt non-critical processes. The BS:25999 norm describes guidelines on how to implement BCM.

4.4.4.2   Disaster Recovery Planning

Disaster recovery planning (DRP) contains a set of measures to take in case of a disaster, when (parts of) the IT infrastructure must be accommodated in an alternative location.

An IT disaster is defined as an irreparable problem in a datacenter, making the datacenter unusable. In general, disasters can be classified into two broad categories. The first is natural disasters such as floods, hurricanes, tornadoes or earthquakes. The second category is manmade disasters, including hazardous material spills, infrastructure failure, or bio-terrorism.

In a survey performed under eighteen very experienced IT professionals, I found that a disaster as defined above is very unlikely in western Europe. In Figure 13, the estimated occurrence of disasters is shown. Based on this figure, disasters in western Europe are expected to happen no more than once every 30 years.

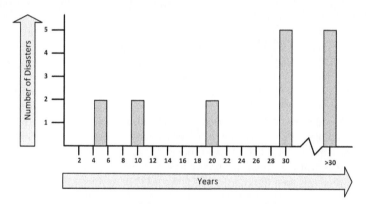

Figure 13: Estimated occurrence of disasters

The IT disaster recovery standard BS:25777 can be used to implement DRP. DRP assesses the risk of failing IT systems and provides solutions. A typical DRP solution is the use of fallback facilities and having a Computer Emergency Response Team (CERT) in place. A CERT is usually a team of systems managers and senior management that decides how to handle a certain crisis once it becomes reality.

The steps that need to be taken to resolve a disaster highly depend on the type of disaster. It could be that the organization's building is damaged or destroyed (for instance in case of a fire), maybe even people got hurt or died. One of the first worries is of course to save people. But after that, procedures must be followed to restore IT operations as soon as possible. A new (temporary) building might be needed, temporary staff might be needed, and new equipment must be installed or hired. After that, steps must be taken to get the systems up and running again and to have the data restored. Connections to the outside world must be established (not only to the internet, but also to business partners) and business processes must be initiated again.

4.4.4.3   RTO and RPO

Two important objectives of disaster recovery planning are the Recovery Time Objective (RTO) and the Recovery Point Objective (RPO). Figure 14 shows the difference.

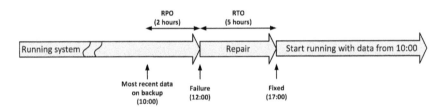

Figure 14: RTO and RPO

The RTO is the maximum duration of time within which a *business process* must be restored after a *disaster*, in order to avoid unacceptable consequences (like bankruptcy). RTO is only valid in case of a disaster and not the acceptable downtime under normal circumstances. Measures like failover and fallback must be taken in order to fulfill the RTO requirements.

The RPO is the point in time to which *data* must be recovered considering some "acceptable loss" in a disaster situation. It describes the amount of data loss a business is willing to accept in case of a disaster, measured in time. For instance, when each day a backup is made of all data, and a disaster destroys all data, the maximum RPO is 24 hours – the maximum amount of data lost between the last backup and the occurrence of the disaster. To lower the RPO, a different back-up regime could be implemented.

5

PERFORMANCE CONCEPTS

5.1 Introduction

Performance is a typical hygiene factor. Nobody notices a highly performing system. But when a system is not performing well enough, users quickly start complaining.

As an example, according to Equation Research[8]:

- 78% of website visitors have gone to a competitor's site due to poor performance during peak times

- 88% are less likely to return to a site after a poor user experience

- 47% left with a less positive perception of the company

In a similar investigation in 2010, Akamai and PhoCusWright[9] found that 57% of online shoppers will wait three seconds or less before abandoning the site and 65% of 18- to 24-year-olds expect a site to load in two seconds or less.

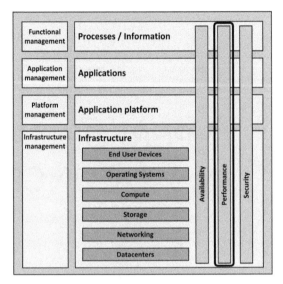

Figure 15: Performance in the infrastructure model

5.2   Perceived performance

Perceived performance refers to how quickly a system *appears* to perform its task. Most people understand that running a very complex report takes longer than opening an e-mail. But while people have implicit expectations about performance, they are seldom expressed in hard figures. And in general, people tend to overestimate their own patience.

People tend to value predictability in performance[10]. When the performance of a system is fluctuating, they remember a bad experience, even if the fluctuation is relatively rare. For instance, even when the system has a bad response time only once a week, in the perception of the users the system is often slow, even if the rest of the time the system is performing well. It is therefore important for a system to have a predictable and consistent performance.

If a certain task takes a long time, it helps to inform the user about how long it will take. When users are aware they have to wait for 40 seconds to get a task done, and are informed about it (for instance by showing a progress bar), they accept the waiting time more easily. On the other hand, when the system seems unresponsive with no apparent reason, people get irritated very quickly.

Picture 3: Progress bar

Increasing the real performance of a system is one way to increase the perceived performance. But when real performance cannot be increased (because of physical limitations for instance), or if the cost of improving the performance is very high, some techniques can be used to increase perceived performance. Two of those techniques are splash screens and progress bars.

Picture 4: Splash screen of a relatively slow starting application

Of course, the amount of time an application takes to startup, or the time it takes for a set of files to copy, is not made any faster by showing a splash screen or a progress bar. Showing these screens, however, satisfies a typical human need: they provide visual feedback to inform the users that the system is handling their request and is busy working for them.

Drawing and refreshing a progress bar while loading a file satisfies the user who is waiting, but steals time from the process that is actually performing the work. Usually this is only a very small amount of time and the benefit of a satisfied user is much higher.

> *A nice example of handling perceived performance is implemented by YouTube. Many of the videos on YouTube are stored on slow storage systems – some of them are even stored on powered down disks.*
>
> *The time it takes to spin the disk and fetch the video is hidden by showing commercial ads in the meantime.*

5.3 Performance during infrastructure design

Most IT systems will respond to increased load with some degree of decreasing performance. Designing for performance ensures that a solution is designed, implemented, and supported to meet the performance requirements, even under increasing load.

When designing a system, performance must be considered not only when the system works as expected, but also when the system is in a special state. When for instance:

- Parts have failed (like the failure of a server in a cluster).

- The system is in maintenance (for instance implementing a patch in an operating system).

- A backup is performed.

- Batch jobs are running.

Calculating performance of a system in the design phase is extremely difficult and very unreliable. Only on very small parts of the system, with predictable load, the performance can be calculated by analyzing each and every step of the implemented process. Because this is a complex, time consuming, and costly process, usually other means are used to determine the performance of a system. Some generic ways to do this are:

- Benchmarking

- Using vendor experience

- Prototyping

- User Profiling

5.3.1   Benchmarking

With today's complex infrastructures it is difficult to compare the performance of various components simply by looking at their specifications. Benchmarks can be used as an alternative.

A benchmark uses a specific test program to assess the relative performance of an infrastructure component. Benchmarking is used to assess the performance characteristics of computer hardware, for example, the floating-point operation performance (Floating Point Operations Per Second – FLOPS) or the number of instructions per second (Million Instructions Per Second – MIPS) of a CPU. Benchmarks provide a method of comparing the performance of various subsystems across different system architectures.

Many benchmark programs perform only a small subset of tasks that only test one small part of an infrastructure, like the CPU, memory, or disk drives. They measure the raw performance, not taking into account the typical usage of such components. Therefore, benchmarks are only useful for comparing the raw speed of parts of an infrastructure (like the speed difference between processors or between disk drives).

5.3.2   Using vendor experience

The best way to determine the performance of a system in the design phase is to use the experience of vendors. Vendors of applications and infrastructure components like IBM, Oracle, Dell, SAP, HP, HDS, EMC or Microsoft, all have a lot of experience running their products in various infrastructure configurations. Usually they can provide tools, figures, and best practices to help design the appropriate infrastructure for their products. Using their experience is extremely valuable. I strongly recommend using it.

5.3.3   Prototyping

To measure the performance of a system at an early stage, a prototype can be built. For infrastructure systems, this could be done by hiring equipment from suppliers, by using datacenter capacity at a vendor's premise or by using cloud computing resources. I strongly recommend prototyping in order to find potential performance issues as early as possible in the design process.

Prototyping should focus on those parts of the system that pose the highest risk. An example from my own experience is described below.

In 2002, I was involved in a project to create a Business Intelligence system for a Short Message Service (SMS) texting system.

The system would insert a copy of the log records from the SMS system into an Oracle database, and would use that data to create reports for the marketing department of the telecom provider (for instance to find patterns in demographics, like "At what time do most teenagers use SMS to text their friends?").

The database was to be used by the helpdesk of the telecom provider as well, to answer questions of end users (for instance, when a text message was sent but not delivered, why it was not delivered?).

The project was already running for a few months, and BI specialists were working on data models, reporting, and user interfaces, when I was asked to look at the infrastructural aspects. One of the first questions I asked was how many log records the system was supposed to insert in the Oracle database for processing. The answer was stunning.

10,000 records per second.

The system was supposed to insert 10,000 records in an Oracle database each and every second 24/7. Of course, the next question was how they were going to do this. The answer was also stunning.

By inserting them in the database one by one.

The project members didn't have a clue that this was quite a challenge (certainly in 2002!). When looking for information on the maximum speed at which records could be inserted in an Oracle database, I found that the maximum speed reported at that time was around 1,000 inserts per second; 10 times too slow for us. I suggested to the project team to build a prototype to find out how fast we could actually insert records in our database setup. The outcome: 500. A factor twenty too slow. A bit disappointing and clearly a project risk!

We eventually reached an acceptable solution by doing some fancy Oracle tricks. After using the same prototype setup, we eventually reached an acceptable 5,000 inserts per second (it may have been a world record at the time).

Apparently, the project needed an infrastructure architect to show them the highest risk of the project (low performance). A small prototype setup was enough to show the actual performance of the system. Obviously, such a prototype should have been one of the first activities in the project.

I have positive experiences with using prototypes (also known as proof of concepts) in projects. A proof of concept should be used to test the most challenging parts of your solution early in the project. This is not a natural thing to do. Most people start with the part of the project they feel most comfortable with. The more challenging part usually is addressed at a later stage. But these challenging parts need to be addressed anyway, and could lead to a delay in the project or even a halt. A proof of concept shows this at a time not too much money is spent yet and shows to both the project team and the customer that the project's highest risk has been taken care of.

5.3.4   User profiling

User profiling can be used to predict the load a new software system will pose on the infrastructure, and to be able to create performance test scripts that put representative load in the infrastructure before the software is actually built.

In order to predict the load on the infrastructure, it is important to have a good indication of the expected usage of the system. This can be done by defining a number of typical user groups of the new system (also known as personas) and by creating a list of tasks they will perform on the new system.

As a first step, a limited list of personas must be defined. Representatives of these persona groups must be interviewed to understand how they will use the new system. A list can be compiled with the main tasks (like login, start the application, open a document, create a report, etc.) they will perform when the system is in operation.

For each of these tasks, estimations can be made on how, and how often they will use the system's functionality to perform the task. Based on these estimations, and the number of users the personas represent, a calculation can be made on how often each system task is used in a given time frame, and how these relate to infrastructure load. A very simplified example is given in the following table.

Persona	Number of users per persona	System task	Infrastructure load as a result of the system task	Frequency
Data entry officer	100	Start application	Read 100 MB data from SAN	Once a day
Data entry officer	100	Start application	Transport 100 MB data to workstation	Once a day
Data entry officer	100	Enter new data	Transport 50 KB data from workstation to server	40 per hour
Data entry officer	100	Enter new data	Store 50 KB data to SAN	40 per hour
Data entry officer	100	Change existing data	Read 50 KB data from SAN	10 per hour
Data entry officer	100	Change existing data	Transport 50 KB data from server to workstation	10 per hour
Data entry officer	100	Change existing data	Transport 50 KB data from workstation to server	10 per hour
Data entry officer	100	Change existing data	Store 50 KB data to SAN	10 per hour
Data entry officer	100	Close application	Transport 500 KB configuration data from workstation to server	Once a day
Data entry officer	100	Close application	Store 500 KB data to SAN	Once a day

Table 6: Personas and tasks

This leads to the following profile for this persona group:

Infrastructure load	Per day	Per second
Data transport from server to workstation (KB)	10,400,000	361.1
Data transport from workstation to server (KB)	2,050,000	71.2
Data read from SAN (KB)	10,400,000	361.1
Data written to SAN (KB)	2,050,000	71.2

Table 7: Infrastructure tasks

Of course, in real life, this exercise is much more complicated. There might be many personas, complex tasks, tasks are spread in time, or show hotspots (like starting the application or logging in, which typically happens at the start of the day), the system can have background processes running, and the load on the system for a specific task can be very hard to predict.

But as this very simplified example shows, user profiling can help determining the load on various parts of the infrastructure, even before the application software is written.

5.4 Performance of a running system

5.4.1 Managing bottlenecks

The performance of a system is based on the performance of all its components, and the interoperability of various components. Therefore, measuring the performance of a system only has value if the complete system is taken into account. For instance, building an infrastructure with really fast networking components has little benefits when the used hard disks are slow.

A performance problem may be identified by slow or unresponsive systems. This usually occurs because of high system loads, causing some component of the system to reach some limit. This component is referred to as the bottleneck of the system, because the performance or capacity of the entire system is limited by a single component, slowing down the system as a whole. To find this bottleneck, performance measurements are needed.

Only when we know where in the system the bottleneck occurs, we can try to improve performance by removing that bottleneck.

When a bottleneck is removed, usually another bottleneck arises. In fact, no matter how much performance tuning is done, there will always be a bottleneck somewhere. According to the Bottleneck law[11], every system, regardless of how well it works, has at least one constraint (a bottleneck) that limits its performance. This is perfectly okay when the bottleneck does not negatively influence performance of the complete system under the highest expected load.

Benchmarking is a way to measure individual components, while system performance tests measure the system as a whole.

5.4.2   Performance testing

There are three major types of performance tests for testing complete systems:

- **Load testing** - This test shows how a system performs under the expected load. It is a check to see if the system performs well under normal circumstances.

- **Stress testing** - This test shows how a system reacts when it is under extreme load. Goal is to see at what point the system "breaks" (the breakpoint, as shown in Figure 16) and *where* it breaks (the bottleneck).

- **Endurance testing** - This test shows how a system behaves when it is used at the expected load for a long period of time. Typical issues that arise are memory leaks, expanding database tables, or filling disks, leading to performance degradation.

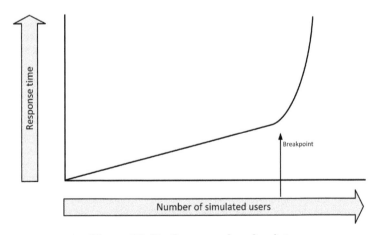

Figure 16: Performance breakpoint

Performance testing software typically uses one or more servers to act as injectors – each emulating a number of users, each running a sequence of interactions (recorded as a script, or as a series of scripts to emulate different types of user interaction). A separate server acts as a test conductor, coordinating the tasks, gathering metrics from each of the injectors, and collecting performance data for reporting purposes.

The usual sequence is to ramp up the load – starting with a small number of virtual users and increasing the number over a period of time to some maximum. The test result shows how the performance varies with the load, given as number of users versus response time.

Performance testing should be done in a production-like environment. Performance tests in a development environment usually lead to results that are highly unreliable. To reduce cost, sometimes it is advisable to use a temporary test environment, for instance one hired from your hardware vendor that comprises the same components as the production environment. If the test environment has a lower capacity (the machines are not as fast as production, the disks are of a different type, etc.) the test results cannot be relied upon, as that they are not comparable to the production environment. Even when underpowered test systems perform well enough to get good test results, the faster production system could show performance issues that did not occur in the tests.

> *I have experienced such a situation: A production system was much faster than the test system we used. While the tests showed no performance issues on the slower test system, the application performed badly on the faster production systems.*
>
> *The reason was a network protocol that could not receive network packages as fast as the production systems could provide it.*

5.5 Performance patterns

There are various ways to improve the performance of systems. This section describes caching, scaling, load balancing, high performance clusters, grids, designing for performance, and capacity management.

But first a quick word on increasing performance on other levels than the infrastructure.

5.5.1 Increasing performance on upper layers

Experience learns that 80% of the performance issues are due to badly behaving applications. While much effort can be put in optimizing infrastructure performance, it is good practice to first check for performance optimizations in the upper layers. Database and application tuning typically provides much more opportunity for performance increase than installing more computing power. Especially in the interfaces between applications and underlying databases much performance gain can be achieved.

I have seen a management report that used to run for 45 minutes. After tuning the database, it ran in 3 minutes, just by optimizing some SQL queries and adding a database index. Increasing the performance that much in the infrastructure layer instead is not only very complicated but also very expensive!

Another example was a badly programmed application where each read and write to disk opened and closed the file, instead of opening the file at the start of the application and keeping it open until the application is stopped.

Since opening and closing files is much slower than the actual reading or writing of data, just keeping files open vastly increased the performance of the application!

Application performance can benefit from prioritizing tasks, working from memory as much as possible (as opposed to working with data on disk), and making good use of queues and schedulers.

Of course, bad behaving applications can only be fixed when you have access to the application's source code. For commercial off-the-shelf software, this is usually not feasible. Tuning the databases used by the application, by for instance adding indexes, can be an opportunity to significantly improve performance. Fortunately, today's databases use automated query optimizing, where the performance of often used queries automatically gets better over time.

In the current era of multi-core processors, it is important for application developers to understand how applications work on a multithreaded system. Unfortunately, this is not always the case and many applications run on only one of the available cores of the CPU.

Intel introduced circuitry in its latest processors that can boost the clock speed of one of the cores when a running single threaded application is detected. This boost of the clock speed would normally introduce too much heat in the processor, but since the other cores are not performing any work in a single threaded application, the overall temperature of the CPU stays within range.

5.5.2   Caching

Caching improves performance by retaining frequently used data in high speed memory, reducing access times to data.

Some sources that provide data are slower than others. The approximate speed of retrieving data from various sources is shown in Table 8.

Component	Time it takes to fetch _1 MB_ of data (ms)
Network, 1 Gbit/s	675
Hard disk, 15k rpm, 4 KB disk blocks[12]	105
Main memory DDR3 RAM[13]	0.2
CPU L1 cache[14]	0.016

Table 8: Approximate speeds of fetching data

Especially in situations where retrieving data takes relatively long (for instance reading from hard disk or from the network), caching in memory can significantly improve performance.

5.5.2.1   Disk caching

Disks are mechanical devices that are slow by nature. To speed up the reading of data from disk, disk drives contain cache memory. This cache memory stores all data recently read from disk, and some of the disk blocks following the recently read disk blocks. When the data is read again, or (more likely) the data of the following disk block is needed, it is fetched from high speed cache memory.

Disk caching can be implemented in the storage component itself (for instance cache used on the physical disks or cache implemented in the disk controller), but also in the operating system. The general rule of thumb that adding memory in servers improves performance is due to the fact that all non-used memory in operating systems is used for disk cache. Over time, all memory gets filled with previously stored disk requests and prefetched disk blocks, speeding up applications.

5.5.3   Web proxies

Another example of caching is the use of web proxies. When users browse the internet, instead of fetching all requested data from the internet each time, earlier accessed data can be cached in a proxy server and fetched from there. This has two benefits: users get their data faster than when it would be retrieved from a distant web server, and all other users are provided more bandwidth to the internet, as the data did not have to be downloaded again.

5.5.4   Operational data store

An Operational Data Store (ODS) is a read-only replica of a part of a database for a specific use. Instead of accessing the main database for retrieving information, often used information is retrieved from a separate small ODS database, not degrading the performance of the main database.

A good example of this is a website of a bank. Most users want to see their actual balance when they login (and maybe the last 10 mutations of their balance). When every balance change is not only stored in the main database of the bank, but also in a small ODS database, the website only needs to access the ODS to provide users with the data they most likely need. This not only speeds up the user experience, but also decreases the load on the main database.

5.5.5   Front-end servers

In web facing environments storing most accessed (parts of) pages on the web front-end server (like the static pictures used on the landing page) significantly lowers the amount of traffic to back-end systems. Reverse-proxies can be used to automatically cache most requested data as well.

5.5.6   In-memory databases

In special circumstances, entire databases can be run from memory instead of from disk. These so-called in-memory databases are used in situations where performance is crucial (like in real-time SCADA systems). Of course, special arrangements must be made to ensure data is not lost when a power failure occurs.

As an example, in 2011 SAP AG introduced HANA, an in-memory database for SAP systems.

5.5.7   Scalability

Scalability indicates the ease in with which a system can be modified, or components can be added, to handle increasing load. A system whose performance improves after adding hardware, proportionally to the capacity added, is considered to scale well.

In general, there are two ways to increase the scalability of a system: vertical scaling and horizontal scaling. Vertical scaling (also known as scale up) means adding resources to a single component in a system, typically adding CPUs or memory to a server. While vertical scaling is easy to do, there is always a limit to how far a system can be expanded. There is only so much memory a system board supports and the number of CPUs is also limited.

An alternative to vertical scaling is horizontal scaling. Horizontal scaling (also known as scale out) means adding more components to the infrastructure, such as adding a new web server in a pool of web servers, or adding disks in a storage system. As a drawback, larger numbers of components also mean increased management complexity, as well as a more complex programming model and issues such as throughput and latency between nodes. But while horizontal scaling is more complex to implement than vertical scaling it pays off in the long run, as it is possible to scale up much more since there is a much higher upper limit.

Horizontal scalability works best when the system is partitioned. This way, parts of the system can scale independently of other parts of the system. Below is a typical example of a partitioned system.

Figure 17: Partitioned system

When more load is placed on the system, somewhere in the system a bottleneck will occur. At that point additional infrastructure components are added to cope with the load. In Figure 18, additional web servers are implemented.

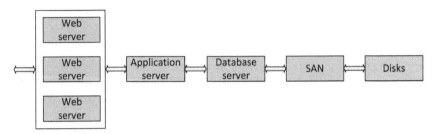

Figure 18: Added web servers

When needed, the system can be expanded further, either in the same tier, or on another tier, as shown in Figure 19.

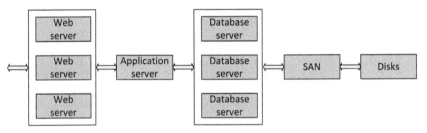

Figure 19: Added database servers

Doubling the number of components does not necessarily double the performance. Because of overhead (for instance, the extra scheduling needed in multiprocessor systems, or buffering and link state issues in network connections) doubling components usually only provides about 70% to 80% performance increase. Adding more components leads to even more diminishing returns.

5.5.8   Load balancing

To make optimal use of a horizontally scaled system, typically some form of load balancing is needed to spread the load over various machines.

Load balancing uses multiple components – usually servers – that perform identical tasks. Examples would be a web server farm, a mail server farm, or an FTP (File Transfer Protocol) server farm. A load balancer automatically redirects tasks to members in the server farm.

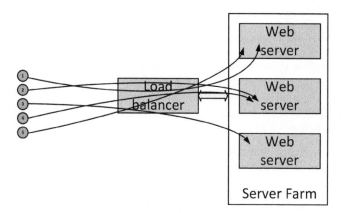

Figure 20: Load balancer

The load balancer checks the current load on each server in the farm and sends incoming requests to the least busy server. More advanced load balancers can spread the load based on the number of connections a server has, or the measured response time of a server. A load balancer also increases availability: when a server in the server farm is unavailable, the load balancer notices this and ensures no requests are sent to the unavailable server until it is back online again. Of course, the availability of the load balancer itself becomes very important in this setting and load balancers are typically setup in a failover configuration.

It is also important to realize that server load balancing introduces new challenges. The servers must be functionally identical to each other. For instance, each web server in a load balancing situation must be able to provide the same information. Furthermore, the application running on a load balanced system must be able to cope with the fact that each request can be handled by a different server. The application (or at least the load balanced parts of the application) must be stateless for this to work.

A typical example is a web application asking the user for a username and password. When the request is sent from web server number one, and the reply (the filled-in form) is sent to web server number two by the load balancer, the web application must be able to handle this. If this is not the case, the load balancer must be made more intelligent; being able to contain the states of the application.

Using for instance a session directory or affinity settings, the load balancing mechanism can arrange that a user's session is always connected to the same server. Of course, if a server in the server farm goes down, its per-session information becomes inaccessible, and sessions depending on it are lost.

In the network realm, load balancing is done to spread network load over multiple network connections. For instance, most network switches support port trunking (also known as Fast Ethernet Channel or bonding). In such a configuration, multiple Ethernet connections are combined to get a virtual Ethernet connection providing higher throughput. For instance, a network switch can trunk three 1 Gbit/s Ethernet connections to one (virtual) 3 Gbit/s connection. The load is then balanced over the three connections by the network switch.

In storage systems, multiple connections are also common. Not only for increasing the bandwidth of the connections, but also to increase availability.

5.5.9   High performance clusters

High performance clusters provide a vast amount of computing power by combining many computer systems. Usually a large number of cheap off the-shelf servers are used, connected by a high-speed network like gigabit Ethernet or InfiniBand. Such a combination of relatively small computers can create one large supercomputer.

High performance clusters are used for calculation-intensive systems like weather forecasts, geological, nuclear, or pharmaceutical research. The challenge is to have all systems doing useful calculations all of the time, without wasting too many resources and too much time communicating to other systems in the cluster.

On www.top500.org a list of the world's 500 most powerful computers is published. Most of these systems are in fact high performance clusters, based on a large number of smaller systems. Many of these systems run Linux. A well-known high performance open source project for Linux is Beowulf.

5.5.10 Grid Computing

A computer grid is a high performance cluster that consists of systems that are spread geographically. The limited bandwidth is the bottleneck when architecting grid systems. Therefore, grids can only be used for specific tasks.

The best known (and relatively old) example of a grid is the SETI@HOME project in which a large number of PCs of internet users are searching for extraterrestrial life. These types of grids utilize the unused computer time of PCs (for instance when the computer is displaying its screensaver). Tasks are distributed through the internet and are calculated on the idle PCs. When a piece of calculation is finished, the result is sent back via the internet and a new task is retrieved. A more serious example of a grid is a project that is searching for a cure for cancer and a project to perform the analyses of the human DNA. And the LHC Computing Grid consists of 140 computing centers in 35 countries that was designed by CERN to handle the significant volume of data produced by Large Hadron Collider (LHC) experiments.

Broker firms exist for commercial exploitation of grids. People and organizations can get paid for contributing computer time, and other organizations pay money to get computer time on the grid. This way organizations can have access to a virtual supercomputer for a relatively small amount of money, and just for the time they need it.

An important aspect of a grid is its security. PCs running calculations must be sufficiently secured against illegal use by third parties. Also, it should not be possible to alter data that is sent through the grid and the grid infrastructure must ensure the PCs calculate their tasks as expected. One way of handling this is to have each calculation executed twice, by two different PCs in the grid, and check for mismatches.

5.5.11 Design for use

Special performance measures must be taken when an infrastructure is to support performance critical applications. Here are some tips:

- In general, it must be known what the system will be used for. A large data warehouse needs a different infrastructure design than an online transaction processing system or a web application. Interactive systems have other performance characteristics and need different infrastructure solutions than batch systems or systems that must support high peak demands.

- In some cases, special products must be used for certain systems. Real-time operating systems, in-memory databases, or even specially designed file systems can be a solution for special performance sensitive systems.

- Most vendors of databases, web servers, operating systems, and storage or network solutions have standard implementation plans that are proven in practice. In general, try to follow the vendor's recommended implementation. It is also always a good idea to have the vendors check the design you created. Not only can they approve your design, they can also suggest improvements that you might not have considered. I have good experiences with having vendors check my designs!

- When possible, try to spread the load of the system over the available time. Maybe it is not such a great idea to have a complex batch job running at 09:00 AM when all people get to work and start-up their

PCs. Making certain that a backup job is not scheduled when some critical report is compiled is also a good idea.

- To increase performance, sometimes it is possible to move rarely used data from the main systems to other systems. Large databases are slower than small ones. Moving old data to a large historical database can speed up a smaller sized database.

5.5.12 Capacity management

To guarantee high performance of a system in the long term, capacity management must be implemented. With capacity management, the performance of the system is monitored on a continuous base, to ensure performance stays within acceptable limits. Trend analyses can be used to predict performance degradation before users start to notice it. This enables systems managers to take action to ensure sustained high performance. And regular communication with the business allows systems managers to anticipate on business changes (like forthcoming marketing campaigns).

6

SECURITY CONCEPTS

6.1 Introduction

Creating secure IT systems is more important than ever. Year after year IT gets more complex, more business processes rely on it, and attacks are getting more sophisticated.

In general, information systems security can be defined as the combination of availability, confidentiality, and integrity, focused on the recognition and resistance of attacks.

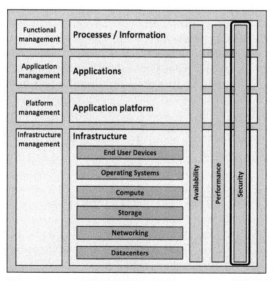

Figure 21: Security in the infrastructure model

Computer crimes use some form of gaining control over – in the context of this book – IT infrastructures. There are various reasons for committing crime against IT infrastructures:

- **Personal exposure and prestige**. In the past, the hacker community was very keen on getting personal or group exposure by hacking into a secured IT infrastructure. When hackers proved that they could enter a secured system and made it public, they gained respect from other hackers. While nowadays most hacking activity is done for other reasons, there are still large communities of hackers that enjoy the game.

- **Creating damage** to organizations to create bad publicity. For instance, by defacing websites, bringing down systems or websites, or making internal documents public.

- **Financial gain**. For instance, by holding data hostage and asking for ransom, stealing credit card data, changing account data in bank systems, or stealing passwords of customers and ordering goods on their behalf.

- **Terrorism**. The main purpose of terrorism is creating fear in a society. A well-planned attack targeted at certain computer systems, like the computer system that manages the water supply or a nuclear power plant, could result in chaos and fear amongst citizens.

- **Warfare**. Certain governments use hacking practices as acts of war. Since economies and societies today largely depend on the IT infrastructures, bringing important IT systems down in a certain country could cause the economy to collapse. Bringing down the internet access of a country for example means: no access to social media, no e-mails, no web shops, no stock trading, no search engines, etc.

In this chapter, security is explained from a risk management perspective. Security patterns like identity and access management, layered security, and cryptography are explained as well.

6.2 Risk management

Managing security is all about managing risks. If there are no risks, we don't need any security controls. The effort we put in securing the infrastructure should therefore be directly related to the risk at hand. Risk management is the process of determining an acceptable level of risk, assessing the current level of risk, taking steps to reduce risk to the acceptable level, and maintaining that level.

A risk list can be used to quantify risks. Such a list can be compiled in a Business Impact Analysis (BIA) workshop with all relevant stakeholders. A risk list contains the following parts:

- **Asset name**: the component that needs to be protected.

- **Vulnerability**: a weakness, process or physical exposure that makes the asset susceptible to exploits.

- **Exploit**: a way to use one or more vulnerabilities to attack an asset.

- **Probability**: an estimation of the likelihood of the occurrence of an exploit (how often do we estimate this will happen). For example:
  - o 5: Frequent
  - o 4: Likely
  - o 3: Occasional
  - o 2: Seldom
  - o 1: Unlikely

- **Impact**: the severity of the damage when the vulnerability is exploited. For example:
  - o 4: Catastrophic: Complete mission failure, death, bankruptcy
  - o 3: Critical: Major mission degradation, major system damage, exposure of sensitive data
  - o 2: Moderate: Minor mission degradation, minor system damage, exposure of data
  - o 1: Negligible: Some mission degradation

- **Risk** = Probability × Impact.

A typical risk list would look like this (P=Probability; I=Impact; R=Risk):

Asset	Vulnerability	Exploit	P	I	R
Laptop	Laptop gets stolen	Sensitive data on hard disk is exposed	5	3	15
Printer	Printer hard disk contains sensitive data	Repair man could swap hard disk and the hard disk could get on the market with sensitive data	1	3	3
Work-stations	Virus attack unknown to virus scanner	Unavailability or disclosure of data	2	3	6
SAN storage system	Data protection via LUN masking contains error	Data could get exposed to wrong server	1	2	2

Table 9: Example of part of a risk list

Controls mitigate these risks. For example, a control for the risk of laptops with sensitive data getting stolen is to encrypt the hard disk to make the data unreadable for anyone but the owner. Controls can be designed and implemented based on the identified severity of the risk in the risk list.

6.2.1   Risk response

For each risk, the risk response must be decided upon by senior management. There four risk responses:

- **Acceptance** of the risk – for instance, the risk could be accepted if the risk is very unlikely to happen *and* the costs of the damage imposed by exploitation of the risk is low *and* the cost of mitigating the risk is high.

- **Avoidance** of the risk – do not perform actions that impose risk (for instance, don't host your own website or e-mail server).

- **Transfer** of the risk – for instance transfer the risk to an insurance company (if it happens, the insurance company will pay for the damage).

- **Mitigation** of the risk and accepting the residual risk. Some ways of doing this are:

o   Design for minimum risk. Design the system to eliminate as much vulnerabilities as possible. This can for instance be done using source code analysis in software development and by running critical systems stand-alone instead of connected to other systems.

o   Incorporate safety devices. Reduce risk using devices like firewalls and hardened screened routers. These devices usually don't affect the probability, but reduce the severity of an exploit: an automobile seat belt doesn't prevent a collision, but reduces the severity of injuries. A firewall does not prevent attacks, but reduces the chance of an attacker connecting to sensitive parts of the network.

o   Provide warning devices. Warning devices may be used to detect an undesirable condition, and to alert staff, or take automated actions. An example is an Intrusion Detection System that alerts systems managers when a system is under attack (see section 8.6.2 for more information on IDSs).

o   Implement training and procedures. These can mitigate risks that are people-bound like social engineering attacks.

6.2.2   Exploits

Information can be stolen in many ways. Here are some of the more common exploits related to infrastructure:

- Key loggers can be maliciously installed on end user devices. They can send sensitive information like passwords to third parties.

- Network sniffers can show network packages that contain sensitive information or replay a logon sequence by which a hacker can successfully authenticate to an IT system.

- Data on backup tapes outside of the building can get into wrong hands.

- PCs or disks that are disposed of can get into the wrong hands.

- Corrupt or dissatisfied staff can copy information.

- End users are led to a malicious website that steals information (also known as phishing).

6.2.3   Security controls

CIA is short for the three core goals of security: Confidentiality, Integrity, and Availability of information. Security controls must address at least one of these.

- **Confidentiality** prevents the intentional or unintentional unauthorized disclosure of data.

- **Integrity** ensures that:

     o   No modifications to data are made by unauthorized staff or processes.

     o   Unauthorized modifications to data are not made by authorized staff or processes.

     o   Data is consistent.

- **Availability** ensures the reliable and timely access to data or IT resources by the appropriate staff.

While availability is considered part of security, for IT infrastructures availability is a non-functional attribute in its own right. In this chapter, availability is only considered where security is involved. Availability of IT infrastructure is explained in much more detail in chapter 4.

Information can be classified based on CIA levels, typically between one and five. An example of a set of CIA levels is given in the following tables.

Confidentiality Level	Description
1	Public information
2	Information for internal use only
3	Information for internal use by restricted group
4	Secret: reputational damage if information is made public
5	Top secret: damage to organization or society if information is made public

Table 10: Confidentiality levels

Integrity Level	Description
1	Integrity of information is of no importance
2	Errors in information are allowed
3	Only incidental errors in information are allowed
4	No errors are allowed, leads to reputational damage
5	No errors are allowed, leads to damage to organization or society

Table 11: Integrity levels

Availability Level	Description
1	No requirements on availability
2	Some unavailability is allowed during office hours
3	Some unavailability is allowed only outside of office hours
4	No unavailability is allowed, 24/7/365 availability, risk for reputational damage
5	No unavailability is allowed risk for damage to organization or society

Table 12: Availability levels

For each application or data set the CIA classification should be determined. For instance, for a mail server the CIA criteria can be classified as:

- C = 3: Information for internal use by restricted group.

- I = 3: Only incidental errors in information are allowed.

- A = 3: Some unavailability is allowed only outside of office hours.

Based on the CIA classification and the risk list, controls can be implemented to mitigate the identified risks. A sample list of CIA based infrastructure specific controls is provided next.

Control	C1	C2	C3	C4	C5		I1	I2	I3	I4	I5		A1	A2	A3	A4	A5
Standard security policy	X	X	X	X	X		X	X	X	X	X		X	X	X	X	X
Central archiving of documents		X	X	X	X												
User based password protection		X	X	X	X			X	X	X	X			X	X	X	X
Anti-virus measures		X	X	X	X			X	X	X	X			X	X	X	X
Classification of information			X	X	X				X	X	X						
Strong authentication			X	X	X				X	X	X				X	X	X
Restricted remote access			X	X	X				X	X	X				X	X	X
Internal firewalls			X	X	X				X	X	X				X	X	X
Screensaver lock when leaving workplace			X	X	X				X	X	X						
Webmail not allowed			X	X	X												
Logging of authentication and authorization requests			X	X	X				X	X	X				X	X	X
Secured datacenter and systems management room				X	X					X	X					X	X
Encrypted laptops				X	X												
Security key management				X	X												
No single sign on based on operating system credentials				X	X					X	X						
Two factor authentication				X	X					X	X						

Control	C 1	C 2	C 3	C 4	C 5		I 1	I 2	I 3	I 4	I 5		A 1	A 2	A 3	A 4	A 5
Specific passwords for critical systems				X	X					X	X					X	X
Encrypted network communication				X	X												
Digital signatures				X	X					X	X						
No remote access for third parties				X	X					X	X					X	X
Penetration hack-tests				X	X					X	X					X	X
IDS systems				X	X					X	X					X	X
Internet access limited to specific sites				X	X					X	X					X	X
Encrypted e-mail				X	X												
Printing only allowed in specific closed rooms				X	X												
Systems managers cannot read unencrypted data				X	X												
Testing only allowed with test data, not production data				X	X												
Double check on authorization requests (4 eyes principle)				X	X					X	X						
Staff screening					X						X						X
No remote access					X						X						X
Encryption based on specific hardware					X						X						
Network physically separated from					X						X						X

Control	C 1	C 2	C 3	C 4	C 5		I 1	I 2	I 3	I 4	I 5		A 1	A 2	A 3	A 4	A 5
other environments																	
No internet access					X					X							X
Redundant local systems																X	X
Systems management with on demand stand- by 24/7/365 support																X	X
Dual datacenter																	X
On-going and online backup																	X
Systems management with on-site 24/7/365 support																	X

Table 13: Example of CIA based controls

Using such a list makes it clear to all stakeholders (designers, project managers, systems managers, and auditors) how risks are controlled. Auditors can use the list to check if all controls are implemented, and project managers can use the list to calculate the effort needed to make a system secure. The shown list is just an example. In every situation, tailored controls must be considered.

6.2.4   Attack vectors

Attacks on the infrastructure can be executed using malicious code, denial of service attacks, social engineering, and phishing.

6.2.4.1 Malicious code

Malicious code are applications that, when activated, can cause network and server overload, steal data and passwords, or erase data.

Malicious software can come in multiple forms, such as viruses, Trojan horses, and worms.

- **Worms** are self-replicating programs that spread from one computer to another, leaving infections as they travel.

- A **virus** is a self-replicating program fragment that attaches itself to a program or file enabling it to spread from one computer to another, leaving infections as it travels.

- A **Trojan Horse** appears to be useful software but will actually do damage once installed or run on your computer. Those on the receiving end of a Trojan Horse are usually tricked into starting them because they appear to be receiving legitimate software or files from a legitimate source. Trojan horses can be used to deliver viruses or worms.

Users can be tempted to run an application, when it is sent to them in an irresistible format. The best-known case is that of the Anna Kournikova virus in 2001. It was designed to trick e-mail users into opening a mail message purportedly containing a picture of Anna Kournikova, a young and attractive tennis player at the time.

The Kournikova virus tempted users with the message: "Hi: Check This!" with what appeared to be a picture file labeled "AnnaKournikova.JPG.vbs".

But when a user clicked on it, the file did not display a picture of Anna Kournikova, but launched a viral Visual Basic Script that forwarded itself to everybody in the Microsoft Outlook address book of the victim.

Since more than 90% of all PCs run on Microsoft Windows, this operating system is a very attractive platform for malicious software programmers. Most malicious code can be detected and removed by virus scanners. In an ever-enduring battle between virus programmers and anti-virus programmers, virus programmers constantly try to find new vulnerabilities in the Windows operating system or in applications running on top of it like Internet Explorer or Microsoft Outlook. When such vulnerability is found, and malicious software is set free to exploit the vulnerability, anti-virus software companies try to detect the virus and warn users to stop the virus from spreading.

While most malware is still targeted at Microsoft Windows, Apple iOS, Linux and Google's Android are increasingly becoming attractive targets as well.

Detecting viruses is mostly done using a so-called virus signature– a unique string of bits that identifies a part of the virus. When a file contains this signature, it is assumed that the file is infected with the viral code.

To be pro-active, anti-virus detection software also uses techniques like heuristic scanning. Heuristic scanning looks for certain instructions or commands within a program or script that are not found in typical applications. This way, viruses can be detected even before their signature is known to the anti-virus software vendor.

6.2.4.2   Denial of service attack

A Denial of Service (DoS) attack is an attempt to overload an infrastructure to cause disruption of a service. This overload can lead to downtime of a system, disabling an organization to do its business.

To perform a DoS attack, an attacker fires off a large number of (often malformed) requests to a server reachable from the internet – typically a web server. Because of the high load the server needs to process, or because the requests fill up the request queues, the server either crashes, or performs so slow that in effect it is not functioning anymore.

Because usually one attacking computer alone has insufficient power or bandwidth available to bring down a server, most of the time a Distributed Denial of Service (DDoS) attack is used. In this case the attacker uses many computers to overload the server. Since nowadays attackers are often professionally organized, they use groups of computers that are infected by malicious code, called botnets, to perform an attack.

Some preventive measures to a DDos attack are:

- Split business and public resources so that in case of an attack the business processes are not effected

- Move all public facing resources to an external cloud provider

- Setup automatic scalability (auto scaling, auto deployment) using virtualization and cloud technology

- Limit bandwidth for certain traffic – for instance limit the bandwidth or the maximum number of calls per second on ports 53 (DNS) and 123 (NTP), as not much data is exchanged using these ports in normal situations

- Lower the Time to Live (TTL) of the DNS records to be able to reroute traffic to other servers when an attack occurs

- Setup monitoring for early detection on:

  o Traffic volume

  o Source and number of requests

    o   Transaction latency

There is not much that can be done about a DDoS attack when it occurs. When a DDoS attack actually occurs, some actions could be:

- Immediately inform your internet provider and ask for help

- Run a script to terminate all connections coming from the same source IP address if the number of connections is larger than ten

- Change to an alternative server (with another IP address)

- Scale-out the public facing environment under attack

- Reroute or drop suspected traffic

A worldwide distributed Content Distribution Network (CDN) can be used to route traffic to your website. When a DDoS attack occurs CDNs can take mitigating actions, for instance by limiting the requests coming from certain parts of the world.

More recent attacks show an alternative DDoS attack, called Low & Slow, where a website is used in a normal way (low key), but at an extremely slow pace. In this type of attack, legitimate data is sent to a webserver (using a HTTP POST command), but only one byte at a time, with a long wait time between the bytes.

The web server keeps on waiting for bytes, while keeping a channel occupied and busy. Eventually, this will drain application level resources, as a large number of connections are open, which effectively halts the service to other users.

This type of attack takes relatively few attacking machines. Low & Slow attacks are typically not detected by DDoS monitors, as they break no networking rules. It is therefore important to implement specific monitoring for this type of attack, checking application level resources.

6.2.4.3   Social engineering

In social engineering, social skills are used to manipulate people to obtain information, such as passwords or other sensitive information, which can be used in an attack.

All social engineering techniques are based on specific attributes of human decision-making, known as cognitive biases. In short: by nature, people want to help other people. If someone from the systems management department calls and asks for your help in solving a computer issue, most people tend to help the caller, without checking if he or she really is a systems manager. When the caller asks the user to click on a link that was sent via e-mail, most users will do so, installing malicious software without realizing it.

6.2.4.4 Phishing

Phishing is a technique of obtaining sensitive information. Typically, the phisher sends an e-mail that appears to come from a legitimate source, like a bank or credit card company, requesting "verification" of information. The e-mail usually contains a link to a fraudulent web page that seems legitimate — with the company logo and content on it — and has a form requesting everything from a home address to an ATM card's PIN.

6.2.4.5 Baiting

Baiting uses physical media, like an USB flash drive, and relies on the curiosity of people to find out what is on it.

For instance, an attacker leaves a malware infected USB flash drive in some location where it will be easily found, like the elevator or the parking lot of an organization it wants to attack. The device is given a legitimate looking label to increase the curiosity of anyone finding it. For instance, the organization logo could be put on the device, or a label called "Financial year results". The attacker hopes some employee picks up the device and brings it inside the organization. When the device is put into an organization owned PC, malicious software is installed automatically.

The effect of this kind of attack can largely be mitigated by switching off the "auto-run" feature on all organization PCs.

6.3 Security Patterns

6.3.1 Identity and Access Management

Identity and Access management (IAM) is the process of managing the identity of people and systems, and their permissions. The IAM process follows three steps:

- Users or systems claim who they are: *identification* – they provide their identity, typically their name.

- The claimed identity is checked: *authentication* – identities provide for instance a password, which is checked.

- Permissions are granted related to the identity and the groups it belongs to: *authorization* – identities are allowed into the system.

Most systems have a way to connect identities and their permissions. For instance, the kernel of an operating system owns an administration of users and a list of user rights that describes which identities are allowed to read, write, modify, or delete files. This is primary task of the kernel and the basis of security of the operating system – the so-called Trusted Computing Base (TCB).

IAM is not only used on the operating system level, but also in applications, databases, or other systems. Often these systems have their own stand-alone IAM system, which leads to users having to log in to each and every system they use.

With Single Sign-On (SSO), a user logs in once and is passed seamlessly, without an authentication prompt, to SSO enabled applications. SSO provides ease of use, but does not necessarily enhance security – when the login credentials of a user are known, an attacker gains access to all SSO enabled systems for that user. SSO is typically implemented using identity providing systems like LDAP, Kerberos, or Microsoft Active Directory. Users authenticate to these identity providers, and applications trust the identity provider, so they allow access when a user is authenticated.

Federated identity management extends SSO above the enterprise level, creating a trusted identity provider across organizations. In a federated system, participating organizations share identity attributes based on agreed-upon standards, facilitating authentication from other members of the federation and granting appropriate access to systems.

In the IAM process, users can be authenticated in one of three ways:

- Something you *know*, like a password or PIN

- Something you *have*, like a bank card, a token or a smartphone

- Something you *are*, like a fingerprint or an iris scan

Many systems only use a username/password combination (something you know), but more and more systems use multi-factor authentication, where at least two types of authentication are required. An example is an ATM machine, where both a bank card is needed (something you have) and a PIN (something you know).

Typically, identities are members of one or more groups (typically related to their roles in the organization) and, instead of granting permissions to individual identities, groups are granted permissions. And since groups can be nested (a group is member of another group), this so-called Role Based Access Control (RBAC) model is very powerful and used in almost all organizations.

6.3.2 Segregation of duties and least privilege

Segregation of duties (also known as separation of duties) assigns related sensitive tasks to different people or departments. The reasoning is that if no single person has total control of the system's security mechanisms, no single person can compromise the system.

This concept is related to the principle of least privilege. Least privilege means that users of a system should have the lowest level of privileges necessary to perform their work, and should only have them for the shortest length of time.

In many organizations, a systems manager has full control of the system's administration and security functions. In general, this is a bad idea. Security tasks should not automatically be given to the systems manager. In secure systems, multiple distinct administrative roles should be configured, like a security manager, a systems manager, and a super user.

The security manager, systems manager, and super user may not necessarily be different people (but this would be preferred of course). But whenever for instance a systems manager takes the role of the security manager, this role change is controlled, logged, and audited. While it may be cumbersome for the person to switch from one role to another, the roles are functionally different and must be executed as such in order to maintain a high level of security.

In addition, a two-man control policy can be applied, in which two systems managers must review and approve each other's work. The purpose of two-man control is to minimize fraud or mistakes in highly sensitive or high-risk transactions. With two-man control, two systems managers are needed to complete every security sensitive task.

6.3.3 Layered security

A layered security strategy is a good practice to enhance the overall IT security. The essence of layered security (also known as a Defense-In-Depth strategy) is to implement security measures in various parts of the IT infrastructure. This approach is comparable with physical security.

If a burglar wants to steal money from your house, he has to climb over the fence in the garden, then he has to get through a closed front door with locks, then he has to find the safe with the money, he has to break into the safe, get the money, and leave the premise. All of this must be done without being seen or heard; he must not be noticed by anyone during all of these steps.

It is obvious why this layered security works so well:

- Many barriers must be crossed (fence, door, safe).

- Opening every barrier takes different technical skills (climbing over the fence, lock picking a door with a mechanical lock, opening a safe with a digital lock).

- The burglar is slowed down by every barrier he tempts to cross, which increases the possibility of detection.

- The burglar doesn't know in advance how many barriers he has to cross, how much time each barrier takes, and which knowledge is needed for every barrier.

- The chance of getting caught is present in every step.

- When one barrier is crossed, the security of all other barriers is still intact.

In IT infrastructure, instead of having one big firewall and have all your security depend on it, it is better to implement several layers of security. Preferably these layers make use of different technologies, which makes it harder for hackers to break through all barriers; they will need a lot of knowledge for each step.

Each layer can be integrated with an Intrusion Detection System (IDS – see section 8.6.2) or some other system that detects break-ins, which increases the chance of getting caught. On top of this, more layers introduce uncertainty for the hacker: it is unknown many barriers must be passed to get to the data, and how long will this take, leading to demotivation. And if one layer is passed unnoticed, or if one security layer contains a vulnerability, the total security is still intact, albeit with less layers.

A disadvantage of implementing layered security is that it increases the complexity of the system. Every security layer must be managed, and systems managers must have knowledge about all used technologies.

6.3.4 Cryptography

Cryptography is the practice of hiding information using encryption and decryption techniques. Encryption is the conversion of information from a readable state to apparent random data. Only the receiver has the ability to decrypt this data, transforming it back to the original information.

A cipher is a pair of algorithms that implements the encryption and decryption process. The operation of a cipher is controlled by a key. The key is a secret only known by the sender and receiver, much like the key of a mechanical lock.

Two types of ciphers exist: block ciphers and stream ciphers. A block cipher takes as input a block of plaintext and a key, and outputs a block of cipher text. Several block-encryption systems have been developed. The Data Encryption Standard (DES) and the Advanced Encryption Standard (AES) are the most popular block cipher designs. Despite its deprecation as an official standard, DES (especially its still-approved and much more secure triple-DES variant) remains quite popular. It is used across a wide range of applications, from ATM machine data encryption to e-mail privacy and secure remote access.

Stream ciphers create an arbitrarily long stream of key material, which is combined with the plaintext bit-by-bit or character-by-character. Stream ciphers are used when data is in transit using a network. In a stream cipher, the output stream is created based on a hidden internal state which changes as the cipher operates. That internal state is initially set up using a secret key. RC4 is a widely-used stream cipher.

6.3.4.1 Symmetric key encryption

Symmetric key encryption is an encryption method where both the sender and receiver share the same key.

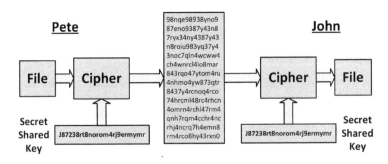

Figure 22: Symmetric key encryption

In Figure 22, Pete sends a file to John and encrypts it before sending using a cipher and a secret shared key. Upon receiving the file, John's cipher decrypts the data stream using the same key, leading to the original file. Both ciphers use the same secret shared key, only known by Pete and John.

A significant disadvantage of symmetric key encryption is the key management necessary to use them securely. *Each pair* of communicating parties must share a *different key*. The number of keys required or a group of N systems is $N \times \frac{N-1}{2}$. With three systems, this leads to $3 \times \frac{3-1}{2} = 3$ keys. With four systems, this leads to $4 \times \frac{4-1}{2} = 6$ keys. Table 14 shows the number of keys needed with an increasing number of systems.

Number of systems	Number of keys
2	1
3	3
4	6
5	10
6	15
7	21
8	28
9	36
10	45

Table 14: Number of keys needed for symmetric key encryption

This effect very quickly requires complex key management schemes to keep them all aligned, correct, and secret.

The difficulty of securely establishing a secret key between two communicating parties, when a secure channel does not already exist between them, also presents a chicken-and-egg problem.

6.3.4.2 Asymmetric key encryption

In asymmetric key cryptography, two different but mathematically related keys are used: a public key and a private key. The public key may be freely distributed and is for instance published on the organization's website. Its paired private key must remain secret by the organization.

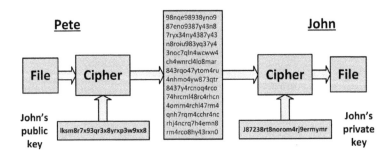

Figure 23: Asymmetric key encryption

In Figure 23, Pete sends a file to John and encrypts it before sending using a cipher and *John's* public key. The encrypted file can only be decrypted using John's private key (which must be kept a secret to everyone but John). Upon receiving the file, John's cipher decrypts the data using his private key, leading to the original file.

When John wants to send a file to Pete, Pete's public and private keys are used.

Because public key cryptography is a very slow process (about 1000 to 10,000 times slower than symmetric key encryption), it is mostly used to setup a channel between two parties, to safely exchange a new, temporary symmetric key, solving the chicken-and-egg problem and key management mentioned in the previous section. After exchanging symmetric keys, the rest of the communication is done using much faster symmetric key encryption.

Here is how it works:

- Pete creates a random secret key and encrypts it using the public key from John.

- The encrypted secret key is sent to John using an open channel (like the internet).

- John is the only party that can decrypt the message, because he has the private key that is related to the public key. John decrypts the message and now knows the secret key.

- Pete and John start communicating using symmetric key encryption, using the exchanged secret key.

- When the communication is finished, the shared key is no longer valid and is deleted.

Diffie–Hellman and RSA algorithms are the most widely used algorithms for public key encryption.

6.3.4.3 Hash functions and digital signatures

Hash functions take some piece of data, and output a short, fixed length text string (the hash) that is unique for that piece of data and which can be used to validate the integrity of the data.

It is practically impossible to find two pieces of data that produce the same hash. If the hash of a piece of data is known, and the hash is recalculated later and it matches the original hash, the data must be unaltered. An example:

The input string "hello world" produces the following MD5 hash:

```
5eb63bbbe01eeed093cb22bb8f5acdc3
```

The input string "hallo world" produces the following MD5 hash:

```
5fd591a948dc76dd731f8998e19c773a
```

While only one letter was changed, the hash is completely different.

The length of this hash will not grow, even if the input for the hash function is the entire text of this book, yet it will be nearly impossible to find another input that produces the exact same hash output.

MD5 is a very popular hash function. SHA1 and SHA512 are also widely used and more secure than MD5.

To create a digital signature, a hash is created of some text (like an e-mail) and encrypted with the private key of the sender. The receiver decrypts the hash key using the sender's public key. The receiver also calculates the hash of the text and compares it with the decrypted hash to ensure the text wasn't tampered with. Since the hash was encrypted using a private key, it is guaranteed that the hash was created by the owner of the private key – the only person that could have created the encrypted hash.

Digital signatures are central to the operation of public key infrastructures and many network security schemes (like SSL/TLS and many VPNs).

6.3.4.4 Cryptographic attacks

It is common knowledge that every encryption method can be broken. Yet this is not entirely true. It is scientifically proven that a so-called one-time pad cipher is unbreakable, provided the key material is truly random, never reused, kept secret from all possible attackers, and of equal or greater length than the message. But it is very impractical, as the key must be exchanged between sender and receiver in a safe way, and the key has the same length as the data to be transferred. So, you might as well exchange the data in a safe way instead of the key.

Most ciphers, apart from the one-time pad, can be broken given enough computational effort by what is known as a brute force attack. A brute force attack consists of systematically checking all possible keys until the correct key is found. The amount of effort needed, however, is usually exponentially dependent on the size of the key. Effective security could be achieved if it is proven that no efficient method (as opposed to the time consuming brute force method) can be found to break the cipher.

Most successful attacks are based on flaws in the implementation of an encryption cipher. It is extremely difficult to create a flawless cipher and it is therefore absolutely not recommended to create your own. To ensure a cipher is flawless, the source code is usually open source and thus open to inspection to everyone. Experience shows that open source ciphers are the most secure ones, while closed source ciphers tend to be breakable.

PART III
–
ARCHITECTURE BUILDING BLOCKS

DATACENTERS

7.1   Introduction

Most IT infrastructure hardware, except for end user devices, are hosted in datacenters. A datacenter provides power supply, cooling, fire prevention and detection, equipment racks, and other facilities needed to host the installed infrastructure components.

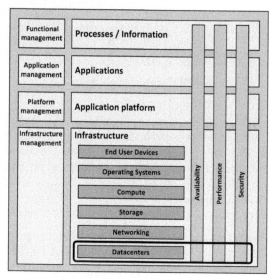

Figure 24: Datacenters in the infrastructure model

Early datacenters (or computer rooms as they were called at the time) were designed and built for large mainframe systems. In those days, a single mainframe, together with its peripheral systems like punch card readers and tape units easily filled up a fairly large computer room.

Picture 5: Computer room in 1962

Individual terminals of all end users in the offices were connected directly to the mainframe, leading to large cable bundles in the computer room. Apart from these terminal cables, power cables were installed to connect power to all equipment and data connection cables to connect the peripheral equipment with the communications units of the mainframe. To store all of these cables, computer rooms were equipped with a raised floor (also known as a computer floor). Cables were installed in cable trays underneath this raised floor.

Since the mainframe and peripheral equipment used to run quite hot, they were cooled using water cooling systems. Water pipes used for this water cooling were installed under the raised floor as well. Many datacenters today still use raised floors for cabling and cooling purposes (although not using water cooling anymore).

Because most peripheral equipment was installed in the computer room, operators had to be present in the computer room most of the time. They had to perform tasks like loading punch card decks, replacing paper in printers, switching tapes in tape units, or collecting printed paper.

With the emergence of smaller midrange and x86 based systems, datacenters got equipped with standardized 19" racks that could house servers, storage devices, and network equipment. These racks were installed in rows forming corridors between them.

Picture 6: Computer racks[15]

More flexible air cooling replaced the traditional water cooling and sophisticated fire prevention, detection and extinguishing systems were installed. Because almost all work on the servers could be done without touching the physical equipment, lights-out datacenters were introduced, where during normal operations no people are needed inside the datacenter, and the lights could thus be switched off.

The pace of innovation in datacenters is increasing. There has been more innovation in the last ten years than in the previous decades. This innovation is driven by cloud service providers and large scale datacenters running internet applications like search engines, video streaming, and social media.

Very large datacenters today contain shipping containers packed with thousands of servers each. When repairs or upgrades are needed, entire containers are replaced (rather than repairing individual servers).

7.2   Datacenter building blocks

7.2.1   Datacenter categories

A datacenter can occupy one room in a building, one or more floors, or an entire building. Below are four typical datacenter categories.

- **Sub Equipment Room (SER)** – a SER is also known as a patch closet. They contain patch panels for connections to wall outlets in offices and some small equipment like network switches.

- **Main Equipment Room (MER)** – a MER is a small datacenter in the organization's subsidiaries or buildings.

- **Organization owned datacenter** – a datacenter that contains all central IT equipment for the organization. An organization can have multiple datacenters, often with failover and fallback capabilities.

- **Multi-tenant datacenter** – this datacenter category is used by service providers that provide services for multiple other organizations. These datacenters are typically the largest.

If the datacenter is used for one organization only, it makes sense to install the datacenter inside one of the office buildings. But when the datacenter is used by multiple organizations, like in case of an internet service provider, choosing a location of the datacenter is more difficult.

7.2.2   Location of the datacenter

Finding a good location to build a datacenter can be a nontrivial task. Many variables should be considered to determine where a datacenter could be installed.

Below is a checklist that can be used as guidance when choosing a location for a datacenter:

- Environment
  - Is enough space available to expand the datacenter in the future? The initial datacenter should be designed with enough free space and spare capacity in utilities to allow for growth.
  - Is the location vulnerable to flooding? Some countries are below sea level, are in a vulnerable delta, or are close to a river. In that case make sure the datacenter is not located at

the ground floor or (worse) the basement, but for instance on the third floor.

In 2015, outside of the Amsterdam AMC hospital a large water supply pipe broke. The water flooded not only the ground floor of the hospital, but also the basement, that hosted steam systems needed to sterilize the hospital's tools. All patients in the hospital were evacuated immediately and the hospital was closed for two weeks, leading to multi-million dollar damages.

Later, the hospital management acknowledged that putting critical systems in the basement was a design flaw in the building's architecture.

- o Is the datacenter located in a hurricane prone area?

- o What is the chance of an earthquake?

- o What is the climate like? Datacenter cooling can be easier accomplished and is much cheaper in places with a low ambient temperature with low temperature fluctuations.

- o Is the datacenter close to possible external hazards like fireworks storage, a waste dump, or a chemical plant?

- o What is the crime rate? Are there many burglaries in the neighborhood? What about vandalism or the possibility of terrorism?

- o Is the datacenter near an airport (chance of crashing airplanes)?

- o Is the datacenter near an area that is likely to be closed because of unforeseen circumstances (like a car crash on a nearby highway, a forest fire, a military location, or a nuclear plant)?

- o Is the location close to the home or office of maintenance staff, systems managers, and external expertise?

- o Can the datacenter be reached easily in case of emergencies?

- o Are hospitals, police, and fire fighters located in the vicinity?

- Visibility

    - o Is the location of the datacenter included in public maps (like http://www.datacentermap.com)?

- o Does the building have windows? Windows are not preferred as they are easy to break into the building.

- o Are markings on the building showing that this building contains a datacenter?

- Utilities

  - o Is it possible to have two independent power providers and internet providers?

  - o Can cabling routes to the building be determined? Is it possible to have double power and data connections leave the building from two different places?

  - o Can cabling routes inside the building be determined in a flexible way? Are there multiple paths available to the patch panels, floors, and end users?

  - o Is the datacenter located in a shared building? What if the building must be evacuated? What if the power must be shut down due to maintenance activities performed by another user of the building?

  - o Is enough power available to supply the datacenter? How reliable is the power supply?

  - o Is cheap power available? Can the datacenter use renewable energy like wind or water generated power?

  - o What is the available bandwidth of the external data connections? Is the datacenter close to an internet exchange point? Are dark fiber connections possible? How reliable are the data connections?

- Foreign countries

  - o Can the country be reached at all times?

  - o Is the country politically stable? Are there specific laws and regulations you need to adhere to or be aware of?

  - o Does the country have a high level of corruption? How reliable is the staff?

  - o What is the legal status of the data and the datacenter itself?

7.2.3   Physical structure

The physical structure of a datacenter includes floors, wall, windows, doors, and water and gas pipes. These components, together with the layout of the rooms around the actual computer room, are discussed in this section.

7.2.3.1   Floors

In datacenters, the floor is quite important, mostly because of the weight of the installed equipment. In a typical datacenter, the floor must be able to carry 1500 to 2000 kg/m^2. For instance, one fully filled 19" computer rack weighs up to 700 kg. The footprint of a rack is about 60x100 cm, leading to a floor load of 1166 kg/m^2. By comparison, in office buildings typically the floor can carry approximately 500 kg/m^2.

Many datacenters have raised floors. Raised floors consist of a metal framework carrying removable floor tiles. These tiles are usually 60×60 cm in size. Tiles can be lifted individually to reach cables installed under the raised floor. To lift the tiles, a "floor puller" or "tile lifter" is used, as shown below.

Picture 7: Removable tiles in a raised floor

Raised floors are typically installed at heights between 40 cm and 120 cm. Vents in the raised floor provide cool air flow to the racks placed on the floor. Under the raised floor, data and power cables are installed (usually in cable trays).

It is important to keep data cables and power cables separated from each other, as electrical current flowing through the power cables can interfere with data being sent through the data cables. A rule of thumb is to keep one phase electricity and data 20 cm apart from data cables, and 3 phase power and data cables 60 cm apart.

Not all datacenters use raised floors anymore, since raised floors have the following disadvantages:

- Raised floors are expensive.

- The total available height in the datacenter is decreased, which could lead to regulation problems and problems installing large equipment.

- The maximum floor load is limited.

- Doors and equipment loading slopes are hard to install due to the difference in floor height.

- Under the raised floor fire, for instance caused by a short circuit, could easily spread through the entire datacenter.

Instead of installing cables under raised floors, overhead cable trays can be used.

In either situation, cable trays can be installed with several layers. For instance, the bottom layer can be used for data copper UTP cables, the middle layer for fiber cables, and the top layer for power cables.

7.2.3.2 Walls, windows, and doors

Because of fire safety and physical intrusion prevention, walls should reach from the floor to the building's ceiling. Walls should have an adequate fire rating to serve as a physical firewall.

Windows in the outside of the building, facing the computer room, are not desirable in a datacenter. If they are present however, they must be translucent and shatterproof, and it must be impossible to open them.

Doors in the datacenter must resist forced entry and have a fire rating equal to the walls. Emergency exits must be clearly marked, monitored, and alarmed. Doors should be large enough to have equipment brought in, with a minimal width of 1 m and a minimal height of 2.10 m.

7.2.3.3   Water and gas pipes

When the datacenter is part of a larger building, water or gas pipes may have been installed under the floor, in the walls, or (even worse) above the ceiling of the datacenter. At multiple occasions, I have seen leakage from water pipes in the ceiling of a datacenter that led to damage of equipment. Datacenter operators should know where the shutoff valves are to water or gas pipes in the building.

7.2.3.4   Layout of the datacenter

Figure 25 shows a possible layout of a datacenter. Of course, this is just an example, in practice many considerations lead to an optimal layout for any specific environment.

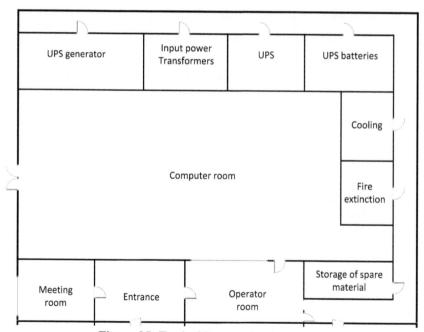

Figure 25: Typical layout of a datacenter

In this example, separate rooms are located around the main computer room providing optimal use of the available space. The datacenter contains:

- **Computer room** – This is where the actual IT infrastructure components like servers, storage, and network equipment are installed.

- **UPS generator** – A diesel generator providing electrical power in case the utility power input fails. The fuel for the generator should be kept outside of the building or in an isolated room, but also close by and secured.

- **Input Power Transformers** – Input transformers from the power utility company.

- **UPS** – The Uninterruptable Power Supply system (see section 7.2.4.2).

- **UPS batteries** – A set of batteries providing short term power used in the system.

- **Cooling** – The cooling systems.

- **Fire extinction** – Fire extinction systems.

- **Operator room** – Room for the datacenter operators. This room has a large window looking into the computer room to spot unusual activity.

- **Storage room for spare material** – Spare hardware and other equipment like tools and boxes can be stored here.

- **Entrance** – Entrance room to the other rooms. This entrance does not have windows.

- **Meeting room** – For staff meetings and visitor meetings. This room has a window to allow direct sunlight, but this window must be secured (shatter proof).

In this example, the datacenter provides three entries:

- One main entry in the entrance room.

- One entry (opposite of the storage room) for utilities maintenance staff (these people cannot enter or pass the computer room).

- One entry directly into the computer room for loading of equipment This entry also serves as an (additional) fire escape.

All entries are secured and can only be opened upon request from inside the building. Camera surveillance (CCTV) is used to monitor activity at all doors.

7.2.4 Power supply

Energy usage is a key issue for datacenters. Power drawn by datacenters ranges from a few kilowatts (kW) for one rack of servers in a small server room, to dozens of megawatts (MW) for large facilities.

7.2.4.1 Power density

The amount of power available in a datacenter is typically expressed as the number of kilowatts (or more accurate: kVA – 1000 * Volt * Ampere) per m^2. A value of between 2 and 6 kW/m^2 is typical in a normal density datacenter. One 19" rack, including its space around it, typically occupies approximately 1 m^2.

For example, a HP DL380 server uses 250W power, which means that only between 8 and 24 servers can be placed in one 19" rack when 2 to 6 kW/m^2 is available, even if the rack could physically hold 40 servers. This means in practice that most server racks cannot be fully equipped.

In a high-density datacenter, the power supply is between 10 and 20 kW/m^2. This allows racks to be filled with approximately 40 to 80 servers.

Blade server enclosures (see section 10.2.1) can hold even more servers in one rack, and because blade servers each can have multiple multi-core CPUs, they could use much more power than a classical rack mounted server as well. This is not only needs to be addressed when designing the power supply and distribution of power to the racks, but also when designing the cooling system!

7.2.4.2 Uninterruptable Power Supply (UPS)

Several types of power issues can occur in the utility power supply, possibly leading to downtime or damage to equipment in the datacenter if not handled properly. Some examples are:

- **Blackout** - A total loss of power (also known as a power failure), which can have many causes, like human errors, lightning strikes or damaged cables as a result of construction work of digging.

- **Surge** - A period of high-voltage (also known as a swell), typically caused due to switching off heavy equipment.

- **Spike** - Instantaneous jumps in voltage, typically caused by lightning strikes.

- **Brownout** - A voltage drop (also known as a sag), usually for a few seconds, typically caused by an overload in the electrical grid caused by switching on heavy equipment.

- **Waveform issues** - Frequency variations or waveform distortion change the shape or frequency of the 50/60Hz AC power, sometimes caused by switching power supplies or rectifier issues in AC/AC converters.

An Uninterruptable Power Supply (UPS) provides high quality electrical power that is independent of the utility power supply. A UPS typically includes filters to reduce the effect of spikes and other power issues. It also provides emergency power to the datacenter in case the utility power supply fails.

A UPS installation consists of filters, a diesel power generator, and a set of batteries or a flywheel system. The batteries or flywheel temporarily power the datacenter during the startup time of the power generator or during short power outages.

7.2.4.3   Power generators

A power generator can power the datacenter for an indefinite period of time (as long as diesel fuel is available), until the utility power supply is restored. A typical power generator can provide between 0.5 and 2 MW of power.

Picture 8: 2 MW diesel generator[16]

Note that diesel cannot be stored forever. After about a year, unused diesel loses some of its calorific value. This means that more diesel fuel is needed by the generator in order to provide the needed electrical power. When diesel is stored for many years, chances are that the diesel generator will not start at all.

A fuel re-circulation/filtration system can be installed to overcome this problem. Regular fuel testing to monitor fuel integrity is a good practice.

Periodically adding fuel stabilizer is another common practice for diesel powered generators.

It is good practice to use the generator regularly and to refill the diesel tanks every two months or so. Because the diesel generator must be tested regularly anyway, I recommend using the testing period for three reasons:

- Test the working of the generator (does it start? can it provide power to the datacenter?).

- Use up "old" diesel to empty the tanks and refill them with new diesel.

- Use the generated power to run the datacenter when a peak load is expected – for instance on Monday morning. At that time the generator can be used to power the datacenter while the office buildings get power from the utility provider. This can prevent costly power peaks from the utility power net leading to reduced cost.

7.2.4.4   Battery powered UPS systems

A battery powered UPS is most common today. In a typical setup, these batteries last about 5 to 15 minutes before they get discharged too much. During this period the power generator must be started and be online in order to take over power supply to the datacenter.

Picture 9: UPS battery array[17]

There are three types of battery powered UPSs:

- **Standby UPS systems** (also known as off-line systems) are typically used in small setups (a few workstations or servers). Incoming utility power is fed to the IT systems and monitored for interruptions. In case of a power interruption, the UPS system provides AC power from a battery using an electronic inverter circuit.

- **Line interactive UPS systems** use a transformer between the utility power and the IT equipment that works as a filter for many of the power issues (like spikes or waveform issues). Like the Standby UPS systems, in case of a power interruption, the UPS system provides AC power from a battery using an electronic inverter circuit.

- **Double conversion UPS systems** convert the AC utility power to DC power and then back to high quality AC power again using an inverter. This way the AC power to the IT systems is always generated locally and is free of most of the power issues. In case of a power interruption, the UPS system uses DC power from a battery instead of the converted DC power from the utility provider. This eliminates (even brief) switch-over moments if the power fails and avoids AC power phase changes.

A battery powered UPS used in a datacenter typically uses a large set of batteries, usually racks full of them. As an alternative, several small battery-powered UPSs can be installed near the servers in the racks.

7.2.4.5   Flywheel UPS systems

Flywheel UPS systems, also known as rotary UPS systems, are relatively new, although the flywheel technology itself is already decades old. Flywheels use kinetic energy stored in a rotating heavy wheel to drive a generator. A motor, which uses electric current from the utility grid to provide energy to rotate the flywheel, spins constantly to maintain a ready source of kinetic energy. A generator then converts the kinetic energy of the flywheel into electricity. To make this system energy efficient the mechanical friction of the flywheel is minimized. Magnetic bearings are used and the flywheel is placed in a vacuum. Flywheels rotate at a speed of between 5,000 and 55,000 rotations per minute.

Flywheels provide power for about 10 to 20 seconds before they get slowed down too much. In this time frame the power generator must be started and brought online. The 10 to 20 seconds is much less than the 5 to 15 minutes available in battery powered UPSs. It is sufficient time, however, to automatically start a generator. But when 10 to 20 seconds is not considered enough, multiple flywheels can be used to extend the failover period.

The flywheel can also be mechanically connected to the diesel generator, acting as startup for the generator, replacing the electric starter motor.

7.2.4.6   UPS maintenance

UPS systems need regular maintenance and attention.

- Batteries are the weakest link in a UPS system and must be replaced at regular intervals, typically every three to five years. Battery capacity can get less over time, especially when they are charged and discharged frequently.

- Flywheels last for 30 years or more, but do need regular maintenance such as bearing replacement.

- Diesel power generators should be preheated (so they can start immediately when needed) and tested regularly (preferably monthly) to ensure proper function and emergency readiness.

For maintenance activities, the UPS should provide a maintenance bypass circuit. Remember: during maintenance, the datacenter is completely dependent on the utility power supply unless multiple UPS systems are used!

7.2.4.7 Power distribution

A power distribution unit (PDU, also known as a Mains Distribution Unit – MDU) is a device with multiple power outlets that distributes power to equipment located in the datacenter. Two types of PDUs exist:

- Large floor mounted PDUs which take main feeds (usually 3 phase power) and distribute it into multiple smaller feeds to computer racks.

- Power Strips, sometimes called Rack-PDUs that feed equipment in racks.

Most servers, network switches, and other infrastructure components can be equipped with two power supplies for redundancy. For availability reasons at least two power strips are needed to power equipment in a rack, each feeding one of the two power supplies in the equipment.

Connecting both power strips to the same UPS will make the UPS a single point of failure. To avoid this, two completely separated UPS systems can be used, but this can be costly. A more cost-effective option is to connect one power supply to the UPS and the other to the utility power, like in Figure 26.

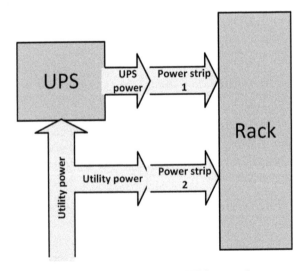

Figure 26: Connecting UPS to rack

Connected this way, two separate distribution paths are created. If the utility power fails, the equipment is still powered by the UPS. If the utility power is available, but the UPS fails (a situation I have seen occur more than once), the equipment keeps running on utility power. This practice also allows maintenance of the UPS during which the datacenter runs on utility power only (but for a limited amount of time of course).

7.2.5   Cooling

More than 90% of all power used by IT infrastructure components is converted into heat. This means that in a 1 MW datacenter, 900 kW of heat is produced, all of which has to be dissipated by a cooling system.

In general, there are two types of cooling systems: CRAC and CRAH. Computer Room Air Conditioners (CRAC) are refrigerant-based units connected to outside condensing units. A Computer Room Air Handler (CRAH) is chilled water based and connected to outside chillers. A chiller produces chilled water via a refrigeration process.

Both CRAC and CRAH units move air through the datacenter via a fan system. They deliver cool air to the racks and exhaust fans remove hot air from the datacenter to the CRAC or CRAH. Most CRAC and CRAH systems include a humidifier that ensures humidity levels are within a specific range.

The efficiency of a cooling system is specified in one of three metrics:

- **EER** - Energy Efficiency Ratio. This is the measure of efficiency at maximum air conditioning load.
  EER is the ratio between output cooling in BTU (British Thermal Unit – a unit of energy equal to about 1,055 joules) per hour and the electric energy input in Watts at a given operating point. For example, if a cooling system provides 20,000 BTU cooling capacity and consumes 1,500 watts of electricity, its EER is $\frac{20,000}{1,500} = 13.3$.

- **SEER** - Seasonal Energy Efficiency Ratio.
  SEER is exactly the same as EER, but seasonal data is used for the measurement; the time of year the cooling system is used most (typically in the summer). The SEER is the output cooling in BTU during summer time divided by the total electric energy input in watt-hours in that period.

- **COP** - Coefficient Of Performance.
  This is the ratio between cooling load in kW and the electric energy input in kW. Normal values are between 3 and 10. For example, to cool 150 kW with a cooling system with a COP of 3.2, the cooling system uses 47 kW of electricity.

7.2.5.1   Operating temperatures

The air temperature in the datacenter usually ranges from 18 degrees to 27 degrees Celsius. The ASHRAE (American Society of Heating, Refrigerating and Air-conditioning Engineers) provides recommendations[18] for air temperature and humidity levels in a datacenter. While a few years ago, the temperature in datacenters was kept as low as 18 degrees Celsius to avoid hotspots in racks and inside infrastructure components, today more efficient cooling allows datacenters to operate at much higher temperatures (up to 27 degrees Celsius). Using higher temperatures saves cooling capacity and power. Raising the temperature in a datacenter with one degree Celsius lowers the cost for cooling by approximately 5%!

But infrastructure components have maximum operating temperatures. If their temperature gets too high, the component gets damaged or is switched off automatically. For instance, some servers will shut themselves down at an air inlet temperature of 40 degrees Celsius to protect the CPU(s) inside the server that might be as warm as 80 degrees Celsius at that moment.

7.2.5.2   Airflow

There are several ways to provide cool air to equipment. An optimized air flow eliminates hot spots in racks and components as much as possible without having to cool the air in the datacenter too much.

One way of providing a good air flow is to have cold air blown through the raised floor using perforated tiles, crating cold isles. The cold air is sucked in by the fans in the components, resulting in air flowing horizontally through the racks. The warm air from the components leaves the racks at the opposite side where it gets sucked back into the cooling unit, as shown in Figure 27.

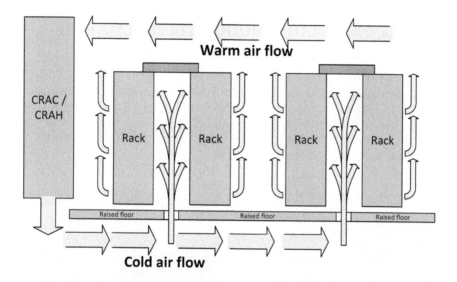

Figure 27: Air flow example

An alternative is to blow air horizontally through each individual rack using one cooling unit per rack. This makes the air flow more precise, but is also more expensive, as more cooling units are needed. The advantage is that this solution is more scalable (an extra rack means an extra cooling unit) and can provide more cooling capacity to high density racks.

7.2.5.3 Humidity and dust

The humidity of the air in a datacenter is critical for the IT infrastructure components. When air is too humid, corrosion of metal parts can occur, especially in printed circuit boards, and tape and disk drives can get mechanical problems. When the air is too dry Electro Static Discharge (ESD) up to thousands of volts can cause damage to integrated circuits on circuit boards. Therefore, the relative air humidity in a datacenter should between 40% and 60%.

Finally, the number of dust particles in a datacenter should be minimized. Not allowing people (visitors) in the datacenter is a good way to avoid dust. And when people need to get in for some reason they should wear dust-free clothing (like white coats) and protective sleeves around their shoes.

7.2.6 Fire prevention, detection, and suppression

Fire is one of the main enemies of a datacenter. Because of the large density of equipment and cables, a short circuit in a cable, or a defect in the equipment can easily lead to fire. And because of the air flow in the datacenter and the frequent use of raised floors fires can spread around very quickly. Even if a fire starts outside of the datacenter's computer room, the smoke of such a fire could damage equipment in the datacenter.

> *I know of situations where the fire was not in the computer room, but in an office in the same building.*
>
> *The smoke was not entering the datacenter at all, but the fire fighters demanded to have the power of the entire building (including the datacenter's UPS) shut down before they could start extinguishing the fire.*

Smoke should be taken seriously as well. Even if there is no fire breakout, smoke exposure alone can cause extensive damage to the electronic equipment within the datacenter.

Suppressing fire in a datacenter consists of four levels:

- **Fire prevention** – measures to avoid a fire in the first place.

- **Passive fire protection** – measures to limit the exposure of the fire once it has started.

- **Fire detection systems** – systems to detect smoke and fire.

- **Fire suppression systems** – systems to extinguish the fire once it is detected.

Each of the levels above should be taken care of. They are described in more detail below.

7.2.6.1 Fire prevention

The best way to avoid fire damage is to ensure fires don't start at all. Respecting regulations and implementing fire prevention guidelines is of course a good practice. In datacenters, the most common source of fires is overheating of equipment or cables. Avoiding "cable spaghetti" is a very useful step in fire prevention, as is not overloading the power supply connections.

7.2.6.2 Passive fire protection

Passive fire protection limits the exposure of fire once it has started. Measures include the installation of fire resistant walls, floors, and ceilings to keep the fire from spreading fast, and firewalls around parts of the datacenter to restrict the fire to a certain datacenter compartment.

Be aware of vulnerable fire entry points, such as cables, coolant tubes, and air ducts. These entry points should be filled with fire resistant material.

7.2.6.3 Fire detection systems

Fire detection systems allow investigation, interruption of power, and manual or automatic fire suppression before the fire spreads too much.

Smoke detectors, flame detectors, and heat detectors should be installed in the datacenter to provide early warning of a developing fire. Installation of these detectors is a delicate task, as the air flow of the datacenter's cooling systems must be considered.

Early warning signs should enable staff to investigate the alarm and if possible stop the fire using for instance hand fire extinguishers, or by simply shutting off the power to overheated equipment.

7.2.6.4 Fire suppression systems

Fire needs three components to exist: heat, fuel, and oxygen. If any of these three lack, a fire will stop.

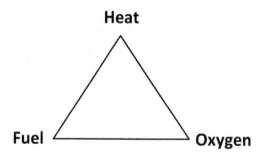

Figure 28: Fire triangle

So, in general there are three ways to stop a fire:

- Reduction or isolation of fuel.

- Reduction of heat.

- Reduction or isolation of oxygen.

Putting out a fire by reducing heat using water (as used by sprinkler systems or by firemen) is not preferred in a datacenter. The damage created by the water might be worse than the fire itself.

Therefore, in the early days of datacenters fire extinguishing was mostly done using Halon gas. Halon extinguishes fire without damaging electronic equipment by replacing the oxygen in normal air with Halon gas. But Halon is bad for people, as it causes dizziness – not a good combination with a spreading fire.

Today most fire extinction systems in datacenters are still gas based, but they use other types of inert gases, like Argon and special patented gas types (usually combinations of Argon and for instance Nitrogen in a special mix). They have all the benefits of Halon but none of its disadvantages.

Picture 10: Argon fire suppression system[19]

Because releasing fire suppression gas in the datacenter increases the air pressure in the datacenter with some 50% in a very short time, the pressure peak can break windows, or hurt people. This means that proper vents must be installed when gas based fire extinguishing is used.

7.2.7   Equipment racks

While mainframes and large midrange systems are typically housed in dedicated floor standing chassis, most x86 and midrange systems today are installed in racks.

A rack is a standardized metal enclosure to house IT infrastructure components. Typically, components placed in the rack have a front panel of 19 inches (49 cm) wide, which is why these racks are also known as 19" racks.

The height of a rack is measured in rack unit or 'U', where one U is 44.5 mm. A typical rack is 42U high and components installed in the rack are usually between 1U and 10U high; rack mountable servers are typically 1U or 2U high, while blade server enclosures are typically 10U high.

Figure 29: 19" Rack

Usually racks are equipped with rack mount rails and cable trays to enable equipment to be sled out of the rack easily for maintenance or upgrades, without cables getting disconnected.

7.2.7.1   Rack design tips

When planning rack placement consider the following:

- Check if the racks will fit through doors and in elevators if needed.

- Make sure the racks are deep enough for the equipment to be installed in them.

- Place racks in the datacenter such that one can walk around them.

- Put the racks in isles and use blind plates in open spaces in the rack to optimize airflow.

- Make sure there is enough room in the datacenter for extra racks and don't fill up the racks completely to enable future expansion.

- Make certain the rack doors can be opened, both on the front side and the back. It should be possible to open doors in neighboring racks as well.

- Usually network equipment like switches and routers are installed at the back of the rack to enable easy handling of the cables. Ensure there is enough room for patch panels in the back of the rack, while not interfering with equipment placed in the front of the rack.

- Non-19" equipment (like modems, keyboard switches, and external disk drives) can be installed in a rack using shelves. Rack manufacturers usually have shelves available that can be mounted in the rack. Ensure that equipment that is placed on shelves is tightened to prevent the equipment from falling off and to prevent cable disconnects.

- Make sure all cables are labeled and fit properly in the rack. This avoids mistakes like pulling a wrong cable, leading to downtime.

- If possible, try to install the heaviest equipment at the lowest position in the rack to provide mechanical stability and to guard the rack from falling over when the equipment is sled out of the rack.

7.2.7.2   KVM switches

When there are a large number of servers in a single rack, it is impractical for each one to have its own separate keyboard, mouse, and monitor. Instead, a KVM (Keyboard, Video, Mouse) switch can be used, combined with a rack mounted keyboard and display.

A KVM switch is a hardware device that allows a user to control multiple servers from a single keyboard, video monitor, and mouse. Control is switched from one server to another by the use of a switch or buttons on the KVM switch.

Picture 11: KVM switch[20]

Most KVM switches also allow control to be switched through keyboard commands (such as hitting a certain key, often Scroll Lock, rapidly two or three times), or via an On-Screen Display (OSD) menu.

Some KVM switches are UTP wired and operate over TCP/IP, allowing a normal PC to work on one of the servers remotely.

7.2.8 Datacenter cabling and patching

In 2005 the Telecommunications Industry Association (TIA) introduced the TIA 942 Telecommunications Infrastructure standards for Datacenters. This standard describes how datacenters should be designed based on a hierarchical cable structure. It defines a standard and structured cabling infrastructure for datacenters.

Cables and patching are discussed in more detail in chapter 8 on networking.

7.2.8.1 Demarcation point

A demarcation point is the point at which the telecom provider's network ends (including its responsibility) and the datacenter network (and responsibility) begins.

The demarcation point is usually a cable strip in a locked location of which one part can only be accessed by the telecom provider and the other part only by the systems managers.

If possible two or more demarcation points should be installed in the datacenter, to avoid a single point of failure. Ensure operators know where the demarcation points are. The cables from the demarcation points should leave the building using different routes.

7.2.9 Datacenter energy efficiency

The US EPA estimates that servers and datacenters are responsible for up to 1.5% of the total US electricity consumption[21]. And according to a study by Gartner[22], IT accounts for approximately 2% of all the world's CO_2 emissions. This is approximately the same volume as all airplanes combined.

The amount of money that can be saved by implementing power efficient IT can be substantial. For instance, during the lifetime of a server the amount of money spent on electricity can be much higher than the cost of the server itself. The price of electricity raised 78% between 2000 and 2015[23], and the electricity bill will probably only go up in the forthcoming years.

It is important to know who pays the electricity bill in an organization. In most cases, the facilities department pays the electricity bill, not the IT department. Often systems managers and architects know pretty well how much a server costs, but they rarely have a clue about the cost of electricity. Do you know how much one kWh cost for your organization?

Apart from the power used by the IT infrastructure components in the datacenter, the datacenter itself uses power as well. Most of this power is used by the cooling system, but power is also needed for lighting, heating of the operator rooms, etc.

To measure the power used by the datacenter the Power Usage Effectiveness (PUE) metric is most used. In a white paper published by the Green Grid in February 2007 called "*Green Grid Metrics: Describing Data Center Power Efficiency*"[24] the use of the PUE metric was introduced.

The PUE is calculated by dividing the amount of power used by the datacenter, by the power used to run the IT equipment in it. PUE is therefore expressed as a ratio, with efficiency improving as the metric decreases towards 1.

For example, running a datacenter with a PUE of 1.5 means that for each watt of power used by the IT equipment an extra half watt is used by the rest of the datacenter. This means that if this datacenter has 1 MW of IT components installed, another 0.5 MW is "wasted" by the datacenter (mainly for cooling, which does not directly lead to better or more customer service).

In this example, with an average electricity cost of $0.12 per kWh[25], every year $500 \text{ kW} \times 24 \text{ hours} \times 365 \text{ days} \times \$0.12 = \$525,500$ is spent on running the datacenter alone (not including the actual IT equipment)!

In this example by optimizing the datacenter's power usage to a PUE of 1.3, $210,240 per year can be saved.

Over the years, the trend has been to decrease the PUE from more than 2 a few years ago to a typical value of 1.7 today[26]. Google claims its datacenters reach a PUE of 1.14[27], and the Facebook datacenter in Prineville even claims to reach a PUE of only 1.06[28], as a result of cooling optimizations and large scale operations. In other words, apart from powering their servers, this Facebook datacenter uses only six percent additional power for all sources of overhead combined.

The best way to lower the PUE of a datacenter is to implement efficient cooling systems. More information on cooling systems is provided in section 7.2.5.

It is important to understand that PUE only measures datacenter power efficiency, and not for instance server efficiency, the efficiency of the power supplies used, let alone the amount of useful work that is done by the IT equipment!

Another thing to remember is that a high PUE is not always bad. If a datacenter uses its IT infrastructure components very efficiently, for instance by virtualizing all servers to a few large physical systems, much energy is saved compared to using many individual servers. The PUE, however, will be relatively high as much cooling is needed for the fully loaded physical machines.

7.3   Datacenter availability

7.3.1   Availability tiers

Some years ago, the Uptime institute[29] introduced an availability classification for datacenters. The classification consists of four tiers, in which a tier 1 datacenter has a lower availability than a tier 4 datacenter. Datacenters can be certified by The Uptime Institute for a certain tier.

Below is a high-level overview of the four tiers, the availability they provide and the measures that must be implemented to reach the classification.

Tier	Measures	Expected downtime
Tier 1 Availability 99.671% Type Basic	Single path for power and cooling distribution No redundant components	Downtime very likely for planned and unplanned maintenance

Tier	Measures	Expected downtime
Tier 2 Availability 99.741% Type Redundant components	Fulfills all Tier 1 requirements Single path for power and cooling distribution Redundant components	Downtime likely for planned and unplanned maintenance
Tier 3 Availability 99.982% Type Concurrently maintainable	Fulfills all Tier 1 and Tier 2 requirements Multiple active power and cooling distribution paths Only one path active Redundant components All IT equipment must be dual-powered	No downtime due to planned maintenance Downtime unlikely for unplanned maintenance
Tier 4 Availability 99.995% Type Fault tolerant	Fulfills all Tier 1, Tier 2, and Tier 3 requirements Multiple active power and cooling distribution paths Redundant components All cooling equipment is independently dual-powered, including chillers and Heating, Ventilating and Air Conditioning (HVAC) systems	No downtime due to planned or unplanned maintenance

Table 15: Datacenter tiers

The table above only describes the highlights of the tier classification. The classification system documentation contains much more detail.

While a datacenter can have different tier levels for different portions of the datacenter, the overall rating of the datacenter is equal to the lowest tier rating. There is no such thing as a tier 2.5 or tier 3+ datacenter.

The tier classification only describes the availability of the datacenter facilities, not the availability of the IT infrastructure components. The availability of the IT infrastructure in a datacenter must therefore be multiplied by the availability of the datacenter to get the overall availability.

For instance, a tier 3 datacenter running an IT infrastructure with an availability of 99.990% will have a total availability of $0.99982 \times 0.9990 = 0.99972 = 99.972\%$

7.3.2   Redundant datacenters

Building a tier 4 datacenter is sometimes not possible, for instance in places with only one power supply company. Tier 4 datacenters are also extremely expensive. There are only a few certified tier 4 datacenters in the world.

Instead of using a Tier 4 datacenter, multiple redundant datacenters can be used to increase availability. Multiple datacenters are a must when higher availability than 99.995% is needed. Typically, two datacenters are used, but highly redundant systems can use as many datacenters as needed.

As an example, if a datacenter with all its equipment has an availability of 99.5% (lower than tier 1), two datacenters can reach an availability of the same level as one tier 4 datacenter: $1 - (1 - 0.995)^2 = 0.99995 = 99.995\%$

(see section 4.2.3 for an explanation of this formula) given that there is no single point of failure for both datacenters, and the uninterrupted availability for the end users is guaranteed if one of the datacenters is available.

Based on the effect of incidents like the 9/11 terrorist attacks in the USA and reports of explosions in factory plants and fireworks storage, the datacenters should be at least 5 km apart.

7.4   Datacenter performance

The datacenter itself does not provide performance to IT Infrastructures, except for the bandwidth of the internet connectivity and the scalability of the location. As explained in section 7.2.2, the location of the datacenter should be chosen with these properties in mind.

7.5   Datacenter security

Datacenter security is mostly a matter of physical security, ensuring that equipment is physically safe behind the datacenter doors. To implement this, doors, windows, and other entry points must be secured.

Physical access to the datacenter must be restricted to selected and qualified staff and an entry registration system should be used. A log should be maintained containing all staff entering and leaving the datacenter.

Doors must be secured using conventional locks (for instance for dock loading doors) or electronic locks. The electronic locks should open only after proper authentication. This can be done using card access control systems using either proximity based cards or swipe cards.

Entry points can be implemented as regular doors, but also as mantraps (where staff is routed through a set of double doors that may be monitored by a guard) or revolving doors, where only one person at a time can enter the datacenter's restricted area. These entries can be equipped with weighing scales to ensure only one person enters the restricted area.

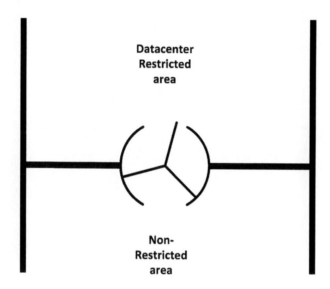

**Datacenter
Restricted
area**

**Non-
Restricted
area**

Figure 30: Revolving door

Doors and windows should have monitoring and preferably CCTV camera surveillance to alert upon opening. Motion detection systems can be used to detect movement inside and outside the building. In general, the number of entry and exit points of the datacenter should be kept to a minimum.

Permanent security guards (possibly with dogs) could be considered if the datacenter is large or contains sensitive information.

Finally, anti-ram raid equipment can be installed to protect from frontal assaults using vehicles.

8

NETWORKING

8.1   Introduction

Mainframe computers in the 1960s were stand-alone machines. They performed computing jobs based on input (usually on punched cards or tapes) and created output, usually on printed paper. Mainframe computers were large expensive systems typically in use at universities and large corporations. Since a university or corporation had only one computer (the mainframe), there was little need to have networking.

Even with time sharing systems like the early UNIX systems in the 1970s, the user's terminals or teletypes were connected to the central computer through serial (RS-232) lines.

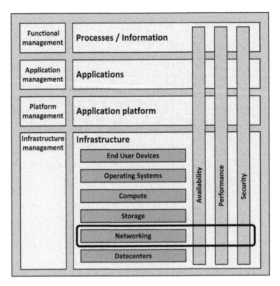

Figure 31: Networking in the infrastructure model

In the late 1960s, for the first time a number of computers were connected by means of the ARPANET – the predecessor of the internet. The ARPANET network consisted of Interface Message Processors (IMPs) which we would now call network routers.

Picture 12: The first IMP[30]

The first e-mail system via ARPANET was implemented back in 1971, and by 1973, the File Transfer Protocol (FTP) was defined and implemented, enabling file transfers over the ARPANET.

In 1973, engineers started to connect the ARPANET to the packet radio network (PRNET) and the Satellite Network (SATNET). They called the connection between these networks inter-networking, or the internet for short.

ARPANET originally used the Network Control Protocol (NCP), which was replaced by TCP/IP in 1983.

When Personal Computers (PCs) found their way into the office in the 1980s, the need arose for sharing data between office PCs. Local Area Networks (LANs) were designed to allow PCs to connect to each other and to shared resources like a file server, a printer or a router to the internet.

In the early years, LANs were built using technologies like ARCNET, Token Ring, Ethernet and others. Most of these technologies are phased out now and today Ethernet is the norm for LANs.

The internet became available for the average business and home user around 1996. One of the reasons was the introduction of Windows 95, which came with a web browser. The first billion internet users were reached in 2005, the second billion in 2010 and the third billion in 2014. It is estimated that in 2017, more than 3.5 billion people use the internet[31].

8.2   Networking building blocks

8.2.1   OSI Reference Model

The architecture of almost every network is based on the Open Systems Interconnection (OSI) standard reference model. The OSI Reference Model (OSI-RM) was developed in 1984 by the International Organization for Standardization, a global federation of national standards organizations representing approximately 130 countries.

A host or node is a component on the network, like a server, a router, a switch or a firewall. The OSI-RM consists of a set of seven layers that define the different stages that data must go through to travel from one host to another over a network. Figure 32 shows these seven layers, including some examples of implementations of that layer.

Layer　　　Implementation

#	Layer	Implementation	
7	**Application**	BOOTP & DHCP DNS & DNS SEC NTP	SNMP
6	**Presentation**	TLS SSL	
5	**Session**	PPTP L2TP VPN	
4	**Transport**	TCP UDP NAT	
3	**Network**	IP (v4, v6, sec) MPLS ICMP	OSPF IGMP
2	**Data link**	Ethernet Wi-Fi X25, ATM	Frame relay WAN GPRS, 3G
1	**Physical**	Cabling & patching UTP Dark fiber	SONET/SDH DSL T and E-carrier

Figure 32: OSI layers

The layers can easily be recalled using the mnemonic:

People Do Need To See Pamela Anderson,

where the first letter of each word is the first letter of each layer, starting from layer one.

The main benefit of implementing the OSI stack is that it allows implementing network components independently of each other, while still ensuring all components work together. For instance, TCP/IP, which is used to send information over the internet, comprises the TCP protocol in layer 4 with the IP protocol in layer 3. Without changing the IP protocol, an UDP/IP stack can be used as well, by just changing the level 4 protocol from TCP to UDP.

Because each layer in the OSI stack can be implemented independently from the layer below and above. This provides freedom to implement the network stack in an optimal way for a certain usage. For instance, local area networks use different building blocks than wide area networks or the internet.

Each layer's payload contains the protocol for the next layer. Consider the example in Figure 33.

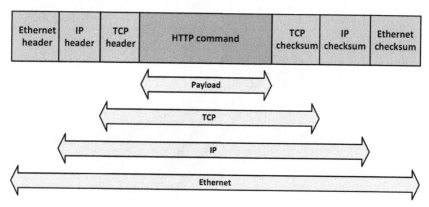

Figure 33: Frames embedded in each other

Figure 33 shows an Ethernet frame with an IP packet in it, with a TCP segment in it, with a HTTP command in it. The nesting of these protocols allows sending HTTP traffic (like web pages) to another computer using an Ethernet network in a reliable way.

This chapter is organized based on the OSI model, starting from the bottom layer and working up to the top of the stack. For each layer the most used implementations are discussed.

8.2.2 Physical layer

The physical layer defines physical hardware components of the network, such as Network Interface Cards (NICs), copper and fiber optic cables, leased lines, cable internet, and DSL.

8.2.2.1 Cables

At the most elementary level, networking is about cables. In early networks coax cables were used to interconnect computers, but most copper based cables today are of the twisted pair type. Apart from copper cabling, fiber optic cabling is used quite often as well.

8.2.2.1.1 Twisted pair cables

Twisted pair cables consist of paired insulated wires that are twisted around each other to prevent interference. A cable contains multiple wire pairs, that can be shielded (Shielded Twisted Pair - STP) or unshielded (Unshielded Twisted Pair - UTP). UTP is the most common cable in networking today.

Picture 13: UTP cable

Having separate pairs of wires for transmitting data (TX) and receiving data (RX) allows for full duplex communication. Full duplex communication means that data may be transmitted and received by a host at the same time.

UTP comes in several quality ratings called categories. The rating is based on how tightly the copper wires are intertwined: The tighter the wind, the higher the rating and its resistance to interference and attenuation. This resistance to interference is crucial for providing higher data rates. Table 16 shows a list of today's most used categories and their maximum bandwidth.

Category	Maximum bandwidth
5 or 5e	1 Gbit/s
6	10 Gbit/s
7	10 Gbit/s
8	40 Gbit/s

Table 16: Twisted pair cables and their bandwidth

8.2.2.1.2 Coax cable

Coax cable consists of an inner conductor surrounded by a flexible, tubular insulating layer, surrounded by a tubular conducting shield.

Picture 14: Coax cable[32]

Historically, coax cable provided the highest bandwidth possible in copper cabling. It is still heavily used by cable companies, but improvements in UTP and STP cables allow higher bandwidths, eliminating coax cables for most other uses.

8.2.2.1.3 Fiber optic cable

A fiber optic cable contains multiple strands of fiber glass or plastic, that each provide an optical path for light pulses. The light source can either be a light-emitting diode (LED) or a laser.

The maximum transmission distance depends on the optical power of the transmitter, the optical wavelength utilized, the quality of the fiber optic cable and the sensitivity of the optical receiver.

Two types of fiber optic cable are most common:

- Multi-Mode Fiber (MMF)
- Single Mode Fiber (SMF)

SMF is used for long distance communication (up to 80 km), and MMF is used for distances of 500m or less, typically used in the datacenter or on a campus setup.

Light waves in Multi-Mode Fiber (MMF) are dispersed into numerous paths, also known as modes, as they travel through the cable's core – hence the name.

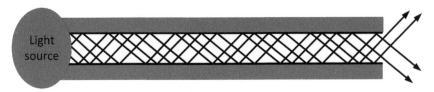

Figure 34: Multi-Mode Fiber

Single-Mode Fiber (SMF) is designed to carry only a single narrow band of ray wavelengths of light (a single mode).

Figure 35: Single-Mode Fiber

SMF requires a light source with a narrow spectral width (typically a laser). SMF has a much smaller core than MMF. The small core and single light-wave virtually eliminates any distortion that could result from overlapping light pulses, providing transmissions over long distances. SMF is more expensive than MMF, not only because of cable costs, but also because of the more expensive interface cards needed to send a single ray of light.

Using one light source, the maximum bandwidth of a fiber optics cable (both MMF and SMF) is approximately 10 Gbit/s. Using Dense Wavelength-Division Multiplexing (DWDM) the capacity of fiber optics cables can be extended. By using multiple light sources, each having a distinct color (wave length), multiple channels can travel though the fiber optics cable simultaneously. This way up to 80 channels can be created, leading to a total bandwidth of 800 Gbit/s for a single strand of fiber cable.

8.2.2.1.4 Vertical and horizontal cabling and patch panels

Cables in buildings are most visible in patch panels. Patch panels are installed in racks in the datacenter and in patch closets (or SERs – see 7.2.1) in various locations in (office) buildings. They are used to connect systems in a flexible way, without having to change the installed cabling in the building.

After the initial installation, over the years, cables in the datacenter and rest of the buildings sometimes have to be added, moved, replaced, or removed. To enable this flexibility, cables are terminated on patch panels; not directly on the network switches, servers or PCs.

Patch panels are passive connecting devices with port locations or jacks, in which so-called patch cables can be plugged. Connecting systems is done by connecting them through the patch panel.

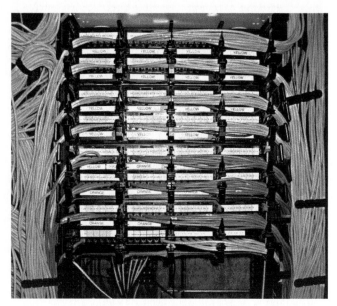

Picture 15: Patch panel[33]

The main distribution cabling in buildings connects the patch panels on the various floors to the patch panels in the datacenter, as shown in Figure 36. This cabling is also known as the vertical cabling, as the cables typically span multiple floors. On the floors, horizontal cabling connects the endpoints in the walls to the patch panels.

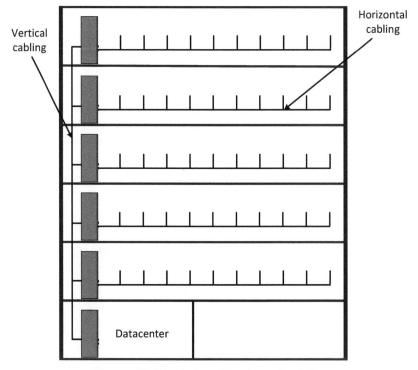

Figure 36: Vertical and horizontal cabling

It is good practice to implement redundant vertical cabling. If possible, try to create two different physical routes for connecting patch panels on each floor to the datacenter, preferably using a ring layout.

Try to avoid having redundant cables using the same physical path. Vertical cabling is sometimes installed in elevator shafts. While this seems like a good (and relatively cheap) idea, when the elevator is repaired, cables can get damaged causing entire floors to become disconnected.

Of course, in buildings with multiple elevators redundant connections can be implemented using multiple elevator shafts. In other situations, alternative paths should be used.

Patch panels usually contain multiple types of patching, including for instance UTP Ethernet patching, analog telephone patching, and fiber optics patching. Using separate patch panels for these types of patch cables is highly recommended, and using color coding of cables is also good practice (for instance green cables for telephony, blue for LAN, orange for fiber optics to the datacenter).

Patch cables can easily become tangled, making them difficult to work with, sometimes resulting in infrastructure components accidentally getting unplugged in attempts to move a cable. Such cases are known as "cable spaghetti".

I have seen this many times in practice. Originally the cables were installed properly, but after some years, and many changes, cable routing got messy.

We found rack doors could not be closed because of excessive bundles of cables hanging out of the rack. At several occasions, we had cleanup sessions (in evenings or weekends) to completely re-cable all racks.

Proper cable management is needed to avoid this situation. It is a good practice to color code patch cables to identify the type of connection and to label them properly. Use cable management trays wherever possible and use different racks for copper and fiber cables patch panels.

8.2.2.2 Leased lines

Leased lines are dedicated data connections between two locations provided by a third party, typically a telecom provider. Leased lines are based on a long-term contract and the physical connection is often created especially for that contract.

Leased lines are based on T or E carrier lines, SONET, SDH, or dark fiber.

8.2.2.2.1 T and E carrier lines

T (USA, Canada, and Japan) and E (most other countries) carrier lines are copper based leased lines. This does not necessarily mean there is an end-to-end copper bundle used, but the end user is connected using copper cables.

There are many types of T and E versions, each providing different bandwidths. In practice, only the following bandwidths are used:

Type	T-Bandwidth	E-Bandwidth
1	1.5 Mbit/s	2 Mbit/s
3	45 Mbit/s	34 Mbit/s
4	275 Mbit/s	140 Mbit/s
5	400 Mbit/s	565 Mbit/s

Table 17: T and E carrier lines

For example, as shown in Table 17, a T3 line has a bandwidth of 45 Mbit/s.

T and E carrier lines actually consist of multiple individual channels. Most telecom providers allow leasing one or more individual channels; this is known as fractional access. T and E carrier lines are symmetric, meaning that their upload and download bandwidths are the same.

T and E definitions are part of the SONET/SDH standard as described next.

8.2.2.2.2 SONET and SDH

Synchronous Optical Networking (SONET) and Synchronous Digital Hierarchy (SDH) are protocols that transfer multiple data streams over optical fiber, for instance bundles of multiple T or E carrier lines in the backbone of a telecom provider.

SONET and SDH are essentially the same. SONET is used most in the United States and Canada, while SDH is used in most of the rest of the world.

Optical Carrier (OC) levels are used to specify the bandwidth of fiber optic networks conforming to the SONET standard, while Synchronous Transport Module (STM) is used in SDH. Commonly used speeds are:

- OC3/ STM1 - 155Mbit/s
- OC12/ STM4 - 622 Mbit/s
- OC48/ STM16 - 2.5 Gbit/s
- OC192/ STM64 - 9.5 Gbit/s
- OC768 / STM256 – 38 Gbit/s

8.2.2.2.3 Dark fiber

Rather than leasing high speed leased line capacity, which requires expensive SONET or SDH equipment, dark fiber provides a dedicated fiber optic connection without management or prescribed protocols between two end points. The user can send anything he or she wants through the fiber, as it is a private link. This allows dark fiber networks to operate using the latest optical protocols, adding capacity where needed. For example, many dark fiber networks use cheap Gigabit Ethernet equipment, rather than expensive SONET systems.

Due to the cost of installing dark fiber networks, they are generally only available in high-population-density areas where fiber optic cables have already been installed.

8.2.2.3   Cable internet access

Cable internet uses the cable television infrastructure, already installed and available in many places. With cable internet, data is transmitted and received using the same cable as analog and digital television signals. The internet connection uses an asymmetric type of transmission. The data from the internet has download data rates up to 400 Mbit/s and data to the internet is sent at upload data rates up to 20 Mbit/s.

The physical coax cable runs to a wiring closet of the cable company (called "the curb"), where the data connection is converted to optical fiber for further transportation.

8.2.2.4   DSL

DSL is an abbreviation of Digital Subscriber Line. It provides data transmission using existing wires of a local telephone network. Since DSL uses normal telephone lines, no dedicated physical cable needs to be installed (like with leased lines). The speed of a DSL line is highly dependent on the quality of the telephone wiring, and the distance between the DSL connection and the telecom provider's equipment (POP – point of presence – or local exchange).

There are various types of DSL connections.

- **Asymmetric DSL (ADSL)** is the most common deployed type of DSL, supporting data rates up to 25 Mbit/s when receiving data (download) and up to 3.5 Mbit/s when sending data (upload).

- **Symmetric DSL (SDSL)** supports data rates up to 3 Mbit/s, both upload and download.

- **Very High DSL (VDSL)** offers fast data rates over relatively short distances. The shorter the distance, the faster the connection rate, providing speeds up to 100 Mbit/s.

8.2.2.5   Network Interface Controllers (NICs)

A network interface controller (NIC) is a hardware component that connects a server or end user device to a physical network cable. NICs can be implemented on expansion cards that plug into the computer's physical PCI bus or built into the motherboard.

The NIC is actually both a physical layer and data link layer device, as it provides physical access to a networking cable and an implementation of a datalink protocol like Ethernet. A NIC has a fixed MAC address that is uniquely assigned to its network interface.

8.2.3   Data link layer

In layer 2, data is encapsulated in the physical protocol, and the type of network and the packet sequencing is defined. Typical implementations are Ethernet, Wi-Fi, switching, and WANs.

8.2.3.1   Ethernet

Ethernet was developed at Xerox PARC between 1973 and 1975 by a team led by Robert Metcalfe. Metcalfe later founded 3Com that built the first 10 Mbit/s Ethernet adapters in 1981.

Ethernet originally employed a shared medium topology, based on coax cable. All machines were connected to a single, shared Ethernet cable that ran around the building, connecting each machine. Later Ethernet used twisted pair cabling with hubs and switches to decrease the vulnerability of the network caused by broken cables or bad connectors.

Ethernet is also the basis for Wi-Fi. Today's speeds are up to 100 Gbit/s for wired Ethernet (with 400 Gbit/s expected by late 2017[34]) and 300 Mbit/s for wireless Wi-Fi.

Each Ethernet adapter is programmed with a 48 bit globally unique number, called a Media Access Control (MAC) address. MAC addresses are used to specify both the destination and the source of each Ethernet packet.

An Ethernet packet starts with a header including the source and destination MAC addresses, followed by the data that needs to be transported (called the payload). The packet ends with a cyclic redundancy check, which is used to detect any corruption of data after it is received.

Preamble	Frame delimiter	Destination MAC address	Source MAC address	Length	Payload	CRC checksum

Figure 37: Ethernet packet

Each network interface listens to all traffic on the Ethernet cable. When it sees an Ethernet packet with its own MAC address in the destination field, it will copy the packet and deliver the payload of the packet to the protocol handler of the higher level OSI layer for further processing.

Network interfaces normally only accept packets addressed to their own MAC address. A packet with a destination address equal to the broadcast MAC address (all 48 bits set to one) is intended for every network interface on the network, and every network interface will process this type of packet.

The Ethernet protocol allows any machine to start transmitting packets when the shared carrier (coax cable, twisted-pair hub or Wi-Fi radio signal spectrum) is not in use. To avoid two systems from sending data at the same time, Ethernet uses carrier sensing circuitry that checks the activity on the carrier. Only when the carrier is not in use a station can start sending its data. When two machines detect that the carrier is not in use, and start to transmit a packet at the same time (which is quite likely with many active machines), a packet collision occurs. When this happens, it is detected by all sending machines and they will stop the transmission immediately. After a short waiting time, they will retransmit their packet when the carrier is not in use anymore. This technology is the basis of Ethernet, and is called Carrier Sense Multiple Access with Collision Detection (CSMA/CD). By nature, CSMA/CD is half-duplex, meaning a station either transmits or receives data, but not both at the same time.

Due to the time required to recover from collisions, the performance of CSMA/CD Ethernet degrades dramatically if too many machines attempt to send packets at the same time. Throughput is therefore limited to 40% to 60% of the available bandwidth.

8.2.3.2   WLAN (Wi-Fi)

A wireless local area network (WLAN) links two or more devices using radio transmissions. Wi-Fi is a term used to describe WLANs that are based on the IEEE 802.11 protocol family.

Wi-Fi is a special implementation of Ethernet. Wi-Fi listens to the shared radio spectrum for radio signals before starting transmitting. If the radio spectrum is occupied, the Wi-Fi radio will not transmit. The source of the signal is of no concern to the Wi-Fi radio. This is why Wi-Fi is still reliable, but very slow in environments with much noise in the radio spectrum, as created by for instance microwave ovens or other sources of interference.

The wireless communication range of Wi-Fi is typically about 30 m. However, the distance limit highly depends on whether the wireless network is used indoors or outdoors and on the type of 802.11 standard used.

Access points are base stations for a wireless network. Wireless clients are usually mobile devices such as laptops, tablets, and smartphones.

Wi-Fi networks work in one of three modes:

- **Basic Service Set** (also known as infrastructure mode), where clients communicate only to the access point and not directly to each other. Clients on the same Wi-Fi network can only communicate to each other through the access point.

- **Independent Basic Service Set** (also known as peer-to-peer or ad-hoc mode), where clients communicate directly to each other. Wireless devices within range of each other can discover and communicate directly without an access point.

- **Extended Services Set**, where a set of access points are connected by a wired LAN, providing roaming of Wi-Fi clients.

Since Wi-Fi uses radio transmissions, data can be received by anyone in the neighborhood. Encrypting data in transit is therefore much more important than in wired networks. Data encryption in Wi-Fi networks is implemented using Wi-Fi Protected Access (WPA). WPA dynamically generates a new key for each packet sent over the Wi-Fi network. WPA also includes a Message Integrity Check to prevent an attacker from capturing, altering and/or resending data packets. WPA version 2 is now widely implemented and considered secure enough for most applications.

8.2.3.3   Switching

To increase usable bandwidth, switches are deployed to split a single network segment into multiple segments, each with fewer devices (usually only one).

When started up, switches send all data to all ports. But after communicating with a port they learn which MAC address is connected to which port. Subsequent packets with the same MAC address are sent only to the correct ports. This way the amount of traffic is reduced – data sent to a certain MAC address will only be forwarded to the switch port that has that MAC address connected. Switches will still forward broadcasts to all connected switch ports.

Switches typically have dozens of physical ports. Specialized hardware components (ASICs) are used to switch the packets, leading to very high throughput and low latency.

Picture 16: Cisco Nexus 7000 enterprise switch[35]

On a switched network, many simultaneous data transfers can take place. Because the only devices on the segments are the switch and the end station, the connection is always collision free. This enables faster communications, without resending packets due to collisions and without having to wait for other stations sending data.

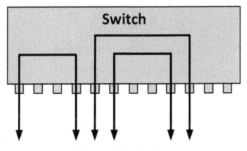

Figure 38: Switch

Switches enable communications using both receive (RX) and transmit (TX) pairs in the UTP cable simultaneously, known as full duplex communication.

8.2.3.4   WAN

Wide Area Networks (WANs) started to appear in the 1980s when organizations started to need a network connection between their central servers and their subsidiaries and (sometimes) to other organizations. The first WANs consisted of point-to-point connections using modems and the analog public telephone system. Modems were connected to routers that routed the data packets between the end points.

Later, telecom providers started to offer dedicated analog leased lines. These leased lines eliminated the need to setup a call and were considerably cheaper in use than dial-up lines. When more and more WAN connections appeared, telecom providers started to offer digital leased lines. Digital leased lines like T1/E1 lines and ISDN (Integrated Services Digital Network) provided higher bandwidths because they eliminated the need for modems to convert digital data to analog frequencies that would fit the characteristics of telephone conversations.

Most WAN connections today are based on packet switching technologies, in which devices transport packets via a virtual point-to-point link across a carrier network. Packet switched networks are very reliable and provide robust WAN connections.

Most Wide Area Network (WAN) connections today are based on packet switching technologies, in which devices transport packets via a virtual point-to-point link across a carrier network. Packet switched networks are very reliable and provide robust WAN connections. While originally Frame Relay and ATM were extensively used technologies for WANs, in recent years most WAN connections have been migrated to VPNs running on one of the following technologies:

- The MPLS network of a network provider (see section 8.2.4.6 for more information on MPLS)

- The internet using IPsec or SSL (see section 8.2.6.1)

- Dark fiber (see section 8.2.2.2.3)

8.2.3.5   Public wireless networks

In the past years, wireless networks have become more popular than wired networks for end user devices. Apart from WLANs based on Wi-Fi, public wireless (mobile) networks are getting more popular every day. The reason is obvious – public wireless networks provide freedom to move around for mobile users and provide connectivity from places where wired connections are impossible (like on the road).

Public wireless networks are much less reliable than private wireless networks. Users moving around will often temporarily lose connectivity, and bad signals lead to frequent re-sending of network packets. The bandwidth is also much lower than when using private networks; noise and other signal interference, usage of available bandwidth by (many) other users and retransmissions lead to low effective bandwidth per end point.

8.2.3.5.1 1G and 2G: GSM, CDMA, GPRS and EDGE

Global System for Mobile Communications (GSM) is the world's most popular standard for mobile telephone systems in which both signaling and speech channels are digital. This technology is also called 1G: the first-generation of mobile technology.

In 1991, 2G was introduced. With 2G, phone conversations were digitally encrypted, and data services for mobile were introduced, starting with SMS text messages.

While GSM is a worldwide standard, an alternative is known as Code Division Multiple Access, or CDMA. It is most popular in the United States and Russia, but it's also used in some Asian and African countries, often alongside competing GSM carriers. GSM and CDMA are not interchangeable and need their own equipment and end points.

General Packet Radio Service (GPRS) is a packet oriented mobile data service providing data rates of 56 to 114 kbit/s based on GSM technology. This technology is also called 2.5G.

Enhanced Data rates for GSM Evolution (EDGE), also known as Enhanced GPRS, allows improved data transmission rates as a backward-compatible extension of GSM. EDGE delivers data rates up to 384 kbit/s.

8.2.3.5.2 3G: UMTS and HSDPA

Universal Mobile Telecommunications System (UMTS) is an umbrella term for the third-generation (3G) mobile telecommunications transmission standard. Compared to GSM, UMTS requires new base stations and new frequency allocations, but it uses a core network derived from GSM, ensuring backward compatibility. UMTS was designed to provide maximum data transfer rates of 45 Mbit/s.

High Speed Downlink Packet Access (HSDPA) is part of the UMTS standard, providing a maximum speed of 7.2 Mbit/s. HSDPA+ is also known as HSDPA Evolution and Evolved HSDPA. It is an upgrade to HSDPA networks, providing 42 Mbit/s download and 11.5 Mbit/s upload speeds.

8.2.3.5.3 4G: LTE

LTE (Long Term Evolution) is a 4G network technology, designed from the start to transport data (IP packets) rather than voice. In order to use LTE, the core UMTS network must be adapted, leading to changes in the transmitting equipment. The LTE specification provides download rates of at least 100 Mbit/s (up to 326 Mbit/s), and an upload speed of at least 50 Mbit/s (up to 86.4 Mbit/s). Today's LTE-Advanced (also known as 4G+) can provide download rates of at least 225 Mbit/s (up to 1 Gbit/s).

LTE is not designed to handle voice transmissions. When placing or receiving a voice call, LTE handsets will typically fall back to old 2G or 3G networks for the duration of the call. In 2017, the Voice over LTE (VoLTE) protocol is launched to allow the decommissioning of the old 2G and 3G networks in the future.

8.2.4   Network layer

The network layer, often referred to as layer 3, defines the route via which the data is sent to the recipient device. The IPv4 and IPv6 protocols and their routing and addressing are implementations of this layer.

8.2.4.1   The IP protocol

The IP protocol is by far the most used layer 3 protocol in the world. IP stands for Internet Protocol. IP in combination with TCP (which is discussed in section 8.2.5.1), was invented by Robert Kahn and Vinton Cerf in 1973. The TCP protocol determines whether a packet has reached its destination, while the IP address is a numeric address that locates a device on a network.

Two versions of IP are used in practice: IPv4 and IPv6. IPv4 is the dominant protocol on the internet today. IPv6 is not used much yet, but it probably will be used much more in the future, due to the almost limitless number of addressable end points. This is needed, since the internet community ran out of available public IPv4 addresses in 2011[36].

The IP protocol assumes that the network is inherently unreliable and that it is dynamic in terms of availability of links and nodes.

IP uses data packets that contain a source and destination address, and some payload data (typically an Ethernet packet). IP routing protocols dynamically define the path of IP packets from source to destination. The destination address of each packet is inspected by each router, which then makes an independent decision on where to send the packet next.

When sending much data, the IP protocol splits the data in multiple smaller IP packets. Since each IP packet is routed individually, the route from source to destination can be different for each IP packet, possibly leading to IP packets arriving at the destination out of order. It is good practice for LAN networks, however, to be configured for packet flows (packets with the same source and destination addresses) to use a consistent network path, thus avoiding (performance) issues caused by re-ordering of packets.

Due to network disruption, IP packets can get lost or corrupted. Corrupted packets are detected by calculating a checksum of each packet at each node the IP packet passes. When an error is detected, the IP packet is dropped by the node that found the error. Because of today's highly reliable network connections, and because checksums are also calculated on lower and higher layers, IPv6 has abandoned this use of IP header checksums for the benefit of rapid forwarding through the network.

The effects of dropped IP packets and IP packets arriving out of order is handled by upper layer protocols like TCP.

8.2.4.2   IPv4

IPv4 addresses are composed of 4 bytes (32 bits), represented by 4 decimal numbers, and divided by a period, for example: 192.168.1.1. Each host (server, switch, router, firewall, etc.) in the IP network needs at least one IP address. Within a network all IP addresses must be unique.

An IP address actually consists of two parts, a network prefix and a host number. For instance, in the IP address 10.121.12.16, the network prefix is 10 and the host number is 121.12.16.

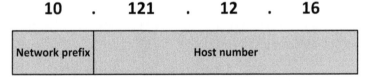

Figure 39: IP network prefix and host number

All hosts with the same network prefix can communicate directly to each other. Hosts in other networks can only be reached using a router.

The first three bits of the first byte of an IP address define the class of the address. Three classes of networks are defined:

Class A

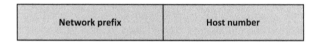

Class B

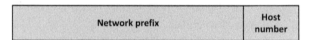

Class C

Network prefix	Host number

Figure 40: IP network Classes

In a typical class C address, like 195.23.221.23, the network is 195.23.221 and the host number is 23.

Class	First byte	Max number of hosts	Number of available networks
A	0–127	16,777,214	128
B	128–191	65,534	16,384
C	192–223	254	2,097,152

Table 18: IP network classes in detail

Table 18 shows that the IP address 170.32.43.12 is a host in a class B network. This network can have 65,534 hosts in it.

The problem is that there are only 16,384 class B networks available worldwide, and only 128 class A networks. Only very large companies (like IBM) and some governments own a class A network. All other organizations sometimes use a class B, and mostly use a class C network.

Classful network design served its purpose in the startup stage of the internet, but it lacked scalability during the rapid expansion of the internet in the 1990s. For instance, when an organization only needs five hosts in their network, they needed to get a class C network, even if they used only five of its 254 available host addresses.

To solve the problem of the inefficient use of IP addresses, the classful system was replaced with Classless Inter-Domain Routing (CIDR) in 1993. CIDR is based on variable-length subnet masking to allow allocation and routing based on arbitrary-length prefixes. This system is also known as subnetting.

8.2.4.2.1 Subnetting

Subnetting is used to split up the host part of an IP network in smaller subnets, each forming a new IP network.

Consider the following example:

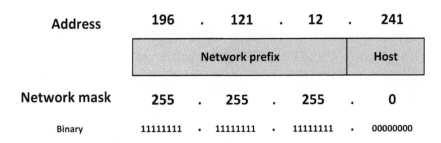

Figure 41: Class C address without subnetting

In this case, the IP address 196.121.12.241 has a network prefix of 196.121.12 and a host number of 241 (in the host range between 1 and 254).

For IPv4 a network mask is a 32-bit number (expressed in four decimals) where bits set to 1 signify the network prefix and bits set to 0 the host part of the address. The default subnet mask of a class C network is therefore 255.255.255.0.

As an alternative, the routing prefix can also be expressed in CIDR notation. It is written as the address of a network, followed by a slash character (/), and ending with the bit-length of the host space. For example, 255.255.255.0 is the network mask for the 192.168.1.0/24 notation.

Now consider the following example using a subnet:

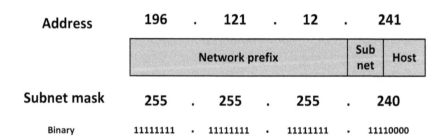

Figure 42: Class C address with subnetting

In this case, the IP address 196.121.12.129 has a network prefix of 196.121.12, a subnet of 240 and a host number of 1 (in the host range between 1 and 14).

Using subnets, the available IP address space can be used much more efficiently, as unused host addresses are not reserved or wasted, but used in a different subnet. In Table 19, the number of hosts that can be used for certain subnet masks is shown.

CIDR prefix	Subnet mask	Available subnets	Hosts per subnet
/24	255.255.255.0	1	254
/25	255.255.255.128	2	126
/26	255.255.255.192	4	62
/27	255.255.255.224	8	30
/28	255.255.255.240	16	14
/29	255.255.255.248	32	6
/30	255.255.255.252	64	2
/31	255.255.255.254	128	2 (only point-to-point)

Table 19: Hosts per subnet mask

To directly connect two routers with each other, a subnet with 4 addresses is needed (each router needs one IP address, plus the subnet needs a broadcast address and a network address), leading to a subnet mask of 255.255.255.252. Point-to-point connections need no broadcast or network address and can use a subnet mask of 255.255.255.254.

Using subnets allows Internet Service Providers to for instance provide 32 organizations with six public IP addresses each and only using one class C IP network for it.

8.2.4.2.2 Private IP ranges

Since the number of unique IP addresses on the internet is limited and because hosts with public internet IP addresses can reach the internet directly, private IP addresses should be used for LANs instead. The following IPv4 address ranges can be used for internal use – so-called private IP address ranges:

- 10.0.0.0 to 10.255.255.255 (class A address range)

- 172.16.0.0 to 172.31.255.255 (class B address range)

- 192.168.0.0 to 192.168.255.255 (class C address range)

These IP addresses are not used on the internet and by default they are not routed by internet routers. This means each organization can use these IP ranges internally without introducing conflicts on the internet.

To maximize the number of IP addresses available in the various LAN segments in an internal network and to minimize the size of routing tables in routers, a well-designed IP addressing plan is needed. In such an addressing plan the available IP ranges of the organization are divided in various subnets, each with its own set of users.

It is a good practice to create separate subnets within the chosen address range for:

- Production environment workstations

- Production environment servers

- Office environment workstations

- Office environment servers

- Development and test environments

- De-Militarized Zone (DMZ – explained in section 8.6.3)

- Systems management network segment

- Printers

- Remote users

- Server clusters

- Guest users' workstations

Routing between these subnets should be done using routers with access-lists, to block undesired network traffic.

8.2.4.3   IPv6

The internet's growth has created a need for more addresses than IPv4 is capable of delivering. IPv6 was introduced in 1998 as a successor of the widely deployed IPv4 to, among other things, solve the problem of limited IP address space.

IPv6 uses 128-bit addresses represented in eight groups of four hexadecimal digits separated by colons, for example:

2001:0bb8:86a2:0000:0000:8b1e:1350:7c34.

IPv6 has the following benefits over IPv4:

- **Expanded address space** - With IPv4, the number of hosts on the internet can theoretically be no more 4 billion (in practice it is much less, due to poor allocation of IP address blocks, with approximately 14% of all available addresses utilized). With IPv6 the maximum number of hosts on the internet is practically unlimited (approximately 3.4×10^{38} or 34 thousand billion billion billion billion).

- **Better support for mobile IP**, which is an important feature for the billions of smartphones in use and the rise of the internet of Things.

- **Fixed header length** - Because IPv6 uses fixed length headers, hardware based routers can be made much more efficient leading to faster networks.

- **Auto configuration** - IPv6 hosts can automatically configure themselves without the need for DHCP servers (see 8.2.8.1).

- **Quality of Service** is built in IPv6, supporting specialized traffic like Voice over IP (VoIP) or streaming video.

- **Security** - IPv6 supports authentication and privacy in the protocol itself.

- **MTU discovery** - Before sending packets from a source to a destination, IPv6 discovers the maximum packet length (MTU) supported in the route, optimizing for the transportation of large files.

While IPv6 has clear advantages over IPv4, and while it is supported by all major operating systems and network equipment today, it is not widely deployed. The main reason for this is that IPv6 is not backwards compatible with IPv4, leading to the need for complex deployments.

The most obvious deployment models for IPv6 are:

- **Use IPv6 on the LAN and on dedicated WAN links** - This is a full IPv6 implementation between multiple locations of an organization, where all locations use IPv6 only and the locations are connected using an IPv6 WAN network. Connection to the internet can be implemented using Protocol Translation.

- **Protocol translation** - In this scenario a separate router runs IPv4 on one port and IPv6 on another. The router performs protocol translation between both ports, much like the way NAT works in IPv4 networks (see section 8.2.5.2).

- **Dual stack** - Dual stack in an operating system implements IPv4 and IPv6 protocol stacks in a hybrid form. Within network equipment dual stack means that the 2 protocols run simultaneously and independently.

- **IPv6 over IPv4 tunnels** - Encapsulating IPv6 packets within IPv4, in effect using IPv4 as a link layer for IPv6. This is also known as "6to4".

Dual stack is the simplest way to begin deploying IPv6. If all the devices in an IPv6-enabled network have dual stacks, they can speak to any destination whether it is IPv4 or IPv6. This is extremely important in the early stages of deployment, when the vast majority of destinations on the public internet are still IPv4-only.

8.2.4.4   ICMP

The Internet Control Message Protocol (ICMP) is an integral part of the IP protocol. It is not used to send data, but to send signals like error messages or test messages related to the network. The best-known use of ICMP are the 'ping' and 'traceroute' commands that use ICMP to check network connectivity and diagnose common network problems.

8.2.4.5   Routing

A router copies IP packages between (sub)networks as discussed in section 8.2.4.2. To be able to make IP packet forwarding decisions between networks, routers compile routing tables. Routing tables determine the network port via which IP packets should exit the router for all destination IP address ranges.

Routing and switching functionality may be combined in one device. A switch capable of handling routing protocols is also known as a layer 3 switch (which is actually an incorrect name – there is no switching on layer 3, just routing. The switching is done on layer 2).

8.2.4.5.1 Routing protocols

In small networks, IP routing tables can be configured manually. In larger networks manually editing these tables is not practical. Instead, dynamic routing protocols automatically create routing tables based on information exchange with neighboring routers. When a network connection experiences problems, the routing protocol automatically reconfigures the routing tables to use alternative routes.

In general, LAN and WAN routing protocols can be divided in three classes:

- Distance vector protocols (like RIP and IGRP)

- Link state protocols (like OSPF and IS-IS)

- Path vector routing (like BGP)

Each of these 3 protocol classes are described in the following sections.

8.2.4.5.2 Distance vector protocols

With distance vector protocols like RIP and IGRP, each router periodically (every 30 or 60 seconds) sends its up-to-date routing table to its immediate neighbors. Once a neighboring router receives this information it is able to amend its own routing table to reflect the changes and then inform its neighbors of the changes. Routers using the distance vector protocol don't have information about the entire path to a destination, but they do know the direction (to which exit interface a packet should be forwarded) and the distance from a destination. Routes are advertised by a Distance Vector protocol as a vector of distance and direction. Direction is the next router hop address (e.g., the destination can be reached via router B), and distance is the router hop count (e.g., the destination via this route is 5 hops away).

8.2.4.5.3 Link state protocols

In a link state routing protocol, each router knows its IP addresses, their connected links, and the state of these links. This information is flooded to all routers in the network if changes in a link state occur (for instance, when a connection to a router goes down). Each router makes a copy of the received information and forwards it to all other routers. Each router then calculates the best path to each destination network, maintaining a map of the network as they see it.

Link state routing is seen as superior to distance vector routing, because of the possibility of routing loops occurring in distance vector routing due to delays.

All routers running a link state routing protocol always have the same (correct) image of the network. While this makes link state protocols better, it also makes them more complex.

8.2.4.5.4 Path vector routing

Distance vector and link state routing are both intra-domain routing protocols. They are used within an organization's network (also known as an autonomous system), but not between autonomous systems. In contrast, path vector routing is very effective for inter-domain routing. The Border Gateway Protocol (BGP) is the best-known path vector protocol and the standard routing protocol on the internet.

Each entry in a BGP routing table contains the destination network, the next router, and the path to reach the destination. BGP makes routing decisions based on path, network policies, and/or rule sets. BGP is a fairly complicated protocol and is therefore seldom used in enterprise networks.

8.2.4.6 MPLS

Multiprotocol Label Switching (MPLS) routes data from one network node to the next with the help of labels. This enables MPLS to carry many different kinds of traffic, including IP packets, SONET, and Ethernet frames. In practice, MPLS is mainly used to forward IP and Ethernet traffic.

In an MPLS network, all data packets are assigned labels. Packet forwarding decisions are made solely on the contents of this label, without the need to examine the packet itself. The MPLS label is stripped from the packet at the end point. This allows setting up end-to-end circuits across any type of physical transport medium, using any protocol.

8.2.5   Transport layer

The transport layer routes data streams coming from multiple applications and integrates them into a single stream for the network layer. At the receiving end the data is split again to be routed to the destination applications. The transport layer can maintain flow control, and can provide error checking and recovery of data between network devices. The most used transport layer protocols are TCP and UDP.

8.2.5.1   TCP and UDP

Applications typically don't use IP directly, but use an upper layer protocol – usually TCP or UDP.

The Transmission Control Protocol (TCP) uses the IP protocol to create reliable transmission of so-called TCP/IP packets. TCP provides reliable, ordered delivery of a stream of data between applications. TCP, however, introduces quite a bit of overhead. Not only because of the introduction of TCP header data, but also because of the acknowledgements the sender requires from the receiver for each packet (or series of packets).

In contrast, the User Datagram Protocol (UDP) emphasizes reduced latency over reliability. It sends data without checking if the data arrived, which reduces much overhead. UDP is typically used when some packet loss is acceptable, like in real-time voice and video streams, or when only small amounts of data are transmitted, that fit in one IP packet (like DNS, where queries must be fast and only consist of a single request followed by a single reply packet). UDP is also used by SNMP and DHCP, explained later in this chapter (17.3).

TCP and UDP use logical port numbers. An application on a host typically binds itself to one logical port number so it can be addressed separately from the other applications on that host. Each side of a TCP or UDP connection uses an associated port number between 0 and 65,535. Received TCP or UDP packets are identified as belonging to a specific connection by its combination of the IP address, and the TCP or UDP port number. For instance: 192.168.1.2:80, where the number after the colon represents the port number.

Servers running a specific service listen to well-known ports, so clients know what port to use to connect to the service. Examples of well-known ports are FTP (port 21), SSH (port 22), SMTP (port 25), DNS (port 53), and HTTP (port 80).

8.2.5.2 Network Address Translation (NAT)

Network Address Translation (NAT) allows the use of a private addressing space within an organization, while using globally unique addresses for routing data to the internet. Typically, NAT is performed by the router connected to the internet. As a packet passes a NAT enabled router from its internal network interface to its internet interface, NAT replaces the packet's private IP address with its public IP address.

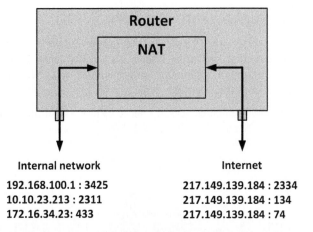

Figure 43: Network Address Translation

TCP and UDP headers support up to 65,536 port numbers, most of which are unused. By mapping an internal address/port combination to an internet address/port combination, NAT can support a large number of sessions with one internet address.

With NAT, all connections from within the organization seem to come from one internet IP address, limiting the number of IP addresses needed by an organization. With NAT, an organization needs a small set of IP addresses, even if they have many systems directly connecting to the internet, as each IP address can be used to setup 64,535 IP connections. In practice, only systems that need to be reachable from the internet, or systems that need to send data directly to the internet, need NAT addresses. Examples are email servers, web servers or web proxy servers. End user workstations typically only indirectly communicate to the internet using one of these servers, so they don't need a NAT address.

8.2.6   Session layer

The session layer provides mechanisms for opening, closing and managing a session between end-user application processes. Session-layer services are commonly used in application environments that make use of remote procedure calls (RPCs). The session layer also implements VPNs using protocols like PPTP and L2TP.

8.2.6.1   Virtual Private Network (VPN)

A Virtual Private Network (VPN) uses a public network to interconnect private sites in a secure way (also known as a VPN tunnel). While VPNs typically use the internet, a VPN could also make use of a telecom provider's backbone separate from the internet – dedicated for business use.

As an alternative to a dedicated leased line, a VPN uses "virtual" connections based on IPsec/SSL (Secure Sockets Layer). Most network providers also offer private VPNs based on MPLS.

Figure 44: VPN tunnel

VPN tunnels can be deployed relatively fast. As soon as an internet connection is available, a remote site can create a VPN tunnel to the organization's headquarters, extending the LAN to the new location.

Since VPNs use strong encryption and strong user authentication, using the internet for transmitting sensitive data is considered safe. The reliability of the internet connections, however, can be a barrier for using VPNs for WAN connections.

VPN tunnels are also often used for remote access to the LAN by users outside of the organization's premises. An internet connection and a computer running VPN client software is all that is required to allow a remote user the same network access as in the office.

The following are the three most common VPN communications protocol standards:

- **The Point-to-Point Tunneling Protocol (PPTP)** is designed for individual client to server connections. It enables only a single point-to-point connection per session. This standard is very common with Windows clients. PPTP uses native Point-to-Point Protocol (PPP) authentication and encryption services.

- **The Layer 2 Tunneling Protocol (L2TP)** was also designed for single point-to-point client to server connections. Multiple protocols can be encapsulated within the L2TP tunnel.

- **IPsec** enables multiple and simultaneous tunnels and can encrypt and authenticate IP data. It is built into IPv6 standard and is implemented as an add-on to IPv4. While PPTP and L2TP are aimed more at VPNs for ad-hoc end user connections, IPsec focuses more on network-to-network connectivity.

8.2.7   Presentation layer

This layer takes the data provided by the application layer and converts it into a standard format that the other layers can understand. Many protocols are implemented in the presentation layer, but SSL and TLS are the most important ones.

8.2.7.1   SSL and TLS

Transport Layer Security (TLS) and Secure Sockets Layer (SSL) – both of which are frequently incorrectly referred to as 'SSL' – are two communication protocols that allow applications to communicate securely over the internet using data encryption. TLS is based on SSL, but has a different initial handshake protocol and is more extensible.

The SSL protocol was originally developed by Netscape. Version 1.0 was never publicly released; version 2.0 was released in 1995 but contained a number of security flaws, which ultimately led to the design of SSL version 3.0, released in 1996. Nowadays, SSL is considered insecure and should not be used.

TLS 1.0 was first defined in 1999 as an upgrade to SSL 3.0. A prominent use of TLS is securing WWW traffic carried by HTTP to form HTTPS. As of 2017, TLS version 1.2 is considered secure and version 1.3 is in a draft state.

TLS relies on an application capable of handling the protocol (like a Web browser) instead of custom VPN clients to logon to the private network. By utilizing the TLS network protocols built into standard Web browsers and Web servers, TLS VPNs are easier to set up and maintain than IPsec VPNs.

8.2.8   Application layer

This is the layer that interacts with the operating system or application whenever the user chooses to transfer files, read messages, or performs other network related activities. Protocols like HTTP, FTP, SMTP and POP3 (e-mail), and CIFS (Common Internet File System) Windows file sharing, also known as SMB (Server Message Block), are all examples of application layer protocols.

This layer also contains the relatively simple infrastructure services like DNS, BOOTP, DHCP, and NTP. These infrastructure services are used by the infrastructure itself, and are not necessarily used by upper layer applications. Please note that if infrastructure services fail usually the entire infrastructure fails! Therefore, these services must be implemented in a high available manner and care must be taken of the performance, as low performing infrastructure services will also stall the rest of the infrastructure.

In the next sections the BOOTP, DHCP, DNS, and NTP protocols are discussed.

8.2.8.1 BOOTP and DHCP

BOOTP was designed in 1984 to automatically assign IP addresses to hosts from a centralized BOOTP server. A BOOTP server uses a list of hardware MAC addresses of the hosts in the network. When a BOOTP enabled host starts up, it sends a BOOTP broadcast packet. The BOOTP server receives the broadcast and looks for the MAC address of the broadcast packet in its list. It then sends the corresponding IP address back to the requesting host. The host uses that IP address for further communications.

The Dynamic Host Configuration Protocol, or DHCP, was defined in 1993 as an extension to BOOTP, mainly because BOOTP required manual configuration for each host in the network, and did not provide a mechanism for reclaiming unused IP addresses. DHCP can dynamically assign the following network related parameters to hosts:

- IP addresses
- Subnet masks
- Default gateway to be used for routing
- DNS server to be used

DHCP superseded BOOTP because it has more options. DHCP provides addresses to hosts from a pre-configured list or range of IP addresses. Typically, DHCP assigns addresses to workstations and remote or mobile devices, while servers, printers, routers, and other network equipment are assigned static IP addresses (with or without the help of DHCP).

Similar to BOOTP, when a new host is connected to the network, the operating system on that host sends a DHCP broadcast to the network asking for a DHCP response. The DHCP server then sends the IP configuration to the client's MAC address. The client configures its IP stack with the received configuration.

In principle, each IP subnet needs a DHCP server, since DHCP broadcasts cannot pass routers. Fortunately, routers can be configured to act as relay agents passing DHCP messages, eliminating the need for a DHCP server on each subnet.

A DHCP assigned IP address has a limited life span, typically a few hours. This is called a lease. When the lease expires, the host can ask for a renewal of the lease to keep its current IP settings. The DHCP server decides if the lease is renewed, or if the host gets new IP settings. When a network connection is lost the host always asks the DHCP server for a renewal. This allows for instance laptops to be reconnected at another network connection without rebooting. The DHCP server of the (sub) network provides the laptop automatically with a new IP address at this new location.

DHCP servers can be configured to provide the same IP address to a certain host at all times (for instance when DHCP is used to provide IP addresses to servers). The MAC address of the host is then bound to a fixed IP address in the DHCP server's configuration.

8.2.8.2   DNS

The Domain Name System (DNS) is a distributed database that links IP addresses with domain names. It translates domain names, meaningful to humans, into IP addresses.

When for instance a web browser tries to connect to *www.sjaaklaan.com*, in the background the web server's hostname www.sjaaklaan.com is sent to a DNS server that translates the hostname to the corresponding IP address (in this case 217.149.139.184). This IP address is then used by the browser to actually connect to the web server. DNS is also used to find mail servers (like when sending an e-mail to *sjaak@sjaaklaan.com*) and aliases to URLs of a certain domain.

The DNS protocol was developed in the early 1980s. Over the years, DNS was implemented on all major operating systems. The most used implementation is BIND (Berkeley Internet Name Domain). BIND was originally created for UNIX systems, but later it was also used on almost all other operating systems. Windows, however, uses its own implementation of DNS.

Before DNS, systems managers kept so-called hosts files that contained the IP addresses of all other hosts a host could connect to. When such a list is relatively small this is a workable solution (hosts files still work in most operating systems, including Windows, UNIX, and Linux). But with the growth of the internet a more scalable solution was needed.

DNS distributes the responsibility of mapping domain names to IP addresses by designating authoritative name servers for each domain. Authoritative name servers are responsible for their particular domains, and in turn can assign other authoritative name servers for their sub-domains. This mechanism has made the DNS distributed and fault tolerant.

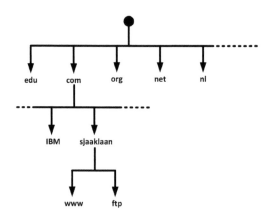

Figure 45: Distributed DNS tree

DNS resolution allows for caching of received records. The period of validity of the cached records is configurable and may vary from seconds to days or even weeks. Because of this caching mechanism, changes to DNS records don't propagate throughout the network immediately, but require all caches to expire and refresh. This means that changes in DNS records can take several hours or even days to propagate through the entire internet.

8.2.8.2.1 DNSSEC

DNS was not designed with security in mind, and it has a number of security issues. For example, updates to DNS records are done in non-encrypted clear text, and the authorization is based on IP addresses only.

To overcome these issues, in 1999 DNS Security Extensions (DNSSEC) was introduced to add security to DNS. DNSSEC is a set of extensions to DNS that provides origin authentication of DNS data and data integrity. By checking the digital signature (see section 6.3.4.3), a DNS resolver is able to verify that the information used by the DNS resolver is identical (correct and complete) to the information on the authoritative DNS server.

DNSSEC does not solve all DNS security issues. For example, it does not provide confidentiality of data – the transferred DNS records are still transferred in clear text. Also, DNSSEC does not protect against DDoS attacks against DNS servers.

While the benefits of using DNSSEC are obvious, it is still not in wide spread use today, mainly because all DNS servers must implement DNSSEC in order to make full use of all benefits.

8.2.8.3   IPAM systems

IP address management (IPAM) systems are appliances that can be used to plan, track, and manage IP addresses in a network. IPAM systems integrate DNS, DHCP, and IP address administration in one high available redundant set of appliances. Functions in the IPAM system are integrated, so that DNS is updated based on IP addresses delivered to clients by DHCP. Most IPAM systems also provide some reporting capabilities on the number of active IP addresses and the usage of subnets.

8.2.8.4   Network Time Protocol (NTP)

The Network Time Protocol (NTP) version 1 was introduced in 1988. It ensures that all infrastructure components use the same time in their real-time clocks. This is particularly important for usage in:

- **Log file analysis** – When tracing information through various infrastructure components, log files show what happened at what point in time. It is crucial for the time stamps in each of the log files of the all infrastructure components to be synchronized and correct.

- **Clustering software** –Clocks of the nodes in a cluster must run as much in sync as possible.

- **Kerberos authentication** – In order for Kerberos authentication to function correctly all clocks must be in sync.

NTP can maintain time to within 10 milliseconds over the internet, and achieves accuracies of 0.2 milliseconds or better in LANs. NTP uses complex algorithms to minimize the influence of network latency introduced by the physical distance of NTP servers.

NTP servers can be implemented as software on most operating systems, routers, and switches, but can also be implemented using dedicated hardware appliances – often using some external signal like long wave radio clocks or GPS clocks. NTP time synchronization services are also widely available on the internet.

NTP operates within a hierarchy, where each level in the hierarchy is assigned a number called the stratum. The stratum defines its distance from the reference clock. Devices such as atomic clocks, GPS clocks, or radio clocks have stratum 0. Stratum 1 NTP servers are directly synchronized with stratum 0 devices. Stratum 2 (secondary) servers are synchronizing to stratum 1 servers and so on.

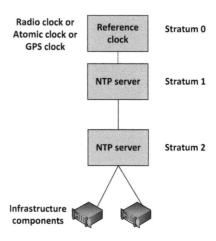

Figure 46: NTP

When the time in an operating system is incorrect, the NTP client in the operating system changes the operating system clock. This is usually not done at once. Sudden changes in time could introduce undesirable results, especially when the clock is set back in time. For instance, log files could start showing double entries and timeouts could get mixed up. Therefore, the time is adjusted in small steps, and the clock "drifts" to the correct time. The amount of time this takes is dependent on the time difference between the NTP time and the operating system time, but it typically takes minutes to hours to complete. When the operating system time is off to a large degree, usually NTP does not try to correct it, but sends a warning to the operating system log files instead.

NTP provides time in Coordinated Universal Time (UTC, previously known as Greenwich Mean Time – GMT). The translation to the local time zone, including the switch to and from daylight saving time, is done at the operating system level, not in NTP clocks.

When using virtual machines (see section 10.2.5.3), each virtual machine should be configured to synchronize the time individually, instead of using tools that synchronize the time with the hardware clock of the physical machine. This makes the time in the virtual machines much more accurate.

8.3 Network virtualization

Network virtualization can be implemented in a number of ways. In this section, we discuss VLANs, virtual switches, software defined networking and network function virtualization.

8.3.1 Virtual LAN (VLAN)

Virtual LANs (VLANs) enable logical grouping of network nodes on the same LAN. VLANs are configured on network switches and operate at the Ethernet level. No extra configuration is needed on hosts using a VLAN.

General purpose of implementing VLANs is to allow segmenting a network at the data link layer without depending on network layer devices, such as routers.

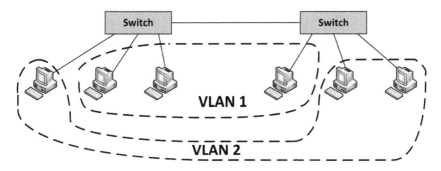

Figure 47: Two VLANs in one LAN

VLANs have the same attributes as a physical LAN, but they allow end stations to be grouped together even if they are not physically connected to the same switch. VLANs offer the flexibility to adapt to changes in network requirements and allow simplified administration.

For VLANs to communicate with each other a router is needed.

Because of the stretched broadcast domain, it is not recommended to have a VLAN spanning multiple locations.

VLANs can enhance security by preventing traffic in one VLAN from being seen by hosts in a different VLAN. It is a weak security control, however, because when traffic is routed between VLANs, or when multi-homed systems are used, VLANs can see each other's traffic again.

8.3.2   VXLAN

Virtual Extensible LAN (VXLAN) is an encapsulation protocol that can be used to create a logical switched layer 2 network across routed layer 3 networks. Like VLANs, only servers within the same logical network can communicate with each other.

VXLANs are heavily used in multi-tenant cloud environments, as they allow many fully separated LAN segments to co-exist in a shared environment. Where VLANs only allow for a maximum of 4,096 network IDs, VXLAN increases the number of available IDs to 16 million.

8.3.3   Virtual NICs

Physical machines contain physical NICs. Virtual machines running on physical machines share these NICs, where the hypervisor (see section 10.2.5.3.3 for more information on hypervisors) provides virtual NICs to the virtual machines, enabling them to communicate to other virtual machines on the same physical machine. Communications between virtual machines on the same physical machine are routed directly in memory space by the hypervisor, without using the physical NIC at all.

When a virtual machine wants to communicate to a virtual machine hosted on another physical machine, the hypervisor routes Ethernet packages from the virtual NIC on the virtual machine to the physical NIC on the physical machine.

Virtual machines are only aware of virtual NICs provided to them. And since physical NICs are invisible to virtual machines, so is the way the physical NICs are connected to the physical network. The hypervisor can use NIC teaming or other technologies to redundantly connect physical machines, while the virtual machines still only see one virtual NIC. This simplifies the network configuration within the virtual machine's operating system.

8.3.4   Virtual switch

In virtual machines, virtual NICs are connected to virtual switches. A virtual switch is an application running in the hypervisor (see section 10.2.5.3.3), with most of the capabilities of a physical network switch. A virtual switch is dynamically configured, and since the ports in the virtual switch are configured at runtime, the number of ports on the switch is in theory unlimited.

In a virtual switch, no transformations to and from physical cables are needed, so no cable disconnects can occur, there is no need for auto-detecting network speed, and a virtual switch doesn't have to learn the MAC addresses of the connected NICs, as they are already known by the hypervisor. This increases speed and reliability, and reduces complexity, compared to physical switches.

Virtual networking also improves security, as there is no easy way to intercept network communications between virtual machines from outside of the physical machine. Virtual networking also improves availability because there are no network hubs, routers, adapters, or cables that could physically fail.

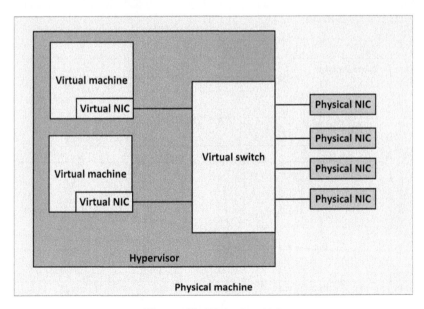

Figure 48: Virtual switch

A virtual switch can be connected to multiple physical NICs, but a physical NIC can only be connected to one virtual switch. This avoids unwanted and illegal network paths.

A tradeoff of a virtual switch is that they are software based only, which is slower than a hardware based switch, as physical network switches benefit from hardware acceleration using specialized hardware circuitry (Application-specific Integrated Circuits – ASICs) for high speed packet switching.

8.3.5 Software Defined Networking

Software Defined Networking (SDN) is a relatively new concept. It allows networks to be defined and controlled using software external to the physical networking devices.

With SDN, a relatively simple physical network can be programmed to act as a complex virtual network. A set of physical network switches can be programmed as a hierarchical, complex and secured virtual network that can easily be changed without touching the physical network components.

This is particularly useful in a cloud environment, where networks change frequently as machines are added or removed from a tenant's environment. With a single click of a button or a single API call, complex networks can be created within seconds.

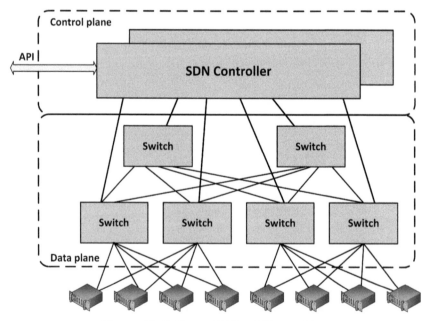

Figure 49: Software Defined Networking

SDN works by decoupling the control plane and data plane from each other, such that the control plane resides centrally and the data plane (the physical switches) remain distributed, as shown in Figure 49.

This way, the SDN can be controlled from a single management console that provides open APIs that can be used to manage the network using third party software.

In a traditional switch or router, network devices dynamically learn packet forwarding rules and store them in each device as ARP or routing tables. In an SDN, the distributed data plane devices are only forwarding network packets based on ARP or routing rules that are preloaded into the devices by the SDN controller in the control plane. This allows the physical devices to be much simpler and more cost effective.

8.3.6 Network Function Virtualization

In addition to SDN, Network Function Virtualization (NFV) is a way to virtualize networking devices like firewalls, VPN gateways and load balancers. Instead of having hardware appliances for each network function, in NFV, these appliances are implemented in virtual machines running applications that perform the network functions.

Using APIs, NFV virtual appliances can be created and configured dynamically and on-demand, leading to a flexible network configuration. It allows, for instance, deploying a new firewall as part of a script that creates a number of connected virtual machines in a cloud environment.

8.4 Network availability

Since networks are one of the basic IT infrastructure components, their reliability is of the utmost importance. High availability in networking is reached through concepts like:

- Layered network topology

- Spine and Leaf topology

- Network teaming

- The spanning tree protocol

- Multihoming

Each of these concepts are discussed in the next sections.

8.4.1 Layered network topology

To improve availability and performance, a network infrastructure should be built up in layers. Figure 50 gives an example of a layered switched network.

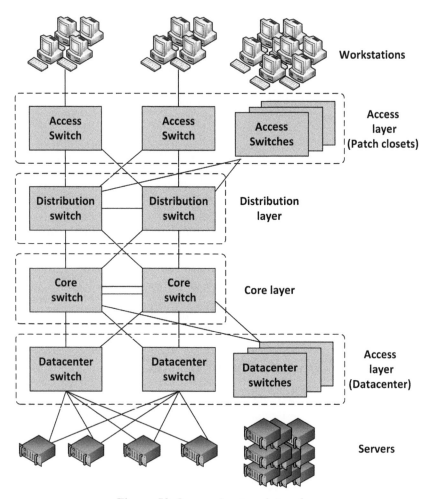

Figure 50: Layered network topology

Layering provides scalability and deterministic routing and avoids unmanaged ad-hoc data streams. Because the layering provides multiple paths to any piece of equipment, the availability of this setup is very high.

The design of a layered network is often driven by the bandwidth and port density required at the top and bottom of the network, but Ethernet broadcast boundaries are also a major design consideration.

Typical layers are:

- **The core layer** - This is the center of the network, providing redundant connectivity to the distribution layer.

- **The distribution layer** - The distribution layer is an intermediate layer between the core layer in the datacenter and the access switches in the patch closets. Because typically many access switches are used in a building and core switch ports are expensive, the distribution layer combines the access layer data and sends its combines data to one or two ports on the core switches.

- **The access layer** - Switches in this layer are used to connect workstations and servers to the distribution layer. For servers, they are typically located at the top of the individual server racks or in blade enclosures. For workstations, these are typically placed in patch closets in various parts of the building (typically each floor in a building has its own patch closet, sometimes more than one).

An oversubscription ratio can be used to handle the increased bandwidth needs when approaching the core of the network. Between the access layer and the distribution layer an oversubscription ratio of 20:1 is common. This means that the bandwidth of the uplink of the access layer to the distribution layer is 20 times less than the combined bandwidth of the connections on the access layer itself.

For instance, with an oversubscription ratio of 20:1, when an access layer switch is equipped with 200 ports of 100 Mbit/s each (a total bandwidth of 20 Gbit/s), an uplink of 1 Gbit/s is needed to the distribution layer switches.

A much-used oversubscription ratio between the distribution layer and the core layer is 4:1.

8.4.2   Spine and Leaf topology

In a Software Defined Network (see section 8.3.5), a simple physical network is used that can be programmed to act as a complex virtual network. Such a network can be organized in a spine and leaf topology, as shown in Figure 51.

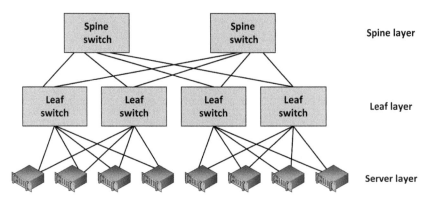

Figure 51: Spine and leaf topology

In contrast with a layered network topology, in a spine and leaf topology, the spine switches are not interconnected. Each leaf switch is connected to all spine switches and each server is connected to two leaf switches.

The connections between spine and leaf switches typically have ten times the bandwidth of the connectivity between the leaf switches and the servers.

This topology has a number of benefits:

- With today's high density switches, typically populated with 48 ports, many physical servers (each containing several virtual servers) can be connected using relatively few switches.

- Each server is always exactly four hops away from every other server, which leads to a very predictable latency.

- The topology is simple to scale: just add spine or leaf servers.

- Since there are no interconnects between the spine switches, the design is highly scalable.

8.4.3   Network teaming

Network teaming, also known as link aggregation, port trunking (see section 5.5.8), or network bonding, provides a virtual network connection using multiple physical cables for high availability and increased bandwidth.

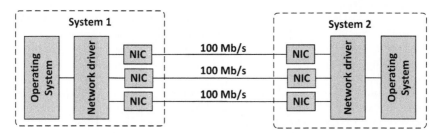

Figure 52: Network teaming

The technology bonds physical NICs (Network Interface Controllers) together to form a logical network team that sends traffic to the team's destination to all NICs in the team. This allows a single NIC, cable, or switch to be unavailable without interrupting Ethernet traffic.

Network teaming allows (physical) network maintenance on active network connections. When maintenance is performed on one cable, the team uses the other cables. And when the first cable is ready, another cable can be taken down for maintenance.

8.4.4   Spanning Tree Protocol

The Spanning Tree Protocol (STP) is an Ethernet level protocol that runs on switches. STP guarantees that only one path is active between two network endpoints at any given time. With STP, redundant paths are automatically activated when the active path experiences problems.

For example, in Figure 53, when Server A wants to communicate with Server B the communication path is:

Server A => Switch 3 => Switch 1 => Switch 4 => Server B

In this situation Switch 1 is the root of the spanning tree.

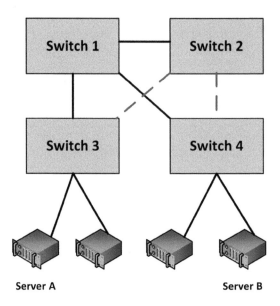

Figure 53: Spanning tree with root switch 1

If switch 1 fails for some reason, the STP protocol reconfigures the network automatically.

In the new configuration, when server A wants to communicate with server B, the communication path is:

Server A => Switch 3 => Switch 2 => Switch 4 => Server B

In this situation switch 2 is the root of the spanning tree.

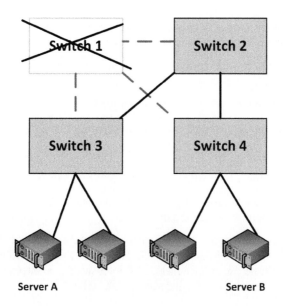

Figure 54: Spanning tree with root switch 2

STP also ensures that no loops are created when redundant paths are available in the network. Without STP, network switches with redundant links can cause broadcasts to continuously circle the network – also known as a broadcast storm. STP avoids this by switching off redundant links when they are not needed.

A disadvantage of using the spanning tree protocol is that it is not using half of the network links in a network, since it blocks redundant paths.

STP was designed at a time when the recovery of connectivity after an outage within a minute was considered adequate. Within datacenters Rapid Spanning Tree Protocol (RSTP) is preferred. The RSTP provides for fast spanning tree convergence after a topology change. While STP can take 30 to 60 seconds to respond to a topology change, RSTP is typically able to respond to changes within 6 seconds, or within a few milliseconds in case of a physical link failure.

8.4.5 Multihoming

Connecting a network to two different Internet Service Providers (ISPs) is called multihoming. Multihoming is a good practice to enhance the availability of internet connectivity by providing redundant internet connections and/or gateways. It also provides network optimization by selecting the ISP or router which offers the best path to an online resource.

In general, there are four options for multihoming, which are (in ascending order of complexity and cost):

- Single router with dual links to a single ISP.

- Single router with dual links to two separate ISPs.

- Dual routers, each with its own link to a single ISP.

- Dual routers, each with its own link to a separate ISP.

While the last option provides the highest availability, it also is the most expensive and complex configuration.

In WANs try to ensure redundant physical cables are used. Since WAN cables are typically installed alongside highways and railway tracks, and because they are used by multiple carrier providers, it is not always guaranteed that multiple network paths actually run on a different set of cables.

8.5 Network performance

Modem and line speeds have become much faster over the years. Nielsen's law states that network connection speeds for high-end home users increase 50% per year, or double every 21 months. Mr. Nielsen predicted this in 1983 and it is still very accurate, as shown in Figure 55.

I remember in 1998 we needed a 2 Mbit/s leased line to a frame relay network, and we had to pay $8,000 per month for that connection!

At the time of writing (2017) my home internet subscription costs me $70 per month, delivering 120 Mbit/s; sixty times as much bandwidth for less than one percent of the cost!

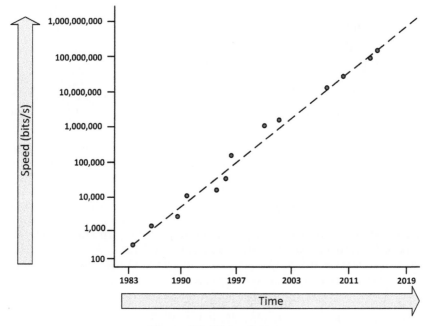

Figure 55: Nielsen's law

There is no reason to assume Nielsen's law will become invalid in the coming years. Regular bandwidths should be 15 Gbit/s in 2025, still for a price of about $50 per month.

There are many ways to measure the performance of a network, as each network is different in design. Throughput, latency, the type of information transmitted, and the way that information is applied all affect the speed of a connection. In the next sections the following concepts are discussed:

- Throughput and bandwidth

- Latency

- Quality of Service (QoS)

- WAN link compression

8.5.1 Throughput and bandwidth

Throughput is the amount of data that is transferred through the network during a specific time interval. Throughput is limited by the available bandwidth. Therefore, the terms 'throughput' and 'bandwidth' are often used interchangeably.

When an application requires more throughput than a network connection can deliver, queues in the network components temporarily buffer data. Buffered data is sent as soon as the network connection is free again. When more data arrives than the queues can store in the buffer, packet loss can occur. To avoid packet loss, the higher layer network protocols typically throttle the data stream.

If possible, try to schedule throughput-intensive applications (like batch jobs and backup jobs) at a time the network is least busy with interactive users.

8.5.2   Latency

Latency is defined as the time from the start of packet transmission to the start of packet reception. Latency is dependent on the distance (in km) that a packet has to travel, given that it travels at nearly the speed of light, and the number of switches and routers the packet has to pass.

As a rule of thumb, latency due to distance is 6 ms per 100 km. In WANs expect each switch in the path to add another 10 ms to the one-way delay, and in LANs add 1 ms for each switch.

In a packet-switched network latency is measured either one-way (the time from the source sending a packet to the destination receiving it), or round-trip (the one-way latency from source to destination plus the one-way latency from the destination back to the source).

Most operating systems and network equipment provide a tool called "ping" that can be used to measure round-trip latency. Ping performs no packet processing; it merely sends a response back when it receives a packet and it is a relatively accurate way of measuring latency.

8.5.3   Quality of Service (QoS)

Quality of service (QoS) is the ability to provide different data flow priority to different applications, users, or types of data. QoS allows better service to certain important data flows compared to less important data flows. This is done by treating high priority traffic different than low priority traffic, for instance by dropping low priority traffic when buffers fill up or by using queues with different priorities.

QoS is mainly used for real-time applications like video and audio streams and VoIP telephony. This allows, for example, a large download via FTP and a VoIP call to use the same bandwidth without causing jittering on the VoIP audio. The FTP download will slow down slightly as bandwidth is needed for VoIP, provided, of course, VoIP was given a higher priority.

There are four basic ways to implement QoS:

- **Congestion management** - This defines what must be done if the amount of data to be sent exceeds the bandwidth of the network link. Packets can either be dropped or queued (using multiple queues for multiple QoS streams). It should be noted that the TCP protocol already automatically slows down when packet loss is detected.

- **Queue management** - When queues are full, packets will be dropped. Queue management defines criteria for dropping packets that are of lower priority before dropping higher priority packets.

- **Link efficiency** - This ensures that the link is used in an optimized way, for instance by fragmenting large packets with a low QoS, allowing packets with a high QoS to be sent between the fragments of low QoS packets.

- **Traffic shaping** – By limiting the full bandwidth of streams with a low QoS to benefit streams with a high QoS, high QoS streams have a reserved amount of bandwidth.

8.5.4   WAN link compression

Data compression can be used to reduce the size of data before it is transmitted over a WAN connection. WAN acceleration appliances can be deployed to provide this compression task and to perform some caching of regularly used data at remote sites.

Note that compression uses CPU resources in the routers handling the compression. When routers are heavily loaded, compression is not recommended.

8.6   Network security

Network security can be implemented using firewalls, DMZs, RADIUS and NAC.

8.6.1   Firewalls

Firewalls separate two or more LAN or WAN segments for security reasons. Firewalls block all unpermitted network traffic between network segments, and permitted traffic must be explicitly enabled by configuring the firewall to allow it. Firewalls can be implemented in hardware appliances, as an application on physical servers, or in virtual machines.

A special type of firewall is a host based firewall, that protects a server or end user computer against network based attacks. This type of firewall is often part of the operating system (like the Windows firewall or Linux' IP tables).

Firewalls use one or more of the following methods to control traffic:

- **Packet filtering** – Data packets are analyzed using preconfigured filters. A typical filter can be: "TCP/IP packets sent to port 80 of any machine to the internet network segment are allowed". This functionality is almost always available on routers and most operating systems.

- **Proxy** (also known as **application layer firewalls**) – A proxy terminates the session on the application level on behalf of the server (proxy) or the client (reverse proxy) and creates a new session to the client or server. Typical use is a HTTP proxy server, which fetches web pages from the internet on behalf of a client in the internal LAN. The application layer firewall needs to have knowledge of the used application protocol and is able to detect anomalies in these protocols.

- **Stateful inspection** – This type of firewall inspects the placement of each individual packet within a packet stream. The firewall maintains records of all connections passing through the firewall and determines whether a packet is the start of a new connection, part of an existing connection, or is an invalid packet.

8.6.2 IDS/IPS

An Intrusion Detection System (IDS) or Intrusion Prevention System (IPS) detects and – if possible – prevents activities that either compromise system security, or are a hacking attempt. An IDS/IPS monitors for suspicious (and possibly hostile) activity and alerts the systems manager when these activities are detected. A typical example of an IDS/IPS alert is the occurrence of a port scan, often used by hackers to find vulnerabilities in internet-attached devices.

IDS monitors a server or a network and provides alerts when something suspicious happens. An IPS, however, can also stop attacks by for instance changing firewall rules on the fly to block detected unwanted traffic. IPS systems are often combined with firewall functionality or have a direct interface to it.

Two types of IDS/IPS systems exist: Network-based IDS (NIDS) and Host-based IDS (HIDS).

- A **NIDS** is typically placed at a strategic point within the network to monitor traffic to and from all devices on that network. A good place would be a central firewall, a core switch or a DMZ router. The NIDS is not part of the network flow, but just "looks at it", to avoid detection of the NIDS by hackers.

- A **HIDS** runs on individual servers or network devices, where it monitors the network traffic of that device. It also monitors user behavior and the alteration of critical (system) files. A good place for a HIDS is a critical (production) server, or a server that can be reached from the internet, like a webserver, an email server or an FTP server.

An IDS system works in one of two ways:

- Looking for specific signatures of known threats; similar to the way antivirus software works (also known as a statistical anomaly-based IDS)

- Comparing traffic patterns against a baseline (the known normal behavior) and looking for anomalies (also known as a signature-based IDS)

8.6.3   DMZ

DMZ is short for De-Militarized Zone, also known as screened subnet, or the Perimeter Network.

> *Originally, DMZ was a term used during the Korean War to indicate a no-man's land where troops residing in North Korea and South Korea were not allowed to enter. The DMZ was a zone of security created to prevent attacks and intrusions from either side.*

In IT networks a DMZ is a network that serves as a buffer between a secure protected internal network and the insecure internet.

Figure 56 shows an example of such a network. It shows segmentation in an internal LAN, a DMZ LAN segment, and the internet.

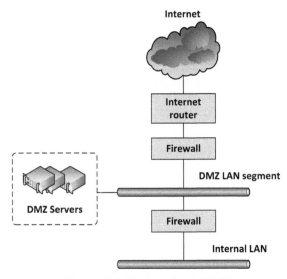

Figure 56: Back-to-back DMZ

Each of the LAN segments is separated from the other segments by firewalls. This is called a back-to-back DMZ. A fast packet filtering router can be set as the outside firewall (connected to the internet) and an application level firewall as the inside firewall (connected to the LAN).

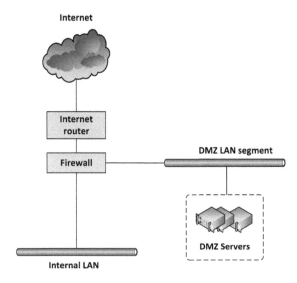

Figure 57: Trihomed DMZ

As an alternative, a Trihomed DMZ uses a single firewall with three interfaces; one interface for the internet, the second for the internal LAN, and the third for the DMZ LAN segment. Separate rules must be configured for each traffic flow based on the origin and the destination.

While a trihomed firewall solution is cheaper than using two firewalls, I don't recommend it. If, by chance, the systems manager makes a mistake when configuring the firewall, the security of the whole network could be compromised. Using two firewalls at least keeps basic security in place in such cases.

No *direct* traffic is allowed from the internal LAN to the internet (or other external networks) and vice versa. This traffic must be terminated on a system in the DMZ (like a web server, a mail relay, or a web browsing proxy server).

While in practice exceptions will occur to this rule (when a "hole" is created in the firewall), these exceptions should be kept to a minimum. Typically, all sessions initiated by external systems trying to connect to internal systems are strictly forbidden.

The servers in the DMZ should preferably have no data storage to lower the risk of data exposure when a server in the DMZ is compromised. But when data *must* be stored in the DMZ, an isolated SAN should be used, or better: only use direct attached storage (local disks) to avoid attacks through the Fibre Channel interfaces. All devices in the DMZ should be hardened with limited functionality.

Windows servers in the DMZ should not be part of the Windows domain of the servers in the internal LAN. Preferably the servers should not be part of any domain, but if they must, a separate Windows domain should be created that is used only in the DMZ LAN segment.

8.6.4 RADIUS

Remote Authentication Dial In User Service (RADIUS) is a networking protocol that provides centralized user and authorization management for network devices such as routers, modem servers, switches, VPN routers, and wireless network access points.

RADIUS is supported by virtually all network components. These devices generally cannot deal with a large number of users and specific authorization details, since that would require more storage than most devices have.

RADIUS authenticates users or devices before granting them access to a network and authorizes users or devices for certain network services. A RADIUS client sends encrypted user credentials to a RADIUS server. The

RADIUS server authenticates and authorizes the RADIUS client request, and sends back a RADIUS message response (accepted or rejected).

The RADIUS client and the RADIUS server use encryption based on a shared secret. The shared secret is commonly configured as a text string on both the RADIUS client and server.

8.6.5   Network Access Control (NAC)

Network Access Control (NAC) is used at the network end points, where end user devices (like laptops) can be connected to the network. It allows predefined levels of network access based on a client's identity (is the laptop known to the organization?), the groups to which a client belongs, and the degree to which a client's device complies with the organization's governance policies (does it run the most recent virus scanner?).

If a client device is not compliant, NAC provides a mechanism to automatically bring it into compliance, for instance by installing the latest virus scanner updates while connected on an isolated LAN segment. After the update finishes, access is granted to the rest of the network.

9

STORAGE

9.1 Introduction

Every day, approximately 15 petabytes of new information is generated worldwide, and the total amount of digital data doubles approximately every two years[37]. About 70% of this data is unstructured (office files, audio and video, e-mail), the rest is structured (stored in databases). To store all this data, storage systems are used.

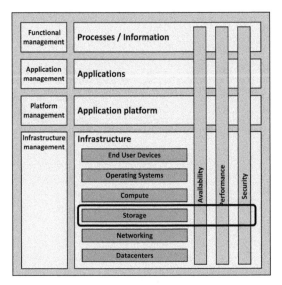

Figure 58: Storage in the infrastructure model

Early computers used a very basic persistent storage system, based on punched cards or paper tape. Each time these computers were switched on, instructions were loaded in main memory and executed by manually flipping physical switches. These keyed-in instructions instructed the computer to load an application program in main memory from a paper tape or from punched cards. Input data was also stored on paper tape or punched cards and output was printed on paper.

Drum memory was one of the first magnetic read/write storage systems. It was widely used in the 1950s and into the 1960s. For many computers in those days, the drum formed the main working memory of the machine.

Picture 17: Drum memory

Drum memory consisted of a large rotating metal cylinder that was coated on the outside with magnetic recording material. Multiple rows of fixed read-write heads were placed along the drum, each head reading or writing to one track. The drum could store 62 kB of data.

Later, hard disks were constructed with a set of rotating disk platters and magnetic read/write heads mounted on a movable arm. This made the construction much smaller than drum memory, and still allowed the read/write heads to reach any place on the disk.

Picture 18: RAMAC 350 Random Access Magnetic Disk Drive[38]

The first commercial digital disk storage device was part of the IBM RAMAC 350 system, shipped in 1956. It could store approximately 5 MB of data, was composed of fifty 61 cm diameter disks, and weighed over a ton. In contrast, in 1980, Seagate Technology created the first hard disk drive that fit in a PC, also with a 5MB capacity.

Over the years, the physical size of hard disks shrunk, disk capacity increased because of increased magnetic density, the rotation speed increased from 3,600 rpm to 15,000 rpm, and seek times lowered as a result of using servo controlled read/write heads instead of stepper motors. But the fundamental design of a hard disk has not changed.

Tapes are another popular type of magnetic storage.

The IBM 726, introduced in 1952, was one of the first magnetic tape systems. It could store 2 MB per 20-centimeter-diameter reel of tape – an enormous amount at the time. Reel tapes were used until the late 1980s, mostly in mainframes.

Picture 19: Reel tape[39]

In 1984, DEC introduced the Digital Linear Tape (DLT) cartridge, superseded by Super DLT (SDLT) tape cartridges, that can store up to 300 GB of data.

Linear Tape Open (LTO) was originally developed in the late 1990s. LTO cartridges look similar to SDLT cartridges, and have roughly the same size, but they are not interchangeable. The most recent version (LTO version 7) was released in 2015 and can hold up to 6 TB of data[40].

Picture 20: LTO tape cartridge[41]

Today, the only alternative to LTO in capacity and performance is the Oracle/StorageTek T10000 tape, that can store 8.5 TB[42].

9.2   Storage building blocks

Servers can use internal storage only, but most use external storage, sometimes combined with internal storage. A model of storage building blocks is shown in Figure 59. Each building block is discussed in detail in de subsequent sections, starting at the lowest building blocks.

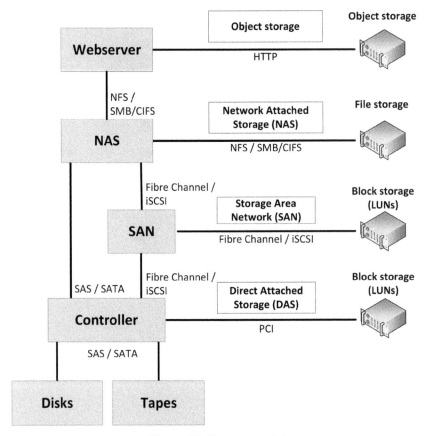

Figure 59: Storage model

9.2.1 Disks

Two types of disks are in use today:

- Mechanical hard disks
- SSD disks

Disks are connected to disk controllers using a command set, based on either ATA or SCSI.

9.2.1.1   Command sets

Disks communicate with disk controllers using a protocol based on either the ATA or SCSI command set.

Advanced Technology Attachment (ATA), also known as IDE, uses a relatively simple hardware and communication protocol to connect disks to computers (mostly PCs). For many years, ATA provided the most common and the least expensive disk interface.

Small Computer System Interface (SCSI) is a set of standards for physically connecting and transferring data between computers (mostly servers) and peripheral devices, like disks and tapes. The SCSI standard defines command sets for specific peripheral device types. The SCSI command set is complex - there are about 60 different SCSI commands in total.

The need for increased bandwidth and flexibility in storage systems made the original parallel SCSI and ATA standards an inefficient option. Serial interfaces replaced the parallel interfaces, but the disk commands are still the same.

9.2.1.2   Mechanical hard disks

Mechanical disks consist of vacuum sealed cases with one or more spinning magnetic disks on one spindle and a number of read/write heads that can move to reach each part of the spinning disks. Picture 21 shows a mechanical hard disk with its cover removed,

Picture 21: Hard disk internal mechanical construction

In today's systems, three mechanical (spinning) disk types are most common, depicted by their used interface:

- Serial ATA (SATA) disks

- Serial Attached SCSI (SAS) disks

- Near-Line SAS (NL-SAS) disks

SATA disks are low-end high-capacity disks. SATA disks are ideal for bulk storage applications (like archiving or backup) as they have a low cost per gigabyte. SATA disks are also often used in PCs and laptops. SATA disks use the SMART command set to control the disk. This command set is limited, but easy to implement.

SAS disks are relatively expensive, high end disks with spinning disk platters with a rotational speed of 10,000 or 15,000 rpm. This makes them very fast, but they typically have 25% of the capacity of SATA or NL-SAS disks.

SAS disks are high-end disks, because they have better error correction capabilities than SATA disks, and can move erroneous disk sectors to spare sectors automatically, making the disks very reliable. In addition, SAS uses the SCSI command set that includes error-recovery and error-reporting and more functionality than the SMART commands used by SATA disks.

NL-SAS disks have a SAS interface, but the mechanics of SATA disks. Because NL-SAS disks use the SAS protocol, they can be combined with faster SAS disks in one storage array. They are used for bulk storage applications as they can store much data, have a low cost per gigabyte and use much less energy than SAS disks, as they typically spin at just 7,200 rpm.

9.2.1.3 Solid State Drives (SSDs)

A Solid State Drive (SSD) is a disk that doesn't have moving parts and is based on flash technology. Flash technology is semiconductor-based memory that preserves its information when powered off. SSDs are connected using a standard SAS disk interface.

SSD's main advantage is performance. SSDs have no moving parts, so data can be accessed much faster than using mechanical disks (microseconds vs. milliseconds). Most storage vendors now offer all-flash arrays – storage systems using only SSD disks. For high-demanding Online Transaction Processing (OLTP) systems, these all-flash arrays are the preferred choice today, because of their high performance.

Picture 22: SSD disk[43]

SSDs consume less power, and therefore generate less heat, than mechanical disks. And since they have no moving parts, they generate no vibrations that could influence or harm other components, or shorten their lifetime.

The main disadvantage of SSDs is their price per gigabyte, which is considerably higher than mechanical disks, although their price per GB is dropping fast.

Another disadvantage of SSD is that the used flash memory can only be rewritten a limited number of times – the disks "wear out" more rapidly than mechanical disks. To overcome this disadvantage, SSDs keep track of the number of times a sector is rewritten, and map much used sectors to spare sectors if they are about to wear out. It is important to monitor the wear level of heavily used SSDs, so they can be replaced before they break.

SSDs are constructed of flash technology using either Single Level Cell (SLC) or Multi-Level Cell (MLC) architectures. SLC stores one bit per memory cell, while MLC has four states per cell that enables them to store 2 bits. MLC based SSDs therefore typically have double the storage capacity, but also double the access time of their SLC counterparts. Technology is moving fast in this area, so more advanced flash storage technologies are expected in the forthcoming years.

Some SSDs utilize RAID technology internally (RAID is discussed in section 9.2.3.1), to distribute data over the available flash chips on the SSD disk. The more RAID channels are available, and the bigger the number of flash chips, the faster the SSD disk can deliver data and the more reliable the SSD becomes.

9.2.1.4 Disk capacity - Kryder's law

Since the introduction of the first disk drives, physical disk sizes shrunk and disk capacity increased every year.

Figure 60 shows that the average disk capacity has followed a logarithmic increase in size for the last 30 years (note that the Y-axis is logarithmic instead of linear).

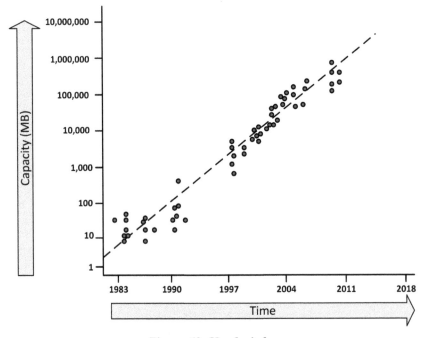

Figure 60: Kryder's law

Kryder's law[44] states that "*the density of information on hard drives has been growing at a rate, increasing by a factor of 1000 in 10.5 years, which roughly corresponds to a doubling every 13 months*". When Kryder's law holds true, an average single disk drive in 2025 will hold more than 20,000 TB (20 PB) of data!

Picture 23: 8 bytes versus 8 GB[45]

Picture 23 illustrates Kryder's law – it shows the physical size of 8 bytes of core memory from the 1960s, and a micro SD flash card containing 8 GB of memory from the 2010's – 1,000,000,000 times as much storage in 50 years.

When designing an infrastructure, it is good to be aware of Kryder's law (as well as Nielsen's law and Moore's law). It makes sense to not purchase too much spare capacity in advance, but instead to purchase and implement new disks "just in time". To have full benefits of Kryder's law, the storage infrastructure should be designed to handle just in time expansion using technologies like thin provisioning (more on that in section 9.2.3.4).

9.2.2 Tapes

When storing large amounts of data, tape is the most inexpensive option. And since tapes can store much data in a relatively small form factor, they can be used as a cheap archive medium. Tapes are suitable for archiving, since tape manufacturers guarantee a long life expectancy. For instance, DLT, SDLT, and LTO Ultrium cartridges are guaranteed to be readable after 30 years on the shelf[46].

Tapes can be stored offsite to protect data in case of disasters like fires. And, unlike online backups and archives, if the tapes are stored offsite, they are not corruptible by viruses and worms and they use no power.

Tapes have some disadvantages as well. Tapes are fragile. Manual handling can lead to mechanical defects due to tapes dropping on the floor, bumping, or bad insertions of tapes in tape drives. Since tapes contain mechanical parts, manually changed tapes get damaged easily. Frequent rewinding of the tape causes stress to the tape substrate, leading to lower reliability of data reads.

Compared to disks, tapes are extremely slow. They only write and read data sequentially. When a particular piece of data is required, it must be searched by reading all data on tape until the required data is found. Together with rewinding of the tape (needed for ejecting the tapes) handling tapes is expressed in minutes instead of in milliseconds or microseconds.

(S)DLT and LTO are the most popular tape cartridge formats in use today, where LTO has a market share of more than 80%. The latest LTO-7 tape cartridges can store 6 TB of uncompressed data[47].

Typical tape throughput now is in the 100 to 150 MB/s range. The tape drive interface is capable of even higher speeds. Existing tape drives typically use 4 Gbit/s Fibre Channel interfaces, supporting a sustained throughput of between 350 and 400 MB/s. To use LTO-5 drives, the interface needs 8 Gbit/s FC, to support up to 800 MB/s.

9.2.2.1 Tape library

A tape drive can handle one tape at a time, and tapes must be changed when more, or other data is needed. Tape libraries can be used to automate this tape handling.

A tape library, also known as a tape silo, tape robot, or tape jukebox, is a storage device that contains one or more tape drives, a number of slots to hold tape cartridges, a barcode or RFID tag reader to identify tape cartridges, and an automated method for loading tapes. Picture 24 shows a tape robot with two tape drives installed in the back (and room for four extra tape drives when needed). On the left, the tapes cartridges are stored.

Picture 24: Tape library[48]

As an example, the tape library in Picture 24 stores 150 LTO tapes, each with a capacity of 5 TB, leading to a total storage capacity of 750 TB.

9.2.2.2 Virtual tape library

A Virtual Tape Library (VTL) uses disks for storing backups. A VTL consists of an appliance or server, and software that emulates traditional tape devices and formats. The benefit of using VTLs is that it combines high performance disk based backup and restore with well-known backup applications, standards, processes, and policies.

Most of the current VTL solutions use NL-SAS or SATA disk arrays because of their relatively low cost, and provide multiple virtual tape drives for handling multiple tapes in parallel.

In some cases, data stored on the VTL's disk array is exported to other media, such as physical tapes, for disaster recovery purposes.

VTLs can be synchronized over multiple locations, creating multiple, offsite backups.

9.2.3   Controllers

Controllers connect disks and/or tapes to a server, typically implemented as a PCI expansion boards in the server. Controllers can also be used as part of a NAS or SAN deployment, where they connect all available disks and tapes to redundant Fibre Channel, iSCSI, or FCoE connections (see section 9.2.5.1 for more information on these technologies).

A controller typically implements high performance, high availability, and virtualized storage using RAID (Redundant Arrays of Independent Disks) technology. They can also implement cloning, data deduplication and thin provisioning, each explained in the next sections.

A controller virtualizes all physical disks connected to it, presenting one or more virtual disks, called Logical Unit Numbers (LUNs). This is usually not one-on-one. Instead, the controller splits up all disks in small pieces called physical extents. From these physical extents, new virtual disks (LUNs) are composed and presented to the operating system. The operating system doesn't know about the physical disks; it just works with the LUNs as if they were real disks.

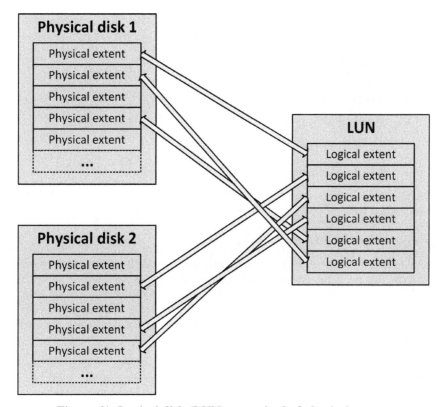

Figure 61: Logical disk (LUN) comprised of physical extents

The controller can make physical disks part of a RAID array for increased availability and/or performance. For instance, six 500 GB physical disks in a RAID 5 configuration can be presented as 1 virtual disk (LUN) of 3 TB to the operating system. The operating system only sees one disk, and has no knowledge that the disk in reality consists of more physical disks. The other way around is also possible; the disk controller can provide the operating system a large number of small sized LUNs, based on a few large physical disks.

9.2.3.1 RAID (Redundant Array of Independent Disks)

Redundant Array of Independent Disks (RAID) solutions can provide high availability of data and/or improvements of performance through the use of redundant disks.

RAID can be implemented in several configurations, called RAID levels, each with their own pros and cons. In practice, five RAID levels are implemented most often:

- **RAID 0** - Striping
- **RAID 1** - Mirroring
- **RAID 10** - Striping and Mirroring
- **RAID 5** - Striping with distributed parity
- **RAID 6** - Striping with distributed double parity

RAID can be implemented in the disk controller's hardware, or as software running in a server's operating system.

9.2.3.1.1 RAID 0 - Striping

RAID 0 (also known as striping) provides an easy and cheap way to increase performance over the use of single disks. RAID 0 uses multiple disks, each with a part of the data on it. When data is read, part of the data comes from one disk, another part from another disk, effectively doubling the read performance. The write performance is faster than using a single disk as well, as different data blocks are written to the disks in parallel.

RAID 0 actually lowers availability – if one of the disks in a RAID 0 set fails, all data is lost. RAID 0 is hardly used in production systems and its use is only acceptable if losing all data on the RAID set is no problem (for instance for temporary data). RAID 0 is often combined with RAID 1 to create a RAID 10 set.

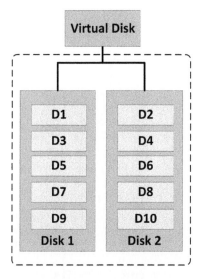

Figure 62: RAID 0

In Figure 62, each D number represents a disk block on one of the physical disks. These disk blocks are combined by the disk controller to represent a virtual disk that is presented to the operating system of a server.

9.2.3.1.2 RAID 1 - Mirroring

RAID 1 (also known as mirroring) is a high availability solution that uses two disks that contain the same data. If one disk fails, data is not lost as it is still available on the mirror disk. In RAID 1, the disk controller (or the operating system driver) writes all data to both disks, and reads data from the first disk that can deliver the data. This is dependent on where the disk's read head is located at that time. Therefore, RAID 1 has a slightly increased read performance over using single disks. The write performance is a bit slower, since writes are only finished after the data is written on both disks.

RAID 1 is thought to be the most reliable RAID level, but its price is relatively high – 50% of the disks are used for redundancy only.

A spare physical disk can be configured (see Figure 63), to automatically take over the task of a failed disk. This enables a quick automatic rebuild to a high available situation after a disk failure. And because most disk arrays support hot-swappable disks, which can be replaced without powering down the disk array, a defective disk can be replaced without causing downtime, restoring high availability of the RAID configuration.

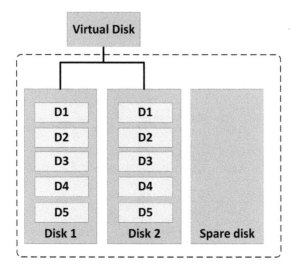

Figure 63: RAID 1

To optimize high availability, it is considered good practice to place the mirror disks in a separate enclosure (and preferably in a separate rack), and to use redundant disk controllers.

9.2.3.1.3 RAID 10 - Striping and mirroring

RAID 10 uses a combination of striping and mirroring, and provides high performance and availability, but at a relatively high price. A RAID 10 set uses at least four disks and only 50% of the disk space is used (the rest of the disk space is used for mirroring).

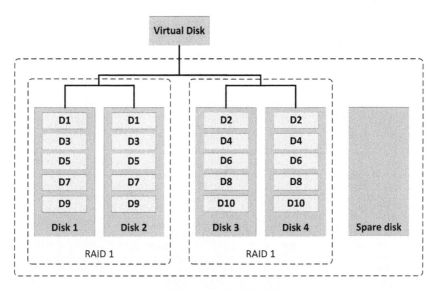

Figure 64: RAID 10

Just like in RAID 1, it is a good practice to place the mirror disks in a separate enclosure (and preferably in a separate rack), and to use redundant disks and disk controllers.

Read performance is high, just like RAID 0, and write performance is a bit slower, just like RAID 1 (but still higher than RAID 5 or 6).

9.2.3.1.4 RAID 5 - Striping with distributed parity

RAID 5 uses striping with distributed parity. Data is written in disk blocks on all disks in parallel (like RAID 0 striping), and a parity block of the written disk blocks is stored as well. This parity block is used to automatically reconstruct data in a RAID 5 set (using a spare disk) in case of a disk failure.

Because RAID 5 uses parity, not all data has to be available twice, like in RAID 1 and RAID 10. Parity blocks use the amount of disk space of one disk in the RAID 5 disk array. So, in a RAID 5 disk array comprising four disks of 500 GB (a total of 2000 GB disk space), the amount of available storage for the virtual disk is three disks (four minus one), so 1500 GB. In a set of eight disks in a RAID 5 configuration, the amount of data on seven disks is available to store data.

RAID 5 spreads the parity blocks over the available disks. This leads to a good spread of disk usage, lowering the risk of a specific disk failing first.

One disadvantage of using RAID 5 is that the parity calculations can dramatically slow down write performance. Because of these calculations, the rebuild time of the spare disk after a disk failure can be substantial.

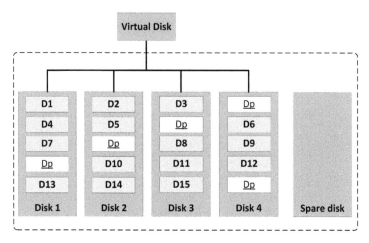

Figure 65: RAID 5

9.2.3.1.5 RAID 6 - Striping with distributed double parity

When a disk fails in a RAID 5 set, the RAID set is reconstructed automatically using the available spare disk. During the reconstruction period, no protection against a disk failure exists. To make things worse, the chance of a second disk failure rises as reconstructing a RAID 5 set requires a lot of disk reads on all still working disks in the RAID set. The larger the disks, the more time is needed for the reconstruction, and the larger the risk of a second disk failing. RAID 6 protects against double disk failures by using two distributed parity blocks instead of one.

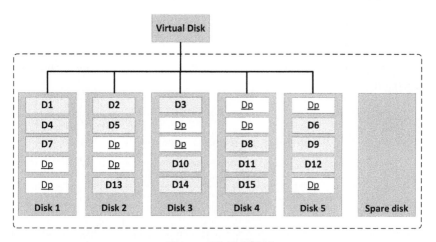

Figure 66: RAID 6

The drawback of RAID 6 is some loss of write performance and increased cost for the storage of extra parity blocks.

9.2.3.2   Data deduplication

Data deduplication searches the storage system for duplicate data segments (disk blocks or files) and removes these duplicates.

Data deduplication typically leads to a 20 to 30% reduction of occupied disk space, but in real-world situations and using highly optimized algorithms, much higher reductions are possible with some types of data. Data deduplication is used in archived as well as in production data.

The deduplication system keeps a table of hash tags (unique calculated data identifiers) to quickly identify duplicate disk blocks. The incoming data stream is segmented (mostly in disk block sizes) and hash tags are calculated of those segments. The hashes are compared to hash tags of segments already on disk. If an incoming data segment is identified as a duplicate, the segment is not stored again, but a pointer to the matching segment is created for it instead.

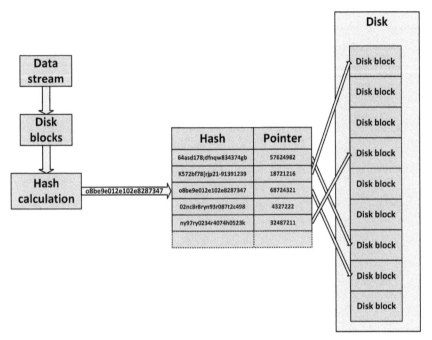

Figure 67: Deduplication

Deduplication can be done inline or periodically. As described above, inline deduplication checks for duplicate data segments before data is written to disk. While this avoids duplicate data on disks at any time, it introduces a relatively large performance penalty.

Another possibility is to write data to disk first, and periodically check if duplicate data exists. Duplicate data is then deduplicated by changing the duplicate data to a pointer to existing data on disk, and freeing disk space of the original block. This process can be done at times when performance needs are low, lowering the performance penalty, but a drawback is that duplicate data will be stored on the disks for some time.

Today's all-flash storage systems' extremely fast read and write speeds make them an ideal candidate for efficient deduplication of data. This enables the all-flash systems to host fewer disks compared to traditional storage system, somewhat compensating the higher price point for the used SSD disks.

9.2.3.3   Cloning and snapshots

All enterprise storage systems provide services called cloning and snapshotting. With cloning and snapshotting, a copy of data is made at a specific point in time that can be used independently from the source data. This is especially useful for creating backups. If a backup is created of one or more disks while those disks are constantly being updated, restoring such a backup could cause problems. Using snapshotting and cloning it is possible to create a backup at a specific point in time, when the data is in a stable, consistent state. Other use cases of cloning and snapshotting are creating test sets of data and an easy way to revert to older data without restoring data from a backup.

With cloning the storage system creates a full copy of a disk, much like a RAID 1 mirror disk. This cloned disk can be split-off at a specific point in time, for instance to make a backup of the data, without touching the original disks that are still on-line.

Snapshotting achieves the same effect as cloning, but is technically quite different. A snapshot represents a point in time of the data on the disks. From that moment on no writing to those disks is permitted anymore, as long as the snapshot is active. All writing is done on a separate disk volume in the storage system. The original disks still provide read-access, but when an operating system reads data that was just written onto the separate disk volume, the data is retrieved from that disk volume automatically and transparently. Since no data is written to the disks during the snapshot period, a backup can be made from the disks, as they contain a consistent state of data. As soon as the snapshot state is ended, all data is written back to the original disks and everything continues as normal.

A big advantage of snapshots compared to cloning is that a clone takes relatively much time to create, and needs a duplication of the disk space. A snapshot is available instantly, and the snapshot doesn't take much additional disk space. This means that when a backup must be made, a snapshot is created (which typically takes less than a second), after which copying the data to a backup system can take as long as needed. No downtime occurs due to the making of a backup, even if making the backup takes several hours.

9.2.3.4   Thin provisioning

Thin provisioning enables the allocation of more storage capacity to users than is physically installed; much like overcommitting memory in virtual machines.

Traditionally, applications are provided with a predetermined amount of physical storage space. The amount needed was defined by the application vendor, or was calculated, estimated, or guessed – often using a worst-case scenario. In practice, experience shows that about 50% of that storage is never used. And in the first years of deployment, the storage is used even less, since the application has only a small set of historic data.

Thin provisioning still provides the applications with the storage needed, calculated, estimated, or guessed. Only the storage is not really available on physical disks. Instead, using automated capacity management the application's real storage need is monitored closely, and physical disk space is added when needed. This means that disk purchases can be deferred until really needed. This way disks are only purchased if really needed and for the latest price, thus providing more storage capacity compared to buying all disks up front.

Typical use of thin provisioning is providing users with large sized home directories. For instance, with thin provisioning, each user can get a home directory of 10 GB or more. Since most users will not fill up their home directories, the combined amount of physical disk space can be much lower than 10 GB for each user. The same principle can be used for email boxes. This provisioning is the reason Dropbox, Hotmail or Google can provide many GB of free disk space to all their users – only a few of them really use all that space, most use much less.

9.2.4   Direct Attached Storage (DAS)

Most PCs use Direct Attached Storage (DAS). DAS – also known as local disks – is a storage system where one or more dedicated disks connect via the SAS or SATA protocol to a built-in controller, connected to the rest of the computer using the PCI bus. The controller provides a set of disk blocks to the computer, organized in LUNs (or partitions). The computer's operating system uses these disk blocks to create a file system to store files.

In servers, DAS is mostly used as a boot device and for caching (to provide quick access to for instance page files). DAS storage is only available to the server that has the DAS storage attached.

9.2.5   Storage Area Network (SAN)

A Storage Area Network (SAN) is a specialized storage network that consists of SAN switches, controllers and storage devices. It connects a large pool of central storage to multiple servers.

A SAN physically connects servers to disk controllers using specialized networking technologies like Fibre Channel or iSCSI. Via the SAN, disk controllers offer virtual disks to servers, also known as LUNs (Logical Unit

Numbers). LUNs are only available to the server that has that specific LUN mounted.

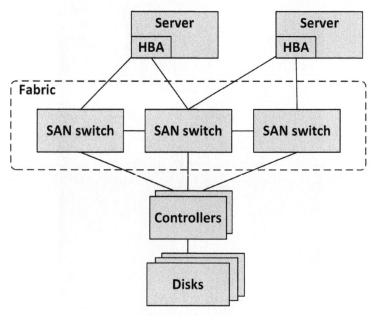

Figure 68: SAN

The core of the SAN is a set of SAN switches, called the Fabric. It is comparable with a LAN's switched network segment.

Host bus adapters (HBAs) are interface cards implemented in servers. They can be compared to network interface controllers (NICs) used in networking. They are connected to SAN switches, usually in a redundant way.

Picture 25: Disks in storage system[49]

Typically, in SANs, a large number of disks are installed in one or more disk arrays. The number of disks varies between dozens of disks and hundreds of disks. With today's disk sizes a SAN can easily contain many hundreds of terabytes (TB) of data or more.

9.2.5.1   SAN connectivity protocols

To connect servers to storage devices using a SAN, connectivity is needed. The most used SAN connectivity protocols are Fibre Channel, FCoE and iSCSI.

9.2.5.1.1 Fibre Channel

Fibre Channel (FC) is a dedicated level 2 network protocol, specially designed for transportation of storage data blocks. It operates at speeds of 2 Gbit/s, 4

Gbit/s, 8 Gbit/s, or 16 Gbit/s. Despite its name, Fibre Channel can run on both twisted pair copper wire (i.e. UTP and STP) and fiber optic cables.

Picture 26: SAN switches[50]

The Fibre Channel protocol was specially developed for the transport of disk blocks. The protocol is very reliable, with guaranteed zero data loss. Each Fibre Channel device has a unique World Wide Name (WWN), which is similar to an Ethernet MAC address.

Fibre Channel can be implemented within three network topologies:

- **Point-to-Point** - Two devices are connected directly to each other.

- **Arbitrated loop** (also known as FC-AL) - In this topology, all devices are in a loop. Most early Fibre Channel systems worked this way.

- **Switched fabric** - All devices are connected to Fibre Channel switches, a similar concept as in Ethernet implementations. Most implementations today use a switched fabric.

9.2.5.1.2 FCoE

Most datacenters use two separate networks – one for Ethernet and one for Fibre Channel. Fibre Channel over Ethernet (FCoE) is a technology that encapsulates Fibre Channel data in Ethernet packets, allowing Fibre Channel traffic to be transported over 10 Gbit or higher Ethernet networks.

FCoE eliminates the need for separate Ethernet and Fibre Channel cabling and switching technology, because it transports regular Ethernet payloads as well as Fibre Channel payloads. While this seems like a good idea, saving costs and reducing complexity, it must be made clear who is responsible for managing the converged network. Storage systems managers, who were once responsible for the complete storage chain, will have to use the available network instead of their own Fibre Channel fabrics.

FCoE is not regular Ethernet. It needs at least 10 Gbit Ethernet with special extensions, known as Data Center Bridging (DCB) or Converged Enhanced Ethernet (CEE). These extensions facilitate:

- **Lossless Ethernet connections** - While in Ethernet networking the risk of losing an Ethernet packet as a result of for example congestion is solved by higher level protocols like TCP/IP, Fibre Channel needs end-to-end lossless connections to function properly on top of Ethernet. This means that a FCoE implementation must guarantee that no Ethernet packets are lost.

- **Quality of Service (QoS)** - QoS allows FCoE packets to have priority over other Ethernet packets to avoid storage performance issues.

- **Large Maximum Transfer Unit (MTU) support** - To be able to fit Fibre Channel frames in one Ethernet packet, large MTU support is required. It allows Ethernet packets of 2500 bytes in size, instead of the standard 1500 bytes. These special Ethernet packets are also known as Jumbo frames.

To use FCoE, specialized Converged Network Adapters (CNAs) are needed. CNAs support the Ethernet extensions described above and present themselves to the operating system as two adapters: an Ethernet Network Interface Controller (NIC) and a Fibre Channel Host Bus Adapter (HBA). To communicate with a CNA, the operating system needs two drivers: one for the NIC part of the adapter, and another for the HBA part (see Figure 69).

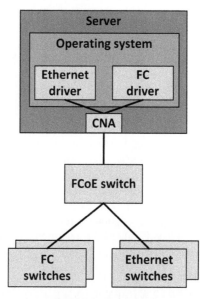

Figure 69: FCoE

FCoE is a switching technology, which means that routing is not part of the protocol (as opposed to IP based networks). Because of the need for DCB or CEE Ethernet, only specialized FCoE enabled switches can be used. And because in many infrastructures networks Fibre Channel switches are already present, FCoE is typically implemented gradually, starting with the host and switch layers. The back-end storage arrays will continue to run native Fibre Channel, and the core network continues to run native Ethernet.

9.2.5.1.3 iSCSI

iSCSI allows the SCSI protocol to run over Ethernet LANs using TCP/IP. iSCSI, also known as IP-SAN, is a protocol to transport data blocks over IP networks, without the need for a specialized network infrastructure, such as Fibre Channel, or the need for more expensive equipment like with an FCoE implementation. The main advantage of using iSCSI is that it uses the familiar TCP/IP protocols and well known SCSI commands.

iSCSI's performance is typically lower than that of Fibre Channel, due to the TCP/IP overhead. But with 10 or 40 Gbit/s Ethernet and jumbo frames, iSCSI is now rapidly conquering a big part of the SAN market.

9.2.6   Network Attached Storage (NAS)

A NAS, also known as a File Server, is a network device that provides a NFS (UNIX and Linux) and/or SMB/CIFS (Windows) shared file system to operating systems over a standard TCP/IP network. A NAS is often an appliance that implements the file services and holds the disks on which data is stored. A NAS appliance could also use external disk storage provided by a SAN.

The difference between a SAN and NAS is the level at which they operate. A SAN offers disk blocks (unformatted disks called LUNs) that can be used by only one server, while a NAS offers a shared filesystem to store files that can be used by multiple servers. There is a difference with respect to security as well. NAS connects to for instance to an LDAP or Active Directory service in order to set file and/or folder permissions, and a SAN doesn't. Where a SAN uses iSCSI, Fibre Channel or FCoE as the communication layer, a NAS uses SMB/CIFS or NFS over TCP/IP.

Picture 27: NetApp NAS[51]

A NAS typically provides redundancy, load balancing, replication of data, and other services, freeing operating systems from these tasks. And since a NAS has knowledge about the files it stores (as opposed to SANs, which only have knowledge of disk blocks), it can optimize file handling in an efficient way and provide file level services. For instance, a NAS can provide snapshot and clone technology at a file level, enabling features like "un-erasing" deleted files by end users.

A clustered NAS is a NAS that uses a distributed file system running simultaneously on multiple servers. The key difference between a clustered and a traditional NAS is the ability to distribute data and metadata across storage devices. A clustered NAS, like a traditional one, still provides unified access to the files from any of the cluster nodes, unrelated to the actual location of the data.

9.2.7   Object Storage

Object storage is a storage architecture that manages data as objects, where an object is defined as a file with its metadata, and a globally unique identifier called the object ID.

Examples of metadata are filename, date and time stamps, owner, access permissions, the level of data protection, and replication settings to for instance a different geography.

Object storage stores and retrieves data using a REST API over HTTP, served by a webserver, and is designed to be highly scalable.

Where a traditional file system provides a structure that simplifies locating files (for example, a log file is stored in /var/log/proxy/proxy.log), in object storage, a file's object ID must be administered by the application using it. Using the object ID, the object can be found without knowing the physical location of the data. For example, an application has administered that its log file is stored in object ID 8932189023.

Using object IDs enables simplicity and massive scalability of the storage system, as the object ID is a link to an object that can be stored anywhere.

Data in object storage can't be modified. Instead, if a file is modified, the original file must be deleted, and a new file must be created, leading to a new object ID. This makes object storage unsuitable for frequently changing data. But it is a good fit for data that doesn't change much, like backups, archives, video and audio files, and virtual machine images.

Object storage allows for high availability using commodity servers with direct attached disk drives. It can be setup to replicate objects across multiple servers and locations (typically, at least three copies of every file are stored in multiple geographical zones). If one or more servers or disks fail, data can still be made available, without impact to the application or the end user.

While object storage was not designed to be used as a file system, some systems emulate a file system using object storage. For instance, Amazon's S3FS creates a virtual filesystem, based on S3 object storage, that can be mounted to an operating system in the traditional way, however, with significant performance degradation. A much better solution is to use object storage with applications designed for it.

9.2.8   Software Defined Storage

Software Defined Storage (SDS) abstracts data and storage capabilities (also known as the control plane) from the underlying physical storage systems (the data plane). This allows data to be stored in a variety of storage systems while being presented and managed as one storage pool to the servers consuming the storage. Figure 70 shows the SDS model.

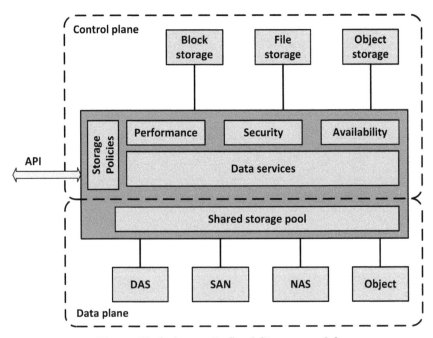

Figure 70: Software Defined Storage model

Heterogeneous physical storage devices can be made part of the SDS system. For instance, SDS enables the use of standard commodity hardware, where storage is implemented as software running on commodity x86-based servers with direct attached disks. But the physical storage can also be a Storage Area Network, a Network Attached Storage system, or an Object storage system. SDS virtualizes all physical storage into one large shared storage pool. From this storage pool, software provides data services like:

- Deduplication
- Compression
- Caching
- Snapshotting
- Cloning
- Replication
- Tiering

SDS provides servers with virtualized data storage pools with the required performance, availability and security, delivered as block, file, or object storage, based on policies. As an example, a newly deployed database server can invoke an SDS policy that mounts storage configured to have its data striped across a number of disks, creates a daily snapshot, and has data stored on tier 1 disks.

APIs can be used to provision storage pools and set the availability, security and performance levels of the virtualized storage. In addition, using APIs, storage consumers can monitor and manage their own storage consumption.

9.3 Storage availability

To increase the availability of storage systems, apart from using RAID technologies, other forms of redundancy and data replication can be used. To save data in case of disaster, it must be backed-up. And for archiving purposes long term storage of data is needed.

9.3.1 Redundancy and data replication

To increase availability in a SAN, components like HBAs and switches can be installed redundantly. Using multiple paths between HBAs and SAN switches, also known as multipathing, failover can be instantiated automatically when a failure occurs, much like in an Ethernet network setup.

To increase redundancy further, multiple storage systems can be used, sometimes installed in multiple locations. Using replication, changed disk blocks from the primary storage system are continuously sent to the secondary storage system, where they are stored as well.

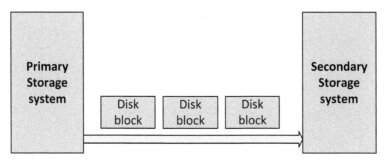

Figure 71: Storage replication

Two types of storage replication are used: synchronous and asynchronous replication.

In synchronous replication, each write to the active storage system and the replication to the passive storage system must be completed before the write is confirmed to the operating system. It ensures data on both storage systems is synchronized at all times and data is never lost. And using the write cache of the secondary storage system, writes can be committed when the data is stored in cache, instead of stored on disk (especially when the write cache is protected with a battery backup). This speeds up the write process. But when the physical cable length between the two storage systems is more than 100 km, latency times get too long, slowing down applications, that have to wait for the write on the secondary storage system to finish. Another issue with synchronous replication is the risk of a failing connection between both storage systems. In this situation, when data is written to the primary storage system, the write is never finished, as the data cannot be replicated. This effectively leads to downtime of the primary storage system.

In asynchronous replication, after data has been written to the primary storage system, the write is immediately committed to the operating system, without having to wait for the secondary storage array to finish its writes as well. Asynchronous replication does not have the latency impact that synchronous replication has, but has the disadvantage of potential data loss when the primary storage system fails before the data has been written to the secondary storage system.

9.3.2   Backup and recovery

Backups are copies of data, used to restore data to a previous state in case of data loss, data corruption or a disaster recovery situation.

Backups are always a last resort, only used if everything else fails, to save your organization in case of a disaster. A well-designed system should have options to repair incorrect data from within the system or by using systems management tools (like database tools).

A common mistake is to mix up backup with archiving. Backup is about protection against data loss, whereas archiving deals with long term data storage, in order to comply with law and regulations (see 9.3.3). Backups are not to be used to view the status of information from the past – it should be possible to retrieve these statuses from the system itself, as no data should ever be deleted in a typical production system (but it could be archived to a secondary system or database).

In general, backups should not be kept for a long time. Because the data copies are only relevant in the event of a disaster, organizations will typically have little use to restore a data backup that is more than a few weeks old.

Restoring a backup takes you back in time. It is like a time machine, but without the rest of the world – like your business partners and customers – going back in time as well.

I see no reason why anyone would want to go back in time for more than 30 days, as the information would be outdated, and of very little use for the survival of the organization.

As an example, I know a large insurance company that keeps no backups older than eight days.

So, saving monthly, or even yearly backups, is really of no use at all. When a disaster strikes, and the organization is restored with last years' databases, it might as well not restore anything at all.

In general, there are two reasons for making backups:

- Because of a technical failure or a user-error files are accidentally deleted or corrupted and must be restored.

- After a physical disaster, data must be recovered (typically on a disaster recovery site).

Backups need to be made at a regular basis: usually daily, but sometimes more often – every hour, or even continuously in highly critical environments.

Please note that storing data on synchronized disks on a disaster recovery site will not necessarily provide enough protection. An example is the case of a virus outbreak. In such a situation, files on the disaster recovery disks are corrupted as well, as they are synchronized immediately as they are changed by the virus. Therefore, it is good practice to have multiple backup copies, and at least one offline.

A good practice is to keep three copies of your data on two different media types, with one copy stored at a separate location. This is known as the 3-2-1 rule.

In case of a disaster, physical media might no longer be available. Therefore, backups must be available at a secondary site for restore. Having a backup copy in the same building as the original (or close to it) is usually a bad idea. Experience with real world disasters (like the 9/11 attacks and bombings) shows it is good practice to have a distance of at least 5 km between the main site and the backup data.

It is important to have backup copies of not only the data, but also copies of the operating system installation disks, and printed procedures on how to build up a new system using the backups. Also, don't forget the license keys of the software (including the restore software)!

It is crucial to test the restore procedure at least once a year, including building up new hardware, to ensure restores work as planned. It would be best to have the restore procedures tested by a third party, or at least by people that have not performed a restore before. Not only does this ensure that the restore procedure is complete and correct, it also ensures no specific knowledge is needed to restore the systems. In case of a real disaster (like a fire or a building collapse), where people are hurt or even killed, we cannot assume that systems managers are able to restore data again. Not only because they might be hurt themselves (and in the hospital), but also because of the stress involved in seeing their colleagues get hurt or killed.

Restore tests where only some files are restored should be performed each month to ensure backup media still work as expected. Do the tapes really contain the expected data?

9.3.2.1   Consistent backups

To create a consistent backup, backup tools and backup agents should be configured to backup open files, and to ensure databases are flushed to disk before making backup copies. For instance, databases back-upped in an inconsistent state can lead to failure to start the database after a restore.

All database transactions in an application must be finished completely before making a backup to prevent a failing application after a restore. An example of something going wrong is a purchase order that states a product came in, where a change in the financial administration for the invoice is missing.

Most systems today hardly ever work in isolation. Usually they are part of a chain of internal and external systems. Purchase orders come in via order intake in an internal SAP system, but can also come in through resellers' web services or via an internet site. These systems are connected, and it seems to make sense to backup them in an integral way.

The question is whether it is useful to force consistencies in backups over multiple applications. In general, this is a very expensive exercise (if possible at all) with little benefit. To create an integral backup, all systems must be in a consistent state. Not only within the application, but the consistency must also be guaranteed between applications. This is only possible when all connected systems are temporarily stopped to create a consistent backup copy. Not only is this most of the time not feasible (an internet site cannot be taken off-line to create a backup), it is also very time consuming. If, for instance, one of the systems in the chain cannot be stopped due to a long running transaction, all other systems must to wait for it in order to get back-upped. And when transactions run between organizations, all organizations must stop working to create chain-consistent backups.

It is important to have backups that are consistent within one application to prevent the problems discussed earlier, but forget consistent backups when more applications are involved.

Remember: a backup should only be used to restore systems that cannot be repaired any other way. Restoring a backup is always a last resort. The decision to perform a restore has great business impact. Restoring a system from backup is always a delicate process that must be taken care of with great caution, especially in a chain of multiple applications or even organizations, even if the backup itself is consistent.

9.3.2.2 Backup schemes

Backups can be made using various backup schemes. A backup scheme describes what data is backed-up, when, and how. Backup schemes can become very complex in large environments with many applications.

In general, four basic backup schemes are possible: full backup, incremental backup, differential backup, and Continuous Data Protection (CDP).

- **Full backup** is a complete copy of all data. In large environments, full backups are only created at relatively large intervals (like a week or a month), since creating them takes much time, disk or tape space, and bandwidth. Restoring a full backup, however, takes the least amount of time.

- **Incremental backups** save only newly created or changed data since the last backup, regardless of whether it is a previous incremental backup or a full backup. Restoring an incremental backup can take a long time, especially when the last full backup is many incremental backups ago. This is because the full backup and all incremental backups since the full backup must be restored (for instance, to perform a restore when the last full backup was made two weeks ago, one full backup and thirteen individual incremental daily backups must be restored).

- **Differential backups** save only newly created or changed data since the last full backup. A differential backup needs more storage space than an incremental backup, since each differential backup stores all changed data since the last full back up. Restoring a differential backup is quite efficient, as it implies restoring a full backup and only the most recent differential backup.

- **Continuous Data Protection (CDP)** guarantees that every change in the data is also simultaneously made in the backup system. In CDP, the RPO (Recovery Point Objective) is set to zero, because each change immediately triggers a backup process. In this regard, CDP is the realization of the backup ideal: Everything is saved – immediately and in its entirety. It is also an expensive technology, and therefore only used in specific situations.

9.3.2.3 Backup data retention time

Backup data retention time is the amount of time in which a given set of data will remain available for restore. It defines how long backups are kept and at which interval. Typically, not all daily backups are kept, as this would use too much storage space.

In practice, a Grandfather-Father-Son (GFS) based schedule is often used:

- Each day a backup is made

- After a week, there are seven backups, of which the oldest backup is renamed to a weekly backup.

- After the second week, the same is done and the daily backups of the week before are deleted.

- Now there are eight backups: seven daily, two weekly.

- Every four weeks, the weekly backup is renamed as a monthly backup and the weekly backups are reused.

The daily backups are the son, the weekly backups are the father, and the monthly backups are the grandfather.

9.3.3   Archiving

Archiving is mostly done for compliancy and regulation reasons.

Noncompliance to law and regulation can lead to serious business disruption, fines, and even jail time.

For example, in the USA, failure to keep personal information secure may result in jail time, and fines up to $500,000. SoX legislation can bring penalties up to 20 years in prison, and fines up to $5,000,000.

In Europe, the EU Data Retention Directive forces all industries with communication services to keep data retention periods.

Regulations can have a great effect on the archiving of data. For example, US regulations require all medical records to be retained for 30 years after a person's death. This means that X-rays taken when a child was born must be kept for as much as 130 years!

Some other examples of data archives are:

- Pension and insurance companies must keep records of their history of people and claims for decades.

- Hospitals store medical information during the lifetime of a patient.

- The Justice department keeps records of crimes (especially if they are not solved) for a long time ("cold cases").

- Newspaper archives, archives of television networks, and government archives are kept for decades.

The ability to make archived data read-only to protect it from being altered is very important for regulatory compliance and non-repudiation. Some archiving systems store data in an encrypted form and use digital signatures to ensure data is not tampered with.

Some systems allow data to be written to it for archiving, but disallow changing or deleting data. A well-known example is the use of write-only optical (Blu-ray) disks. Data can be written to it, but not changed or deleted (except by physical destruction of the medium). For large companies the WORM tape (Written Once Read Many) is a less expensive alternative compared to optical storage, especially in cases where the data needs to be accessed infrequently.

Data must be kept in such a way that it is guaranteed the data can be read after a long time. This means the digital format (like a Microsoft Word file or a JPG file), the physical format (like a DVD or a magnetic tape), and the storage environment (temperature, humidity) must be such, that data can still be retrieved and read after several decades.

A few decades ago, on mainframes data was stored on 2 MB reel tapes. Data was kept in propriety formats, like mainframe database tables specific to a certain application. After mainframes, PCs became the norm, using applications like WordStar, Lotus 1-2-3, WordPerfect, MS-Word, Lotus Notes, Adobe Acrobat, etc. Today we also use a plethora of audio and video formats: BMP, GIF, TIFF, MP3, WAV, MPEG, AVI, etc. The list is very long, and all of this was developed in the last 30 years. It is hard to guarantee that all of this data can be read and interpreted in 50 years' time.

It is therefore good practice to use open standards for storing archived data. Open standards are well documented, implying reading data will always be feasible, using emulation software if needed. Storing all documents in structured human-readable XML text files is one way to ensure data can be read for many decades.

Many archiving technologies are storing data in optical formats. While this is much better than magnetic storage on disk or tape, is it not known if optical media like CDs or DVDs are still readable in many years' time (even if properly stored CDs can last at least 20 years[52]). Therefore, it is good practice to transfer data that is to be kept for a long time to the latest storage media standard every 10 years (from Floppy to CDs to Blu-ray, etc.), or at least to move the data to a new copy (burn a five-year-old CD on a new CD).

9.4   Storage performance

Storage performance is often overlooked. But the effect of storage on the performance of a complete IT system or infrastructure can be very significant!

9.4.1   Disk performance

Disk performance of high-end and low-end disks are quite different. The main differences are disk rotation speed, seek times, and their interface protocol.

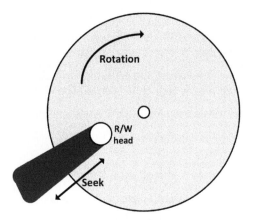

Figure 72: Disk mechanics

When data is to be read, and R/W the head needs to move to the correct location (which takes seek time), and the R/W head needs to wait for the desired data to pass beneath it (rotational delay). Since a high-end disk has a faster rotation speed and somewhat faster head movement mechanics, it can produce more operations per second than a low-end disk.

Rotational delay is proportional to the rotational speed. Some common examples of rotation delay are:

Disk RPM	Average rotational delay (ms)
5,400	5.6
7,200	4.2
10,000	3
15,000	2

Table 20: Disk rotational delay[53]

Disks cannot spin much faster than 15,000 RPM, as at this speed the velocity at the edge of a 3.5" disk is 250 km/h already! Increasing this velocity would physically destroy the disk.

Seek time is the time it takes for the head to get to the right track. Average seek times are about 3 ms for high-end disks and 9 ms for low-end disks.

In general, disk performance is measured in IOPS and interface throughput.

9.4.1.1   IOPS

Input/output Operations Per Second (IOPS) is a measure of how many read and write operations a disk can complete in one second.

To calculate the IOPS of a disk, the following formula can be used:

$$\frac{1000}{\text{Rotational delay (ms)} + \text{Seek time(ms)}}$$

For example, a particular disk has the following average performance characteristics:

- Rotational delay: 3 ms

- Read seek time: 3.5 ms

- Write seek time: 3.8 ms

The maximum number of read IOPS are $\frac{1000}{3+3.5} = 154$.

The maximum write IOPS will be a bit less (147 IOPS) because of the higher write seek time. Writing is typically a bit slower than reading. As a rule of thumb, typical rotational speeds and their equivalent read IOPS are stated in the table below.

Disk RPM	IOPS
7,200	50
10,000	120
15,000	160
SSD	2,500 to 10,000

Table 21: Disk IOPS

Observe the enormous speed increase of SSD disks as opposed to mechanical disks. This is the effect of not having mechanical moving parts.

Of course, real measurements will vary, depending on the physical location of the needed data block, the type of disk controller, the onboard cache algorithm, cache size, and the operating system driver software.

9.4.1.2 RAID penalty

In RAID sets things are a bit different, since multiple disks are used to form one virtual disk (LUN). Because of the multiple disks in the LUN, the number of IOPS of the LUN can be higher than that of the individual disks. How much higher depends on the RAID configuration.

Writing data on multiple disks, however, also introduces some delay. This is known as the RAID penalty. Penalties for various RAID configurations are.

- RAID 0: no penalty

- RAID 1: penalty of 2

- RAID 10: penalty of 2

- RAID 5: penalty of 4

RAID 0 (striping) multiplies the total number of read and write IOPS by the number of disks that are striped. So, if two disks are used, the number of read and write IOPS delivered to the LUN are doubled. There is no RAID penalty with RAID 0.

With RAID 1 (mirroring) and RAID 10 (striping with mirroring), the data is read from one of the two disks in a set and written to both. Hence the RAID penalty on write operations on RAID 1 would be 2.

So, for 15,000 RPM disks, the IOPS for a RAID 1 LUN are still around 150-160 for reads, but only 70-80 for writes, because the write to the LUN is finished only when data is written to both disks.

In a RAID 5 scenario, when a write has to be performed to disks, RAID penalty for write operation would be 4 (read existing data, read parity, write new data, write new parity). As a rule of thumb, in RAID 5 systems with 15,000 RPM disks, the number of read IOPS are somewhere in the 150-160 range, while write IOPS are closer to the 35-45 range.

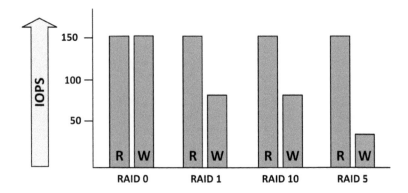

Figure 73: IOPS in RAID

To keep sufficient IOPS in a RAID system, disks can be added to the RAID set. For example, when a RAID 5 set consists of four 15,000 RPM disks (with 160 write IOPS each), the total write IOPS for the LUN is $4 \times \frac{160}{4} = 160$ write IOPS.

But when using six disks in the RAID 5 array, the total write IOPS for the LUN is $6 \times \frac{160}{4} = 240$ IOPS.

9.4.2   Interface throughput

Storage performance is not only measured by how fast physical disks can provide data, but also by how fast the interface can move data from the disks to the systems consuming the data and vice versa. Below is an overview of the various interface speeds.

Interface	Speed
IDE (Parallel ATA)	100 MB/s 133 MB/s
SATA	1.5 Gbit/s (192 MB/s) 3 Gbit/s (384 MB/s)

Interface	Speed
	6 Gbit/s (768 MB/s)
SCSI	160 MB/s (Ultra-160)
	320 MB/s (Ultra-320)
SAS	1.5 Gbit/s (192 MB/s)
	3 Gbit/s (384MB/s)
	6 Gbit/s (768 MB/s)
FC	1 Gbit/s (128 MB/s)
	2 Gbit/s (256 MB/s)
	4 Gbit/s (512 MB/s)
	8 Gbit/s (1024 MB/s)
	16 Gbit/s (2048 MB/s)

Table 22: Disk interface speeds

As long as the interface speed is higher than the speed at which the disks can read or write data, and as long as the interface bus is not shared, everything is fine. For instance, in case of Fibre Channel, using a switched topology (each disk has its own connection to the controller) instead of using an Arbitrated Loop topology (multiple disks sharing the loop's interface, and each disk must wait for a transmission time slot on the loop) can lead to quite a difference in performance.

9.4.3 Caching

To increase performance, most storage vendors implement a caching system in their disk controllers. Cache can improve performance by several orders of magnitude. It can operate on both reads and writes to disk.

Read-cache acts as a buffer for reads. When the same data is read multiple times, it is served from cache. When data is read, the cache system also attempts to read-ahead, anticipating on future read requests from the operating system, and buffering what it expects to be the next blocks of required data. Optimizing read-cache strategies in the disk controller is quite hard, since the disk controller has limited ways of determining what data is needed next.

With writes, the disk controller's cache is typically used in one of two ways: write-through or write-back. In write-through mode, data is written to cache and then to disk, and only acknowledged as written when the data is physically written on the disk. In contrast, write-back mode allows the disk controller to acknowledge the data as written as soon as it is held in cache. This allows the cache to buffer writes quickly and then write the data to the slower disk when the disk is ready to accept new I/O operations.

Write cache usually contains batteries to keep data not yet written to physical disks in RAM cache, in case of a power failure. Some controllers use flash memory as cache to eliminate the use of batteries, but flash memory is slower than RAM. Most disk systems have a local UPS to provide the disk system with enough power to flush the cache to disks immediately after a power failure.

The type and amount of cache needed depends on what applications need. A web server, for instance, will mostly benefit from read-cache, whereas most databases are better off with write cache.

9.4.4   Storage tiering

Tiered storage creates a hierarchy of storage media, based on cost, performance requirements, and availability requirements.

In 1975, mainframes already had Hierarchical Storage Management (HSM), where data was stored on specific storage devices, based on performance requirements. When data was not used for some time, it was compressed and stored on slower disks. When not used for even longer, it was automatically moved to tape.

Information Lifecycle Management (ILM) can be seen as HSM on midrange and x86 platforms. It manages data from its creation to its archiving or deletion and stores the data on various types of media depending on its value and organization policies. Tiered storage is basically the same as ILM (and HSM), but it looks more at the combination of the available hardware and the data usage.

Typically, four to five tiers are defined in a tiered storage environment, for example:

- Tier 1: Production data (SSD and SAS disks)
- Tier 2: Seldom used data, like email archives (NL-SAS disks)
- Tier 3: Backups (Virtual Tape Libraries on NL-SAS disks)
- Tier 4: Archived data (Tape or NL-SAS disks)

The more tiers are used, the more effort it takes to manage the tiers, which can eliminate the cost benefits of using a tiered storage in the first place.

A well-known limitation of tiered storage is the difficulty of categorizing data to determine which tier it belongs in. There is no default way to do this; it depends on the organization's data requirements.

Automated tiering usually checks for file access times, file creation date, and file ownership, and automatically moves data to the storage medium that fits best. Storage vendors each provide their own algorithms to optimize the tiering process.

In practice, automated tiering is often not working as expected. For instance, when a performance test is executed for a few days, test data is moved to the fasted tier at the end of the test, leading to uncertain test results, that cannot be reproduced.

The test data will then be available in the fastest (and most expensive) tier for a number of days, while it will not be used, since the performance test is finished.

Automated tiering always represents the optimal tiering situation from the past; not necessarily the optimal situation at present.

9.4.5 Load optimization

Storage performance is highly dependent on the type of load. For instance, databases perform two types of operations: they randomly write or read data to and from a transactional database file, and they sequentially write data to an archive log file. Because of the different characteristics of these operations, it is good practice to split these operations across separate and different types of RAID sets.

Most vendors recommend a specific storage configuration for their systems or applications. For example, Oracle recommends a combination of RAID 1 and 5 for its database in order to optimize performance.

9.5 Storage security

9.5.1 Protecting data at rest

Data can either be in transit (transported over a network), in use (by an application or a cache), or at rest (on a disk or a tape). Data at rest can be secured using encryption techniques, which prevent reading or writing data to disk or tape without the correct encryption/decryption key.

9.5.1.1   Disk encryption

Encrypting disks located in the datacenter has limited advantages. Since databases and applications need to work with unencrypted data to perform useful work, disk encryption is only useful when the disks are physically lost or stolen; a situation that occurs typically with laptops, desktops, or removable media, but not with disks in the datacenter.

But even when physical security in the datacenter is in place, a disk drive might get in the wrong hands – for instance because it was removed after it was marked "faulty" and was never destroyed. And in case of disk failure, having the data encrypted solves the issue of having potentially sensitive data on a disk that can't be accessed anymore, as it is defective.

Maintenance contracts often require that a failed disk must be sent back to the vendor after replacing it with a new one. Without disk encryption, returning disks may not be possible since a failed disk cannot be erased anymore.

Full disk encryption also makes it harder for an attacker to retrieve data from the "empty" space on the disks, which often contains traces of previously stored data.

Many disk manufacturers offer Self-Encrypting Drives (SEDs) for use in laptops and desktops. In SEDs encryption is built into the disk drive's hardware. When data is written to the disk, it is automatically encrypted before it is stored on the physical disk. Encryption keys are stored on the disk. When an SED is powered up, authentication is required to access data – the user must type in a password to start the boot sequence of the computer.

Some disks provide a feature called Cryptographic Disk Erasure (CDE), which deletes the encryption key on the disk. This has the same effect as erasing all disk contents, as without the key, unencrypted data can no longer be read from the disk.

9.5.1.2   Tape encryption

Because tapes are moved around more easily than disks (and they should), self-encrypting tape drives can be used to encrypt data on the tapes. For instance, today's LTO tape drives come with AES-256 encryption in their hardware.

To access a tape, the original keys must be used to decrypt the data, as without keys, encrypted data becomes inaccessible and is effectively destroyed. It is therefore important to carefully manage keys when tapes are used for backups. When the tape drive or tape robot is destroyed, the key might also get lost. An offsite copy of the decryption key is therefore very important.

9.5.2 SAN zoning

SAN zoning is a method of arranging Fibre Channel devices into logical groups on a SAN fabric for security purposes. Zones are comparable with VLANs in Ethernet networks.

With zoning, Fibre Channel devices can only communicate with each other if they are members of the same zone. Zoning can make it difficult for hackers and viruses to get to all disks in a SAN.

Servers can be part of multiple zones. The SAN switch checks all packets on the fabric and forwards them only to the ports that are allowed to receive them.

Zoning can ensure operating systems only see "their" LUNs, instead of all LUNs in the SAN. This prevents operating systems from altering data on disks that don't belong to them.

Windows is well known for this – when Windows sees a disk, it automatically claims the disk, and puts a Windows volume label on it. If the disk was assigned to another server, the disk's content is probably ruined.

Zoning can prevent this unwanted behavior by making non-Windows disks invisible to the operating system.

9.5.3 SAN LUN masking

In addition to zoning, LUN masking makes a LUN available to some hosts and unavailable to other hosts. LUN masking is implemented primarily at the HBA level, not in the SAN switch.

It is good practice to use a combination of SAN zoning and LUN masking. Using both zoning and LUN masking, two layers of security are implemented. This increases security, but unfortunately also increases systems management effort.

10

COMPUTE

10.1 Introduction

Compute is an umbrella term for computers located in the datacenter that are either physical machines or virtual machines. Physical computers contain power supplies, Central Processing Units (CPUs), a Basic Input/Output System (BIOS), memory, expansion ports, network connectivity, and – if needed – a keyboard, mouse, and monitor.

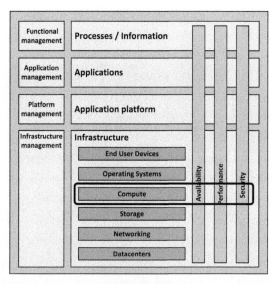

Figure 74: Compute in the infrastructure model

In general, compute systems can be divided into three groups: mainframes, midrange systems, and x86 servers, each with different use cases, history, and future.

Originally the word computer was used for a person who did manual calculations (or computations). Starting from the early 1900s the word computer started to be used for calculating machines as well. The first computing machines were mechanical calculators. Computers as we know them now have two specific properties: they calculate, and they are programmable. Programmable computers only became feasible after the invention of punched cards, which allowed computers to process batches of data.

The British Colossus computer[54], created during World War II, was the world's first programmable computer. Its status was never recognized publicly, however, because information about it was classified under British secrecy laws.

The first publicly recognized general purpose computer was the ENIAC (Electronic Numerical Integrator And Computer). The ENIAC was designed in 1943 and was financed by the United States Army in the midst of World War II. The machine was finished and in full operation in 1946 (after the war) and was in continuous operation until 1955. While the original purpose of ENIAC was to calculate artillery firing tables for the United States Army's Ballistic Research Laboratory, it was actually used first to perform calculations for the design of the hydrogen bomb.

Picture 28: ENIAC[55]

The ENIAC could perform 5,000 operations per second, which was spectacular at the time. However, it used more than 17,000 vacuum tubes, each with a limited life span, which made the computer highly unreliable. The ENIAC got its input using an IBM punched card reader, and punched cards were used for output as well.

As a result of the invention of the transistor in 1956, in the 1960s computers started to be built using transistors instead of vacuum tubes. Transistor-based machines were smaller, faster, cheaper to produce, required less power, and were much more reliable.

The transistor based computers were followed in the 1970s by computers based on integrated circuit (IC) technology. ICs are small chips that contain a set of transistors providing standardized building blocks like AND gates, OR gates, counters, adders, and flip-flops. By combining building blocks, CPUs and memory circuits could be created.

The subsequent creation of microprocessors decreased size and cost of computers even further, and increased their speed and reliability. In the 1980s microprocessors were cheap enough to be used in personal computers.

Today's compute systems include mainframes, midrange systems, and x86 servers. They comprise processors, memory, and interfaces, and they can be implemented as physical or virtual machines.

10.2 Compute building blocks

10.2.1 Computer housing

Originally, computers were stand-alone complete systems, called pedestal or tower computers, which were placed on the datacenter floor. Except for mainframes, most x86 servers and midrange systems are now rack mounted or placed in enclosures as blade servers.

Rack mounted x86 servers are complete machines, typically 1 to 4 Rack Units high (for more information on Rack Units, see section 7.2.7). Since they are complete machines, they need their own power cables, network cables and SAN cables.

Picture 29: A stack of rack mounted servers[56]

Blade servers, on the other hand, are servers without their own power supply or expansion slots. They are placed in blade enclosures, enabling a high server density in a small form factor. Blade servers are connected to shared power supplies, by a wiring system called a backplane.

In general, systems based on blade servers are less expensive than rack mounted servers or pedestal servers because they use the enclosure's shared components like power supplies and fans.

Picture 30: Blade enclosure with one blade partially removed[57]

A blade enclosure typically hosts from 8 to 16 blade servers and provides:

- **Shared redundant power supplies** for all blades.

- **A shared backplane** to connect all blades.

- **Redundant network switches** to connect the blades' Ethernet interfaces providing redundant Ethernet connections to other systems.

- **Redundant SAN switches** to connect the HBA interfaces on the blade servers providing dual redundant Fibre channel connections to other systems.

- **A management module** to manage the enclosure and the blades in it.

The amount of wiring in a blade server setup is substantially reduced when compared to traditional server racks, leading to less possible points of failure and lower initial deployment costs.

A set of blade servers in an enclosure typically uses less electrical power than individual rack mounted servers due to the lower overhead of the shared components in the enclosure. From a deployment perspective, blade servers are also less expensive to install, primarily because the enclosure is a wire-once component and additional blades can be added with a minimum of time and cost.

One often mentioned benefit of using blade servers is that after some years of operation, the blades can be replaced by newer and faster blades. In practice, this is not always the case.

Typically, a blade enclosure is only guaranteed to run one or two generations of server blades. Newer server blades often don't fit, or have additional power, cooling or bandwidth requirements that do not allow them to be used in an existing enclosure.

For example, a blade enclosure's power supply and backplane are designed to provide a maximum number of watts to a blade. If newer blades need more power, then they cannot be used in that blade enclosure, unless the power supplies are replaced as well (if possible).

Newer blades typically also allow for higher network and SAN throughput. The blade enclosure might not allow this, or lowers the network bandwidth to allow running newer and older blade servers together in one blade enclosure.

Enclosures are often not only used for blade servers, but also for storage components like disks, controllers, and SAN switches.

10.2.2 Processors

In a computer, the Central Processing Unit (CPU) – or processor – executes a set of instructions. A CPU is the electronic circuitry that carries out the instructions of a computer program by performing the basic arithmetic, logical, control and input/output (I/O) operations specified by the instructions[58]. Today's processors contain billions of transistors and are extremely powerful.

Picture 31: Intel Xeon Processor[59]

A typical CPU instruction set consists of a fixed number of instructions such as ADD, SHIFT BITS, MOVE DATA, and JUMP TO CODE LOCATION, called the instruction set.

Each instruction is represented as a binary code that the instruction decoder of the CPU is designed to recognize and execute. A program created using CPU instructions is referred to as machine code. Each instruction is associated with an English like mnemonic to make it easier for people to remember them. This set of mnemonics is called the assembly language, which is specific for a particular CPU architecture.

There is a one-to-one correspondence of assembly language instructions to machine code instructions. For example, the binary code for the ADD WITH CARRY machine code instruction may be 10011101 and the corresponding mnemonic could be ADC.

A programmer writing machine code would write the code using mnemonics for each instruction. Then, the mnemonics are passed through a program called an assembler that performs the one-to-one translation of the mnemonics to the machine instruction codes. The machine instruction codes generated by the assembler can run directly on the CPU.

The assembler programming language is the lowest level programming language for computers and very hard for humans to create, understand, and maintain. Higher level programming languages, such as C#, Java, or Python are much more human friendly. Programs written in these languages are translated to assembly code before they can run on a specific CPU. This process is called compiling and is done by a high-level language compiler. It allows higher level languages to be CPU architecture independent.

A CPU needs a high frequency clock to operate, generating so-called clock ticks or clock cycles. Each machine code instruction takes one or more clock ticks to execute. The speed at which the CPU operates is defined in GHz (billions of clock ticks per second). Because of these high clock speeds CPUs are able to execute instructions very fast. An ADD (mnemonic for addition) instruction, for example, typically costs 1 tick to compute. This means a single core of a 2.4 GHz CPU can perform 2.4 billion additions in 1 second!

Each CPU is designed to handle data in chunks, called words, with a specific size. The word size is reflected in many aspects of a CPU's structure and operation; the majority of the internal memory registers in the processor are the size of one word and the largest piece of data that can be transferred to and from the working memory in a single operation is also a word. By using large word sizes larger chunks of data can be read and written to memory in one clock tick.

While the first CPUs had a word size of 4 bits, 8-bit CPUs quickly became much more popular, where numerical values between 0 and 255 could be stored in a single internal memory register.

The first single chip 16-bit microprocessor was the Texas Instruments TMS 9900, but the 16-bit Intel 8086 quickly became more popular. It was the first member of the large x86 microprocessor family, which powers most computers today.

Today's 64-bit CPUs have registers that can hold a single value which can have 2^{64} different permutations. For example, an integer number between 0 and 2^{64} represents a virtual memory address. Therefore, a 64-bit CPU can address 17,179,869,184 TB of memory, as opposed to 32-bit CPUs, which can address 4 GB memory.

10.2.2.1 Intel x86 processors

Following the huge success of the IBM PC architecture, Intel CPUs became the de-facto standard for many computer architectures. The original PC used a

4.77 MHz 16-bit 8088 CPU. The follow-up model IBM PC/AT used the more advanced 16-bit 80286.

A few years later, Intel produced the 32-bit 80386 and the 80486 processors. Since these names all ended with the number 86, the generic architecture was referred to as x86. Later, Intel processors got more marketed names like Pentium (mainly because Intel could not get the numbers patented as a name), but the architecture was still based on the original x86 design. This allowed for backwards compatibility of software; software written for the 8088 could still run on later CPU models without a change.

In 2017, the latest Intel x86 model is the 22-core E5-2699A Xeon Processor, running on 2.4 GHz[60].

10.2.2.2 AMD x86 processors

Advanced Micro Devices, Inc. (AMD) has been, and still is, the largest competitor for Intel. AMD is the second-largest global supplier of microprocessors based on the x86 architecture.

In 1982, AMD signed a contract with Intel, becoming a licensed second-source manufacturer of 8086 and 8088 processors for IBM. IBM wanted to use the Intel 8088 in her IBM PC, but IBM's policy at the time was to require at least two sources for their chips.

Intel canceled the licensing contract in 1986 to prevent AMD from producing a clone of its highly successful 80386 processor. AMD was forced to reverse engineer the 80386 and to create a new 80386 compatible chip from scratch. In 1991, AMD released the AM386, its clone of the Intel 80386 processor. Since this processor was highly successful, AMD performed the same trick for the 80486 and the Pentium processors. Reverse engineering, however, is a very time consuming and costly operation. Today, AMD still produces x86 compatible CPUs, forcing Intel to keep innovating and to keep CPU prices relatively low. In 2017, the latest model is the 16-core AMD Opteron 6386 SE CPU, running on 2.8 GHz[61].

10.2.2.3 Itanium and x86-64 processors

The Itanium processor line was a family of 64-bit high-end CPUs meant for high-end servers and workstations. The Itanium architecture was not based on the x86 architecture; to be able to run x86 based software (like Windows) the Itanium contained an x86 emulator. The architecture jointly developed by HP and Intel. Intel had originally hoped to make Itanium's architecture (IA-64) the replacement for the x86 architecture, but HP was the only company to actively produce Itanium based systems, running mostly HP-UX, and some running

OpenVMS. Although initially Windows could also run on Itanium based systems, Microsoft discontinued Windows support in 2010, due to lack of sales.

In 2005, AMD released the K8 core processor architecture as an answer to Intel's Itanium architecture. The K8 included a 64-bit extension to the x86 instruction set. Later, Intel adopted AMS's processor's instruction set as an extension to its x86 processor line. The first Intel processor to fully implement x86-64 was the Xeon processor.

Because the full x86 16-bit and 32-bit instruction sets remain implemented in hardware, existing x86 applications still run with no compatibility or performance penalty. Today, the x86-64 architecture is used in all Intel and AMD processors.

10.2.2.4 ARM processors

The ARM (Advanced RISC Machine) is the most used CPU in the world, as it is used in billions of mobile phones (like the Apple iPhone, Samsung smartphones, HTC smartphones, and all Nokia phones) and in tablets (like the Apple iPad). The CPU is produced by a large number of manufacturers under license of ARM.

The ARM architecture was originally developed by Acorn Computers in the 1980s, when they needed a more powerful CPU for their BBC home computers. The CPUs available at that time, like the Motorola 68000, were not powerful enough to handle the graphics and GUIs Acorn had in mind. Therefore, Acorn decided to design its own processor. Acorn did not make the chips themselves; VLSI Technology was chosen as the manufacturer. The first processor produced in large series was the ARM2, which shipped in 1986. To develop the third version of the ARM architecture, Acorn went into a partnership with Apple. In 1990, the design was incorporated into the new company Advanced RISC Machines Ltd.

The ARM processor architecture needs a relatively small number of transistors: approximately 34,000 instead of the millions of transistors used in comparable Intel Atom processors. This leads to very low power consumption, which is excellent for use in mobile devices.

In 2013, ARM's customers reported 10 billion ARM processors shipped[62], representing 95% of smartphones, 90% of hard disk drives, 40% of digital televisions and set-top boxes, 15% of microcontrollers and 20% of mobile computers. The processor is also used in Nintendo products and in digital cameras.

Since 2016, ARM is owned by Japanese telecommunications company SoftBank Group[63].

10.2.2.5 Oracle SPARC processors

In 1986, Sun Microsystems started to produce the SPARC processor series for their Solaris UNIX based systems. SPARC is an abbreviation for Scalable Processor ARChitecture. SPARC CPUs were used for the first time in the Sun-4 workstation and server systems.

The SPARC architecture is fully open and non-proprietary (a true open source hardware design). This means that any manufacturer can get a license to produce a SPARC CPU. With the acquisition of Sun by Oracle in 2010, SPARC processors are still used by Oracle in their Exadata and Exalogic products.

In 2017, the latest model is the 32-core SPARC M7 CPU, running on 4.1 GHz[64].

10.2.2.6 IBM POWER processors

POWER (also known as PowerPC) was a series of CPUs, created by IBM, introduced in 1990. The name is an acronym for Performance Optimization With Enhanced RISC. POWER CPUs are used in many of IBM's servers, minicomputers, workstations, and supercomputers.

IBM uses POWER CPUs in many of their high-end server products, including Watson, the supercomputer that won Jeopardy in 2011, which was equipped with 3,000 POWER7 CPU cores.

In 2017, the latest model is the 24-core POWER9 CPU, running on 4 GHz[65].

10.2.3 Memory

Early computers used vacuum tubes, relays, Williams tubes, or magnetic core memory to store data.

The first computers used vacuum tubes. Since a vacuum tube could only store a few bits of data each, this type of memory was extremely expensive, used much power, was very fragile, and generated much heat.

An alternative to vacuum tubes were relays. Relays are mechanical parts that use magnetism to move a physical switch. Two relays can be combined to create a single bit of memory storage. But relays are slow, use much power, are noisy, heavy, and expensive.

Based on cathode ray tubes, the Williams tube was the first random access computer memory, capable of storing several thousands of bits, but only for some seconds.

The first truly useable type of main memory was magnetic core memory, introduced in 1951. Magnetic core memory would become the dominant type of memory until the development of transistor based memory in the late 1960s.

Picture 32: Magnified picture of 2 bytes of core memory[66]

Magnetic core memory uses very small (approximately 0.1 mm across[67]) magnetic rings, called cores, with wires running through them. These wires can polarize the magnetic field one direction or the other (clockwise or counterclockwise) in each individual core. One direction means 1, while the other means 0. Because reading the polarity of the core destroys the information, each read must be followed immediately by a write, to restore the value.

Core memory was non-volatile: the contents of memory were not lost if the power was switched off. Core memory was replaced by RAM chips in the 1970s.

10.2.3.1 RAM

RAM stands for Random Access Memory. "Random" means that any piece of data stored in RAM can be read in the same amount of time, regardless of its physical location. RAM is based on transistor technology, typically implemented in large amounts in Integrated Circuits (ICs). Data stored in RAM remains available as long as the RAM is powered.

RAM either stores a bit of data in a flip-flop circuit, as implemented in SRAM (static RAM), or as a charge in a capacitor, as implemented in DRAM (dynamic RAM).

SRAM uses flip-flop circuitry to store bits, using six transistors per bit. SRAM has faster access times than DRAM and is therefore used mostly in cache memory and video RAM.

The advantage of DRAM over SRAM is that DRAMs only need one transistor and one capacitor to store a bit. The capacitor is either charged (representing a 1) or discharged (representing a 0). The transistor acts as a switch that lets the control circuitry on the memory chip read the capacitor or change its state. DRAM loses its data after a short time due to the leakage of the capacitors. To keep data available in DRAM it must be refreshed regularly (typically around 16 times per second). DRAM uses special hardware circuits to automatically refresh its contents.

10.2.3.2 BIOS

The Basic Input/Output System (BIOS) is a set of instructions stored on a memory chip located on the computer's motherboard. The BIOS is software that controls a computer from the moment it is powered on, to the point where the operating system is started (see chapter 11 for more information on operating systems). The BIOS provides the instructions necessary to access the hard disk, memory, keyboard, monitor, and other hardware.

Today, BIOS memory is mostly implemented in a Flash memory chip installed on the computer's main system board. It is good practice to update the BIOS software regularly. Newer BIOS revisions can increase the stability and performance of the system board and provide new options. Upgrading computers to the latest version of the BIOS is called BIOS flashing.

10.2.4 Interfaces

Connecting computers to external peripherals is done using interfaces. External interfaces like RS-232, USB, and Thunderbolt use connectors located at the outside of the computer case, connecting external hardware devices like printers and hardware tokens.

Internal interfaces, typically some form of PCI, are located on the system board of the computer, inside the case, and connect expansion boards like network adapters and disk controllers.

10.2.4.1 RS-232

One of the first standardized external interfaces was the serial bus based on RS-232. RS-232 (Recommended Standard 232) was introduced in 1962 for communication between electromechanical teletypewriters and modems, and later also for connecting electronic terminals. For many years, an RS-232 compatible port was a standard feature for serial communications, such as modem connections, on almost all computers. It remained in widespread use into the late 1990s. Sometimes RS-232 was preferred because of the long cable length that can be used with these devices, and when a high transfer speed is not necessarily required. Cables up to 15 meters could be used with RS-232, making it a good choice for connecting for instance printers that were placed in a different room than the computers.

RS-232 is still used today in some systems to connect older type of peripherals, industrial equipment, console ports, and special purpose equipment.

Bit rates used with RS-232 are from 75 bit/s to 115,200 bit/s. RS-232 originally used a D-subminiature 25-pin connector for connectivity, but the much smaller 9-pin version was preferred in later designs.

10.2.4.2 USB

The Universal Serial Bus (USB) was introduced in 1996 as a replacement for most of the external interfaces on servers and PCs. Compared with RS-232 and older parallel ports, USB is much faster, uses lower voltages, doesn't need manual configuration, and has connectors that are simpler to connect and use.

The USB interface can provide operating power to attached devices, a feature not found on earlier external interfaces. This enables for instance USB flash disks (also known as memory sticks) to work without an external power source.

Up to seven devices can be daisy-chained, but often hubs are used to connect multiple devices to one USB computer port.

The first widely used version of USB was 1.1, which was released in 1998. It allowed for a 12 Mbit/s data rate for higher speed devices such as disk drives, and a lower 1.5 Mbit/s rate for low bandwidth devices such as keyboards.

The USB 2.0 specification was released in 2000. It provided a maximum data transfer rate of 480 Mbit/s. In 2008, USB 3 was introduced, providing a throughput of almost 5 Gbit/s. USB 3.1, released in 2013, doubled the throughput to 10 Gbit/s. The USB 3.0 and 3.1 implementations and connectors are backward compatible with USB 2.0.

In 2014, USB Type-C (also known as USB-C) was introduced. Its most important feature was a new, smaller connector and the ability to provide more power to connected devices. The connector can for instance be used to charge laptops, like in the latest Apple MacBook, as it is capable of transferring up to 100 W of electricity. USB Type-C is actually only a new connector and cable type, which can be used to run the USB 3.1 protocol. The new connector, however, can also be used for other protocols, like Thunderbolt 3.

10.2.4.3 Thunderbolt

Thunderbolt, also known as Light Peak, was introduced in 2011. It was developed by Intel with technical collaboration from Apple and appeared first on Apple laptops.

Thunderbolt version 1 provides 10 Gbit/s bi-directional data transfers. Up to seven devices can be daisy-chained using optical or copper based cables, but also hubs can be used, like with USB. Also like USB, the copper based cables can provide power to attached devices.

Thunderbolt version 1 and 2 connectors were based on the Mini DisplayPort connector developed by Apple. Thunderbolt 2, released in 2013, allows for a throughput of 20 Gbit/s.

Thunderbolt 3, released in 2015, can provide a maximum throughput of 40 Gbit/s. Thunderbolt 3 can also provide 100 W power to devices. It uses the USB Type-C connector and is backward compatible with USB 3.1.

10.2.4.4 PCI and PCIe

Most x86 servers and midrange systems use PCI for their primary internal expansion slots. PCI stands for Peripheral Component Interconnect. It can be implemented as connectors on the system board for attaching external hardware, or as on-board circuitry to connect expansions like Ethernet or video circuitry on the system board itself.

PCI uses a shared parallel bus architecture, in which only one shared communication path between two PCI devices can be active at any given time. Usually the system board itself is the bus master, exchanging data between the system board and the PCI adapter, but PCI adapters can act as bus masters as well. This enables data exchange between two PCI adapters directly.

Initially, PCI buses were 32 bits wide. The PCI specification included optional 64-bit support, provided via an extended connector with 64-bit extensions.

Apart from the conventional PCI bus, the much faster PCI Express is often used in today's systems.

PCI Express (PCIe) uses a topology based on point-to-point serial links, rather than a shared parallel bus architecture. A connection between any two PCIe devices is known as a link, and is built up from a collection of 1 or more links, called lanes.

All devices must minimally support a single-lane (x1) link. Devices may optionally support wider links, composed of 2, 4, 8, 12, 16, or 32 lanes.

PCIe connections are routed by a hub on the system board acting as a crossbar switch. The hub allows multiple pairs of devices to communicate with each other at the same time. Picture 33 shows various physical PCI and PCIe slots on a system board.

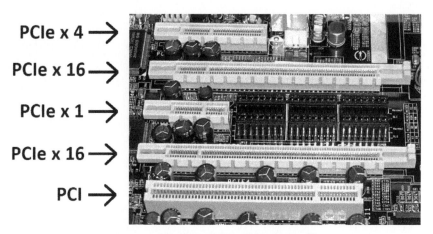

PCIe x 4 →
PCIe x 16 →
PCIe x 1 →
PCIe x 16 →
PCI →

Picture 33: PCI versus PCIe buses[68]

Despite the availability of the much faster PCIe, conventional PCI remains a very common interface in computers. The following table shows the raw speed of the various PCI bus architectures. Since PCIe can handle multiple serial links to exchange data on the same connector, the speed of the combinations is also stated (in Gbit/s).

	Lanes					
	1	**2**	**4**	**8**	**16**	**32**
PCI 32-bit/33 MHz	1					
PCI 32-bit/66 MHz	2					
PCI 64-bit/33 MHz	2					
PCI 64-bit/66 MHz	4					
PCI 64-bit/100 MHz	6					
PCIe 1.0	2	4	8	16	32	64
PCIe 2.0	4	8	16	32	64	128
PCIe 3.0	8	16	32	64	128	256
PCIe 4.0	16	32	64	128	256	512

Table 23: PCI speeds in Gbit/s

10.2.5 Compute virtualization

In traditional computer architectures, the operating system directly interacts with the physical machine, as shown in Figure 75.

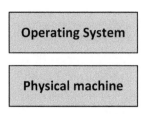

Figure 75: Traditional compute architecture

Compute virtualization, also known as server virtualization or Software Defined Compute, introduces an abstraction layer between physical computer hardware and the operating system using that hardware. Virtualization allows multiple operating systems to run on a single physical machine (see Figure 76).

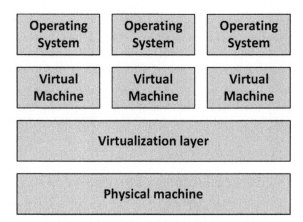

Figure 76: Virtualization architecture

Virtualization decouples and isolates virtual machines from the physical machine and from other virtual machines by means of a virtualization layer. A virtual machine is a logical representation of a physical computer in software.

Virtual machines can be started and stopped independently from each other. And if one virtual machine crashes, the others are isolated from the failure and are unaffected.

Virtualization allows for new virtual machines to be provisioned as needed, without the need for an upfront hardware purchase. This saves a lot of time and money – with a few mouse clicks or using an API, new virtual machines for test or development can be installed in minutes. No purchase order is needed, no waiting time for delivery, no physical hardware needs to be delivered, and no hardware needs to be installed in the datacenter.

In the 1960s, virtual machines were introduced in the experimental IBM M44/44X system. IBM developed the concept and introduced virtualization in the IBM mainframe System/370 in 1972, which was managed by the VM/370, the first virtual machine operating system. All mainframes have been using virtualization since.

In the late 1990s, midrange systems vendors started to implement virtualization, based on Logical Partition (LPAR) technology, which was similar to the technology used in mainframes.

The widespread use of x86 based servers, that gained much more processing power and memory capacity around 2000, started to make virtualization on the x86 platform a viable option. The primary driver was computer consolidation: virtualization allowed a single physical computer to replace multiple underutilized dedicated computers.

VMware became the market leader in x86 virtualization. Their first product, VMware Workstation, was introduced in 1999 and the server product, named VMware GSX, was launched in 2001. Today x86 virtualization is offered by a number of vendors, including VMware, Citrix, Red Hat, and Microsoft.

By consolidating many physical computers as virtual machines on fewer (bigger) physical machines, costs can be saved on hardware, power, and cooling. Because fewer physical machines are needed, the cost of maintenance contracts can be reduced and the risk of hardware failure is reduced.

10.2.5.1 Software Defined Compute (SDC)

Virtual machines are typically managed using one redundant centralized virtual machine management system. This enables systems managers to manage more machines with the same number of staff and allows managing the virtual machines using APIs.

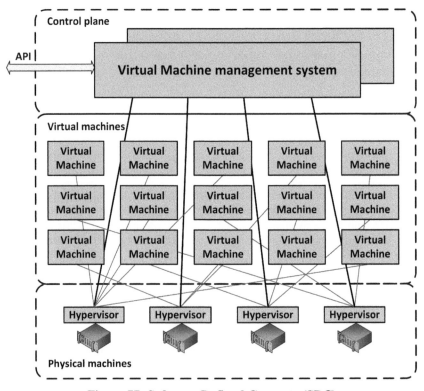

Figure 77: Software Defined Compute (SDC)

Centralized management of resources and (automatic) optimization of resources also eases management efforts. Server virtualization can therefore be seen as Software Defined Compute, as shown in Figure 77.

In an SDC architecture, all physical machines are running a hypervisor and all hypervisors are managed as one layer using management software. Via the hypervisor, CPU, memory, disk, and networking resources can be dynamically allocated to virtual machines, where each virtual machine consumes a percentage of the CPU power, memory, network bandwidth, and storage resources of the underlying physical machine.

Some virtualization platforms, like VMware ESX VMotion, Microsoft Hyper-V Live Migration and Citrix XenServer's XenMotion, allow running virtual machines to be moved automatically between physical machines. This allows virtual machines to be automatically moved to the least busy physical machines, or some physical machines can get fully loaded while other physical machines can be automatically switched off, saving power and cooling cost. It also allows for hardware maintenance without downtime. By moving all virtual machines from one physical machine to other physical machines, the physical machine can be switched off for maintenance without interruption of running virtual machines.

An SDC architecture also provides high availability features. When a physical machine fails, all virtual machines that ran on the failed physical machine can be restarted automatically on other physical machines. Some vendors even provide lockstepping virtual machines, like XenServer Marathon everRun and VMware's Fault Tolerance. Lockstepping keeps the state of two virtual machines in sync, even on memory level. When a server fails, the other takes over without interruption.

When switched off, a virtual machine is nothing more than a file on a disk – the virtual machine image. It is therefore quite easy to create a copy of a virtual machine just before a change, like a patch or a software installation, is performed on the machine. Virtual machine images can be kept for special occasions, for instance, an old version of a virtual machine can be kept to work with old archived data.

10.2.5.2 Disadvantages of computer virtualization

Of course, there are a number of disadvantages to computer virtualization as well.

One pitfall of using virtualization is that it is sometimes too easy to create new virtual machines. Because creating a new virtual machine is so easy, virtual machines tend to get created for all kinds of reasons (usually for testing purposes). This effect is known as "virtual machine sprawl". But all of these virtual machines must be managed; they use resources of the physical machine, and they use power and cooling (ad-hoc created virtual machines tend not to be switched off again). They must be back-upped and kept up to date by installing patches.

Another drawback of using virtualization is that it introduces an extra layer in the infrastructure, which needs to be managed. This layer requires license fees, systems managers training, and the installation and maintenance of additional tools.

Virtualization cannot be used on all servers. Some servers require additional specialized hardware, like modem cards, USB tokens or some form of high speed I/O like in real-time SCADA systems.

While the use of virtualization for database servers is criticized, over the years the performance overhead of the virtualization layer has become low enough to run even high performance databases. But because database servers typically use all resources of a physical machine, running extra virtual machines next to a database virtual machine is impractical. This is the main reason to keep using physical machines for database servers.

Virtualization is not supported by all application vendors. This means that while an application may run fine on a virtual machine; the configuration is not supported by the supplier. When the application experiences some problem, systems managers must reinstall the application on a physical machine before they get support. The main reason for the lack of support is that the application vendor claims to have no control over the total stack – the virtualization layer cannot be influenced (which is not a very good reason of course, since the vendor has no control over the operating system, the hardware or the storage as well). To solve this problem, some application vendors work together with virtualization vendors to provide support. An example is Microsoft, that introduced the Microsoft Server Virtualization Validation Program (SVVP), supporting Microsoft operating systems and applications that run on either VMware or XenServer (and Microsoft's own Hyper-V of course).

10.2.5.3 Virtualization technologies

Many virtualization technologies are in use, each with their own properties. In this section emulation, logical partitions, and various types of hypervisors are described.

10.2.5.3.1 Emulation

An emulator is a piece of software that allows programs to run on a computer system other than the one they were originally intended for. An emulator does this by reproducing the original computer's behavior through a process of translation, called emulation. This allows for instance a mainframe operating systems or OpenVMS to run on an x86 platform.

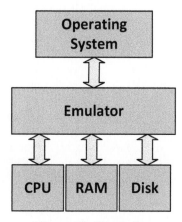

Figure 78: Emulation

Emulators are designed for portability, not necessarily for speed. Emulation is a slow process by nature. The emulator must not only translate CPU instructions from one architecture to another, but must also emulate the behavior of video cards, keyboards, network adapters, disk access, and other devices.

Examples of emulators are Hercules (a mainframe emulator on x86), Charon (a VAX/Alpha emulator on x86), and Bochs (an x86 emulator allowing for instance to run Windows on UNIX systems).

10.2.5.3.2 Logical Partitions (LPARs)

A Logical Partition (LPAR), typically implemented in mainframe and midrange systems, is a subset of a computer's hardware resources, virtualized as a separate computer. Using LPARs, a physical machine can be partitioned into multiple logical partitions, each hosting a separate operating system.

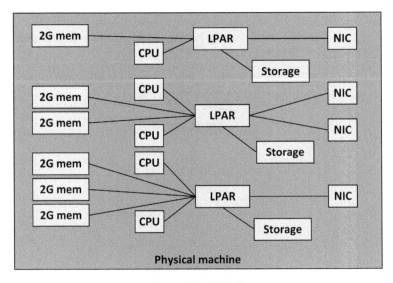

Figure 79: LPARs

Each LPAR is bound to one or more resources, like physical CPUs, network interface controllers (NICs), storage, and memory segments. This means that the number of virtual machines in a LPAR system is limited to the number of physical CPU cores, network cards, and storage connections. A resource allocated to a certain LPAR cannot be used by another LPAR.

10.2.5.3.3 Hypervisors

Hypervisors, also called a virtual machine monitors (VMM), are mostly used in x86 systems and are directly installed on the computer's hardware. Their task is to run and monitor virtual machines. Hypervisors control the physical computer's hardware and provide virtual machines with all the services of a physical system, including a virtual BIOS, virtual devices, and virtualized memory management.

Products like VMware ESX, Citrix XenServer, Red Hat Enterprise Virtualization (RHEV), and Microsoft Hyper-V are examples of hypervisors. They typically run Windows and Linux operating systems in their virtual machines.

While most midrange systems use LPAR technology, HP Integrity Virtual Machines are also hypervisors providing virtualized shared resources. In an Integrity virtual machine, different midrange operating systems can be run, like HP-UX and Linux.

In general, hypervisors can be implemented using the following technologies:

- **Binary translation** – When a hypervisor is used as a layer between the CPU and the virtual machine, not all CPU instructions can be transferred unmodified to the CPU. For example: a HALT instruction normally halts the complete CPU. If a virtual machine would perform a HALT, and that instruction is sent to the CPU unmodified, the physical machine would halt, leading to a halt of all virtual machines on that physical machine. To prevent this from happening, a binary translation hypervisor translates a number of instructions to new sequences of instructions that have the intended effect on the virtual hardware: a HALT only halts the virtual CPU. The remaining instructions run unmodified on the CPU and therefore at native speed. Because binary translation is performed on the binary code that gets executed on the processor, it does not require changes to the operating system running in the virtual machine.

- **Paravirtualization** – Paravirtualization (also known as operating system assisted virtualization) is a virtualization technique where a *modified* operating system communicates to the hypervisor its intent to perform privileged CPU and memory operations. This in contrast to binary translation, where the operating system does not know it runs on a virtual machine. Paravirtualization reduces the number of tasks to be performed by the hypervisor (since the operating system and the hypervisor work together), making the implementation simpler and more efficient than a binary translation hypervisor. Although paravirtualization does not eliminate virtualization overhead, it can greatly improve virtual machine performance.

- **Hardware assisted virtualization** – In hardware assisted virtualization, hardware instructions are implemented in the CPU to assist the hypervisor, allowing virtual machines to run in isolation on the hardware level. Processors with Virtualization Technology have an extra instruction set called Virtual Machine Extensions or VMX. All of today's Intel (VT-x) and AMD (AMD-V) processors provide this hardware support. VMX enabled processors allow trapping of sensitive instructions from virtual machines and handling them safely. This eliminates the need for binary translation or paravirtualization. Like binary translation, hardware assisted virtualization does not require changes to the operating system in the virtual machine. Hardware assisted virtualization is supported by VMware ESX, Citrix XenServer, Red Hat RHEV, and Microsoft Hyper-V and is their default mode of operation.

10.2.5.4 Virtual memory management

Hypervisors manage the memory of the physical computer by dividing the available memory over the virtual machines. The hypervisor uses memory overcommit and memory sharing to make the best use of the available physical memory.

10.2.5.4.1 Memory overcommit

Most operating systems claim more memory than they actually use. With memory overcommit the hypervisor assigns more memory to the combined virtual machines than is physically available in the computer. The assumption is that not all assigned memory will actually be used by all virtual machines at the same time. Some virtual machines may need all of the memory that they have been allocated, while other virtual machines may need considerably less. Most hypervisors can identify idle memory and dynamically reallocate unused memory from some virtual machines to others that need more memory.

The use of memory overcommit is controversial. Some say memory overcommits needs to be avoided as it could lead to problems with virtual machines running out of memory. This can be a problem for example when a physical machine boots up and consequently boots up all virtual machines at the same time. Because all virtual machines claim their allocated memory, they either force the hypervisor to start swapping memory to disk (which makes all starting virtual machines extremely slow, see section 11.4.1) or they might not start at all due to a shortage of memory.

10.2.5.4.2 Memory sharing

Memory sharing maps identical memory pages in one or more virtual machines to a single page of physical memory. With memory sharing the hypervisor scans memory looking for memory pages with identical content and then remaps the virtual machines' pages to a single read-only shared copy of the page. If a virtual machine attempts to write to the shared page, the hypervisor allocates a new copy of the page with read-write permissions for that virtual machine.

Memory sharing can significantly reduce overall memory requirements. For example, if multiple virtual machines are running the same Windows operating system, most their memory pages can typically be shared. This technology is not specific to hypervisors by the way; it is used by the UNIX operating system's fork system call for decades.

10.2.6 Container technology

Originally, operating systems were designed to run a large number of independent processes. In practice, however, dependencies on specific versions of libraries and specific resource requirements for each application process led to using one operating system – and hence one server – per application. For instance, a database server typically only runs a database, while the application server using the database is hosted on another machine.

Compute virtualization, as discussed in section 10.2.5, solves this problem, but at considerable overhead – each application needs a full operating system, leading to high license and systems management cost. And because even the smallest application needs a full operating system, much memory and many CPU cycles are wasted just to get isolation between applications. Container technology is a way to solve this issue.

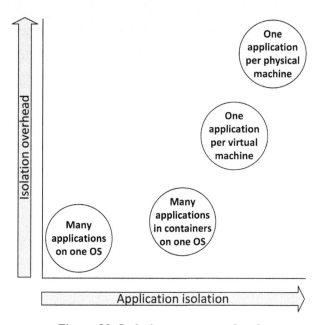

Figure 80: Isolation versus overhead

Figure 80 shows the relation between isolation between applications and the overhead of running the application. While running each application on a dedicated physical machine provides the highest isolation, the overhead is very high, as many physical machines are needed. An operating system, on the other hand, provides much less isolation, but at a very low overhead per application.

Container technology is a server virtualization method in which the kernel of an operating system provides multiple isolated user-space instances, instead of just one. Containers look and feel like a real server from the point of view of its owners and users, but they share the same operating system kernel. This isolation enables the operating system to run multiple processes, where each process shares nothing but the kernel.

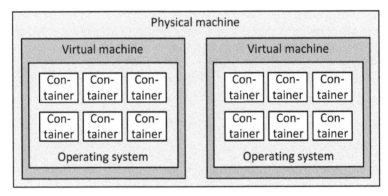

Figure 81: Container technology

Containers are not new – the first UNIX based containers, introduced in 1979, provided isolation of the root file system via the `chroot` operation. Solaris subsequently added many enhancements, and Linux control groups (cgroups) adopted many of these ideas.

Containers are part of the Linux kernel since 2008. But the use of containers to encapsulate all application components, such as dependencies and services is new. And when all dependencies are encapsulated, applications can run in parallel on the same kernel, using their own libraries and dependencies without interfering with each other.

Containers have a number of benefits:

- **Isolation** – applications or application components can be encapsulated in containers, each operating independently and isolated from each other.

- **Portability** – since containers typically contain all components the application needs to function, including libraries and patches, containers can be run on any infrastructure that is capable of running containers using the same kernel version.

- **Easy deployment** – containers allow developers to quickly deploy new software versions, as their containers can be moved from the development environment to the production environment unaltered.

10.2.6.1 Container implementation

Containers are based on 3 technologies that are all part of the Linux kernel:

- **Chroot** (also known as a jail) – changes the apparent root directory for the current running process and its children and ensures that these processes cannot access files outside the designated directory tree. Chroot was available in UNIX as early as 1979.

- **Namespaces** - allows complete isolation of an applications' view of the operating environment, including process trees, networking, user IDs and mounted file systems. It is part of the Linux kernel since 2002.

- **Cgroups** - limits and isolates the resource usage (CPU, memory, disk I/O, network, etc.) of a collection of processes. Cgroups is part of the Linux kernel since 2008.

Linux Containers (LXC), introduced in 2008, is a combination of chroot, cgroups, and namespaces, providing isolated environments.

Docker is a popular implementation of a container ecosystem. It adds Union File System (UFS) to containers – a way of combining multiple directories into one that appears to contain their combined contents. This allows multiple layers of software to be "stacked". Docker also automates deployment of applications inside containers.

10.2.6.2 Containers and security

While containers provide some isolation, they still use the same underlying kernel and libraries. Isolation between containers on the same machine is much lower than virtual machine isolation.

Virtual machines get isolation from hardware - using specialized CPU instructions. Containers don't have this level of isolation. However, there are some operating systems, like Joyent's SmartOS offering, that run on physical machines, and that provide containers with hardware based isolation using the same specialized CPU instructions.

Since developers define the contents of containers, security officers lose control over the containers, which could lead to unnoticed vulnerabilities. This could lead to using multiple versions of tools, unpatched software, outdated software, or unlicensed software. To solve this issue, a repository with predefined and approved container components and container hierarchy should be implemented.

10.2.6.3 Container orchestration

A classical operating system abstracts resources such as CPU, RAM, and network connectivity and provides services to applications. In contrast, container orchestration, also known as a datacenter operating system, abstracts the resources of a cluster of machines and provides services to containers.

A container orchestrator enables containers to be run anywhere on a cluster of machines. It schedules the containers to run on any machine that has resources available and it acts like a kernel for the combined resources of an entire datacenter instead of the resources of just a single computer.

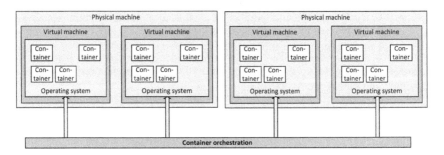

Figure 82: Container orchestration

There are many frameworks for managing container images and orchestrating the container lifecycle. Some examples are:

- Docker Swarm

- Apache Mesos

- Google's Kubernetes

- Rancher

- Pivotal CloudFoundry

- Mesosphere DC/OS

10.2.7 Mainframes

10.2.7.1 History

A mainframe is a high-performance computer made for high-volume, I/O-intensive computing. Mainframes were the first commercially available computers. They were produced by vendors like IBM, Unisys, Hitachi, Bull, Fujitsu, and NEC. But IBM always was the largest vendor – it still has 90% market share in the mainframe market.

Mainframes used to have no interactive user interface. Instead, they ran batch processes, using punched cards, paper tape, and magnetic tape as input, and produced printed paper as output. In the early 1970s, most mainframes got interactive user interfaces, based on terminals, simultaneously serving hundreds of users.

While the end of the mainframe is predicted for decades now, mainframes are still widely used. Today's mainframes are still relatively large (the size of a few 19" racks), but they don't fill-up a room anymore. They are expensive computers, mostly used for administrative processes, optimized for handling high volumes of data.

The latest IBM z13 mainframe, introduced in 2015, can host up to 10TB of memory and 141 processors, running at a 5GHz clock speed. It has enough resources to run up to 8000 virtual machines simultaneously[69].

Mainframes are highly reliable, typically running for years without downtime. Much redundancy is built in, enabling hardware upgrades and repairs while the mainframe is operating without downtime.

All IBM mainframes are backwards compatible with older mainframes. For instance, the 64-bit mainframes of today can still run the 24-bit System/360 code from the early days of mainframe computing. Much effort is spent in ensuring all software continues to work without modification.

Picture 34: IBM z series mainframe

10.2.7.2 Mainframe architecture

A mainframe consists of processing units (PUs), memory, I/O channels, control units, and devices, all placed in racks (frames). The architecture of a mainframe is shown in Figure 83.

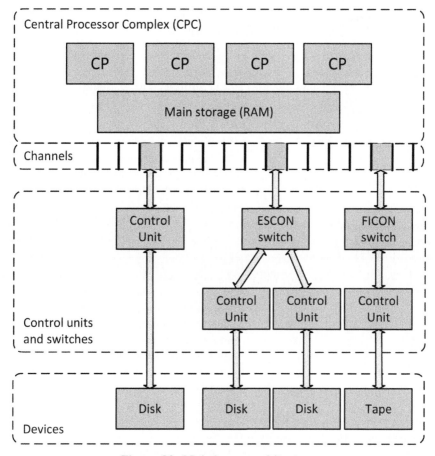

Figure 83: Mainframe architecture

The various parts of the architecture are described below.

10.2.7.2.1 Processing Units

In the mainframe world, the term PU (Processing Unit) is used instead of the more ambiguous term CPU. A mainframe has multiple PUs, so there is no *central* processing unit. The total of all PUs in a mainframe is called a Central Processor Complex (CPC).

The CPC resides in its own cage inside the mainframe, and consists of one to four so-called book packages. Each book package consists of processors, memory, and I/O connections, much like x86 system boards.

Mainframes use specialized PUs (like the quad core z10 mainframe processor) instead of off-the-shelf Intel or AMD supplied CPUs.

All processors in the CPC start as equivalent processor units (PUs). Each processor is characterized during installation or at a later time, sometimes because of a specific task the processor is configured to do. Some examples of characterizations are:

Processor unit (PU)	Task
Central processors (CP)	Central processors are the main processors of the system that can be used to run applications running on VM, z/OS, and ESA/390 operating systems.
CP Assist for Cryptographic Function (CPACF)	CPACF assists the CPs by handling workload associated with encryption/decryption.
Integrated Facility for Linux (IFL)	IFL assists with Linux workloads: they are regular PUs with a few specific instructions that are needed by Linux.
Integrated Coupling Facility (ICF)	This facility executes licensed internal code to coordinate system tasks.
System Assisted Processor (SAP)	A SAP assists the CP with workload for the I/O subsystem, for instance by translating logical channel paths to physical paths.
Spares	Used to replace any CP or SAP failure
IBM System z Application Assist Processors (zAAP)	Used for Java code execution
zIIP	Processing certain database workloads

Table 24: Mainframe processing units

10.2.7.2.2 Main Storage

Each book package in the CPC cage contains from four to eight memory cards. For example, a fully loaded z9 mainframe has four book packages that can provide up to a total of 512 GB of memory.

The memory cards are hot swappable, which means that you can add or remove a memory card without powering down the mainframe.

10.2.7.2.3 Channels, ESCON and FICON

A channel provides a data and control path between I/O devices and memory.

Today's largest mainframes have 1024 channels. Channels connect to control units, either directly or via switches. Specific slots in the I/O cages are reserved for specific types of channels, which include the following:

- **Open Systems Adapter (OSA)** – this adapter provides connectivity to various industry standard networking technologies, including Ethernet.

- **Fiber Connection (FICON)** - this is the most flexible channel technology, based on fiber-optic technology. With FICON, input/output devices can be located many kilometers from the mainframe to which they are attached.

- **Enterprise Systems Connection (ESCON)** - this is an earlier type of fiber-optic technology. ESCON channels can provide performance almost as fast as FICON channels, but at a shorter distance.

The FICON or ESCON switches may be connected to several mainframes, sharing the control units and I/O devices.

The channels are high speed – today's FICON Express16S channels provide up to 320 links of 16 Gbit/s each[70].

10.2.7.2.4 Control units

A control unit is similar to an expansion card in an x86 or midrange system. It contains logic to work with a particular type of I/O device, like a printer or a tape drive.

Some control units can have multiple channel connections providing multiple paths to the control unit and its devices, increasing performance and availability.

Control units can be connected to multiple mainframes, creating shared I/O systems. Sharing devices, especially disk drives, is complicated and there are specialized hardware and software techniques used by the operating system to control updating the same disk data at the same time from two independent systems.

Control units connect to devices, like disk drives, tape drives, and communication interfaces. Disks in mainframes are called DASD (Direct Attached Storage Device), which is comparable to a SAN (Storage Area Network) in a midrange or x86 environment.

10.2.7.3 Mainframe virtualization

Mainframes were designed for virtualization from the start – they typically run multiple virtual machines with multiple operating systems; it is not uncommon for a mainframe to run dozens of virtual machines – each acting as a mainframe in its own right. Mainframes pioneered computer virtualization and their virtualization technology is still very sophisticated today.

Today's mainframes offer logical partitions (LPARs) as the default virtualization solution. LPARs are, in practice, equivalent to separate mainframes. Each LPAR runs its own mainframe operating system. A maximum number of concurrent processors executing in each LPAR can be specified, as well as weightings for different LPARs (e.g. LPAR 1 can use twice the number of PUs as LPAR 2).

The largest IBM mainframe today has an upper limit of 54 LPARs. Practical limitations on the number of available PUs and cores per PU, memory size, I/O availability, and available processing power usually limits the number of LPARs to less than this maximum. A more common number of LPARs in use on a mainframe is less than ten.

Please note that the mainframe operating system running on each LPAR is designed to concurrently run a large number of applications and services, and can be connected to thousands of users at the same time – in an x86 configuration this would typically be split up over many individual operating system and physical and virtual machines. Often one LPAR runs all production tasks while another runs the consolidated test environment.

10.2.8 Midrange systems

The midrange platform is positioned between the mainframe platform and the x86 platform. The size and cost of the systems, the workload, the availability, their performance, and the maturity of the platform is higher than that of the x86 platforms, but lower than that of a mainframe.

Today midrange systems are produced by three vendors:

- IBM produces the **Power Systems** series of midrange systems (the former RS/6000, System p, AS/400, and System i series).

- Hewlett-Packard produces the **HP Integrity** systems.

- Oracle produces the original Sun Microsystems's based **SPARC servers**.

Midrange systems are typically built using parts from only one vendor, and run an operating system provided by that same vendor. This makes the platform relatively stable, leading to high availability and security.

10.2.8.1 History

The term minicomputer evolved in the 1960s to describe the small computers that became possible with the use of IC and core memory technologies. Small was relative, however; a single minicomputer typically was housed in a few cabinets the size of a 19" rack.

The first commercially successful minicomputer was DEC PDP-8, launched in 1964. The PDP-8 sold for one-fifth the price of the smallest IBM 360 mainframe. This enabled manufacturing plants, small businesses, and scientific laboratories to have a computer of their own.

Picture 35: DEC PDP-8[71]

In the late 1970s, DEC produced another very successful minicomputer series called the VAX. VAX systems came in a wide range of different models. They could easily be setup as a VAXcluster for high availability and performance.

DEC was the leading minicomputer manufacturer and the 2nd largest computer company (after IBM). DEC was sold to Compaq in 1998 which in its turn became part of HP some years later.

Minicomputers became powerful systems that ran full multi-user, multitasking operating systems like OpenVMS and UNIX. Halfway through the 1980s minicomputers became less popular as a result of the lower cost of microprocessor based PCs, and the emergence of LANs. In places where high availability, performance, and security are very important, minicomputers (now better known as midrange systems) are still used.

Most midrange systems today run a flavor of the UNIX operating system, OpenVMS or IBM i:

- HP Integrity servers run HP-UX UNIX and OpenVMS.

- Oracle/Sun's SPARC servers run Solaris UNIX.

- IBM's Power systems run AIX UNIX, Linux and IBM i.

10.2.8.2 Midrange architecture

Midrange systems used to be based on specialized Reduced Instruction Set Computer (RISC) CPUs. These CPUs were optimized for speed and simplicity, but much of the technologies originating from RISC are now implemented in general purpose CPUs. Some midrange systems therefore are moving from RISC based CPUs to general purpose CPUs from Intel, AMD, or IBM.

The architecture of most midrange systems typically uses multiple CPUs and is based on a shared memory architecture. In a shared memory architecture, all CPUs in the system can access all installed memory blocks. This means that changes made in memory by one CPU are immediately seen by all other CPUs. Each CPU operates independently from the others. To connect all CPUs with all memory blocks, an interconnection network is used based on a shared bus, or a crossbar.

A shared bus connects all CPUs and all RAM, much like a network hub does. The available bandwidth is shared between all users of the shared bus. A crossbar is much like a network switch, in which every communication channel between one CPU and one memory block gets full bandwidth.

The I/O system is also connected to the interconnection network, connecting I/O devices like disks or PCI based expansion cards.

Since each CPU has its own cache, and memory can be changed by other CPUs, cache coherence is needed in midrange systems. Cache coherence means that if one CPU writes to a location in shared memory, all other CPUs must update their caches to reflect the changed data. Maintaining cache coherence introduces a significant overhead. Special-purpose hardware is used to communicate between cache controllers to keep a consistent memory image.

Shared memory architectures come in two flavors: Uniform Memory Access (UMA), and Non-Uniform Memory Access (NUMA). Their cache coherent versions are known as ccUMA and ccNUMA.

10.2.8.2.1 UMA

The UMA architecture is one of the earliest styles of multi-CPU architectures, typically used in systems with no more than 8 CPUs. In an UMA system, the machine is organized into a series of nodes containing either a processor, or a memory block. These nodes are interconnected, usually by a shared bus. Via the shared bus, each processor can access all memory blocks, creating a single system image.

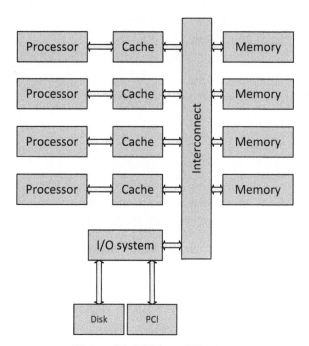

Figure 84: UMA architecture

UMA systems are also known as Symmetric Multi-Processor (SMP) systems. SMP is used in x86 servers as well as early midrange systems.

SMP technology is also used inside multi-core CPUs, in which the interconnect is implemented on-chip and a single path to the main memory is provided between the chip and the memory subsystem elsewhere in the system.

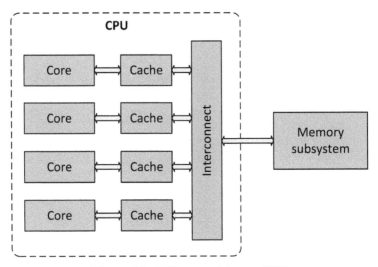

Figure 85: SMP on multi core CPU

UMA is supported by all major operating systems and can be implemented using most of today's CPUs.

10.2.8.2.2 NUMA

In contrast to UMA, NUMA is a computer architecture in which the machine is organized into a series of nodes, each containing processors and memory, which are interconnected, typically using a crossbar. NUMA is a newer architecture style than UMA and is better suited for systems with many processors.

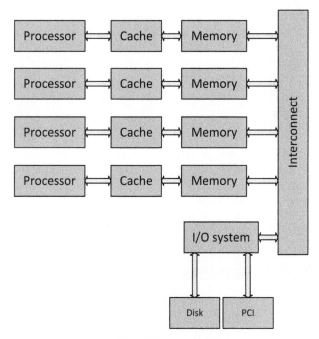

Figure 86: NUMA architecture

A node can use memory on all other nodes, creating a single system image. But when a processor accesses memory not within its own node, data must be transferred over the interconnect, which is slower than accessing local memory. Thus, memory access times are non-uniform, depending on the location of the memory, as the architecture's name implies.

Some of the current computers using NUMA architectures include systems based on AMD Opteron processors, Intel Itanium systems, and HP Integrity and Superdome systems. Most popular operating systems such as OpenVMS, AIX, HP-UX, Solaris, and Windows, and virtualization hypervisors like VMware fully support NUMA systems.

10.2.8.3 Midrange virtualization

Most midrange platform vendors provide virtualization using LPARs as explained in section 10.2.5.3.2. LPARs in the Oracle Solaris operating system are referred to as Logical Domains (LDOMs); they are also a type of hardware partitioning.

IBM AIX offers Workload/Working Partitions (WPARs) as subsystems inside LPARs. IBM's Live Application Mobility technology can transfer a running WPAR from one LPAR to another on the same physical system or to a different physical system without downtime, much like VMware's VMotion of Microsoft's Live Migration's offerings.

HP offers nPARs (comparable with IBM's LPARs) and vPARs (comparable with IBM's WPARs) as virtualization technology in the HP-UX operating system.

Oracle Solaris virtualization provides zones and containers. The terms zone and container can be used interchangeably, although some differences exist. A zone or container is a virtual operating system that provides a protected environment for applications. All zones on the system share a common kernel, but each zone has its own node name, virtual network interfaces, and storage assigned to it.

10.2.9 x86 servers

The x86 platform is the most dominant server architecture today. While the x86 platform was originally designed for personal computers, it is now implemented in all types of systems, from netbooks up to the fastest multi-CPU servers.

x86 servers are produced by many vendors. Best known vendors are HP, Dell, HDS (Hitachi Data Systems) and Lenovo (the former IBM x86 server business that Lenovo acquired in 2014[72]). These vendors typically purchase most server parts (like video graphics cards, power supplies, RAM, and disk drives) from other vendors. This makes x86 server implementations very diverse. So, while the x86 architecture is standardized, the implementation of it is highly dependent on the vendor and the components available at a certain moment.

x86 servers typically run operating systems not provided by the vendors of the hardware. Most often Microsoft Windows and Linux are used, but x86 systems are also capable of running special purpose operating systems.

10.2.9.1 History

Most servers in datacenters today are based on the x86 architecture. This x86 architecture (also known as PC architecture) is based on the original IBM PC. The IBM PC's history is described in more detail in chapter 12.

In the 1990s, x86 servers first started to appear. They were basically PCs, but were housed in 19" racks without dedicated keyboards and monitors.

Over the years, x86 servers became the de-facto standard for servers. Their low cost, the fact that there are many manufacturers and their ability to run familiar operating systems like Microsoft Windows and Linux, made them extremely popular.

10.2.9.2 x86 architecture

The heart of an x86 based system is a CPU from the x86 family (see sections 10.2.2.1, 10.2.2.1, and 10.2.2.2 for descriptions of these CPUs). x86 architectures are defined by building blocks, integrated in a number of specialized chips, known as an x86 chipset.

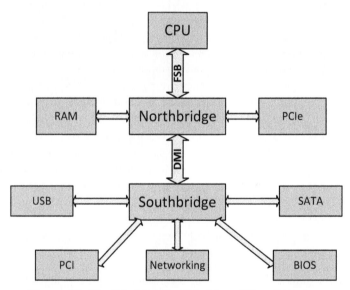

Figure 87: Northbridge/Southbridge x86 architecture

Earlier x86 systems utilized a Northbridge/Southbridge architecture. In this architecture, the data path of the CPU, called the Front Side Bus (FSB), was connected to a fast Northbridge chip, transporting data between the CPU and both the RAM memory and the PCIe bus. The Northbridge was also connected to the Southbridge chip by a bus called the Direct Media Interface (DMI). The relatively slow Southbridge chip connected components with slower data paths, like the BIOS, the SATA adaptors, USB ports, and the PCI bus.

In 2008, the Northbridge/Southbridge architecture was replaced by the Platform Controller Hub (PCH) architecture. In this architecture, the

Southbridge functionality is managed by the PCH chip, which is directly connected to the CPU via the DMI.

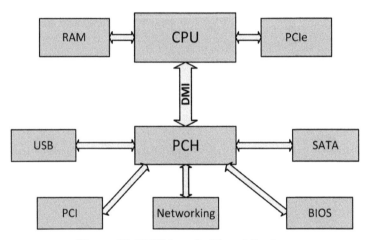

Figure 88: PCH based x86 architecture

Most of the Northbridge functions were integrated into the CPU while the PCH took over the remaining functions in addition to the traditional roles of the Southbridge. In the PCH architecture, the RAM and PCIe data paths are directly connected to the CPU. Examples of x86 architectures that have the Northbridge integrated in the CPU are Intel's Sandy Bridge and AMD's Fusion.

After the PCH architecture, Intel introduced a new architecture and chipsets roughly every two years.

In 2017, the Kaby Lake architecture was introduced. This architecture has the PCH integrated in the CPU, which makes the CPU effectively a full system on a chip (SOC). Rather than DMI, these SOCs directly expose PCIe lanes, as well as SATA, USB, and High Definition Audio connections from integrated controllers.

Multi-CPU x86 servers use architectures based on UMA or SMP (for low end servers), or NUMA (for high end servers), as described in section 10.2.8.2.1.

10.2.9.3 x86 virtualization

Virtualization on the x86 platform can run any operating system that is designed for the x86 platform, but in most cases Windows or Linux are used.

On x86 platforms it is not uncommon that servers only run one application each. A Windows server running Exchange will probably not also run SharePoint, and a Linux server running Apache will probably not also run MySQL. In midrange and mainframe platforms this is highly unusual. The operating systems used on these platforms are designed to run a large number of critical applications in isolation without problems. This is the main reason x86 systems use their hardware much less efficient that midrange systems.

By running multiple operating systems – each in one virtual machine – on a large x86 server, resource utilization can be improved. A strict separation of applications is preserved using a single virtual machine and operating system for each application. The x86 virtualization layer achieves the same isolation of applications that operating systems in midrange and mainframe systems are designed to achieve.

The most used products for virtualization on the x86 platform are VMware vSphere (consisting of ESX, ESXi, and vCenter), Microsoft's Hyper-V, Citrix XenServer, Oracle VirtualBox, and Red Hat RHEV.

10.2.10 Supercomputers

A supercomputer is a computer architecture designed to maximize calculation speed. This in contrast with a mainframe, which is optimized for high I/O throughput. Supercomputers are the fastest machines available at any given time. Since computing speed increases continuously, supercomputers are superseded by new supercomputers all the time.

Supercomputers are used for many tasks, from weather forecast calculations to oil reservoir simulations and the rendering of animation movies.

Originally, supercomputers were produced primarily by a company named Cray Research. The Cray-1 was a major success when it was released in 1976. It was faster than all other computers at the time and it went on to become one of the best known and most successful supercomputers in history. The machine cost $8.9 million when introduced.

Cray supercomputers used specially designed CPUs for performing calculations on large sets of data, together with dedicated hardware for certain instructions (like multiply and divide). The entire chassis of the Cray supercomputers was bent into a large C-shape. Speed-dependent portions of the system were placed on the inner circle of the chassis where the wire-lengths were shorter to decrease delays. The system could peak at 250 MFLOPS (Million Floating Point Operations per second).

Picture 36: Cray-2 supercomputer

In 1985, the very advanced Cray-2 was released, capable of 1.9 billion floating point operations per second (GFLOPS) peak performance, almost eight times as much as the Cray-1. In comparison, in 2017, the Intel Core i7 5960X CPU has a peak performance of 354 GFLOPS[73]; more than 185 times the performance of the Cray-2!

Supercomputers as single machines started to disappear in the 1990s. Their work was taken over by clustered computers – a large number of off-the-shelf x86 based servers, connected by fast networks to form one large computer array. Nowadays high performance computing is done mainly with large arrays of x86 systems. In 2017, the fastest computer array was a cluster with more than 10,000,000 CPU cores, calculating at 125,435,000 GFLOPS, running Linux[74].

In some cases, specialized hardware is used to reach high performance. For example, graphics processing units (GPUs) can be used together with CPUs to accelerate specific calculations.

Where a CPU consists of a few cores optimized for sequential serial processing, a GPU has a massively parallel architecture consisting of thousands of smaller, more efficient cores designed for handling multiple tasks simultaneously.

Picture 37: NVIDIA Tesla P100 GPU

For example, the NVIDIA Tesla GP100 GPU, introduced in 2016, has 3840 cores, runs at 1.3 GHz and – including cache memory – comprises 150 billion transistors[75].

10.3 Compute availability

High availability in servers can be reached by using hot swappable components, parity and ECC memory, and lockstepping.

10.3.1 Hot swappable components

Hot swappable components are server components like memory, CPUs, interface cards, and power supplies that can be installed, replaced, or upgraded while the server is running.

The server must have specific circuitry to power down the connector of the hot swappable component, or the server system board must be equipped with special connectors that physically switch off power to the components while removing the component.

The virtualization and operating systems using the server hardware must be aware that components can be swapped on the fly. For instance, the operating system must be able to recognize that memory is added while the server operates and must allow the use of this extra memory without the need for a reboot.

10.3.2 Parity and ECC memory

To detect memory failures, parity bits can be used as the simplest form of error detecting code. A parity bit is a bit that is added to a byte to ensure that the number of bits with the value '1' in a byte is even or odd.

For instance, with even parity, when a byte of memory contains 1011 0110, the number of ones is five. In this case the parity bit stores a 1, making the number of bits even (six). When the memory contains 1001 0110 the number of ones is four. In the parity bit a 0 is stored, making the number of bits even again (still four).

```
DATA        PARITY
1001 0110   0
1011 0110   1
```

When for some reason one of the data bits or the parity bit itself is "flipped", it can be detected:

```
DATA        PARITY
0001 0110   0 -> ERROR: parity bit should have been 1!
```

Parity bits enable the detection of data errors but cannot correct the error, as it is unknown which bit has flipped.

In contrast, ECC memory not only detects errors, but is also able to correct them. ECC stands for "Error Correction Codes". ECC Memory chips use Hamming Code or Triple Modular Redundancy (TMR) as the method of error detection and correction. Hamming code can correct single bit errors occurring in data. Multi-bit errors in the same memory location are extremely rare and don't pose much of a threat to memory systems. TMR memory, however, is able to repair two failing bits.

Some systems also 'scrub' detected errors, by writing the corrected version back to memory.

The BIOS in some computers, and operating systems such as Linux, count detected and corrected memory errors, to identify and report on failing memory modules before the problem becomes catastrophic.

Memory errors are proportional to the amount of RAM in a computer as well as the duration of operation. Since servers typically contain many GBs of RAM and are in operation 24 hours a day, the likelihood of memory errors is relatively high and hence they require ECC memory.

10.3.3 Lockstepping

Lockstepping is an error detection and correction technology for servers. In lockstepping, multiple systems perform the same calculation, and the results of the calculations are compared. If the results are equal, the calculations were correctly performed. If there are different outcomes, one of the servers made an error.

If two systems are used in a lockstepping configuration, errors can be detected, but not corrected. When more systems are used, errors can be corrected as well; a voting system can be used to determine the correct calculation.

Lockstepping is usually done with systems running in sync per atomic transaction (a step). For each step the results are compared. Lockstepping is very expensive technology, so it is used only in systems that require extremely high reliability.

A practical and low-cost example of lockstepping usage is the SETI@home project, in which multiple computers are performing scientific calculations. Each transaction is sent to at least two nodes by the main computer, thus performing a distributed form of lockstepping. When the results don't match, the calculation is simply performed again by two other nodes.

10.3.4 Virtualization availability

All virtualization products provide failover clustering. When a physical machine fails, the virtual machines running on that physical machine can be configured to restart automatically on other physical machines. And when a virtual machine crashes, it can be restarted automatically on the same physical machine.

Some virtualization products provide monitoring of the operating systems from within the virtual machines' operating system. For instance, VMware provides the VMware-tools application running inside the operating system of the virtual machine. It monitors, among other things, if the operating system is still working. When the operating system crashes, the VMware tools are not reachable anymore and VMware will restart the virtual machine automatically.

Since the virtualization layer has no knowledge of the applications running on the virtual machine's operating system, failover clustering on virtualization level can only protect against two situations:

- A physical hardware failure.
- An operating system crash in a virtual machine.

Since failover clustering on the virtualization layer cannot protect against application failures (like a crashed application process or service), these should be handled by the operating system layer. See the chapter 11 on operating systems for more details.

Both VMware (vSphere with HA/FT) and Citrix (XenServer with Marathon everRun) also provide lockstep technology to keep two virtual machines in sync, effectively providing redundant operating systems. This technology, however, has some technical limitations and uses quite a bit of network bandwidth.

10.3.4.1 Admission

To cope with the effects of a failure of a physical machine, a spare physical machine is needed. For this setup to work, all hypervisors are placed in a virtualization cluster, so they are aware of each other. The hypervisors on the physical machines check the availability of the other hypervisors in the cluster.

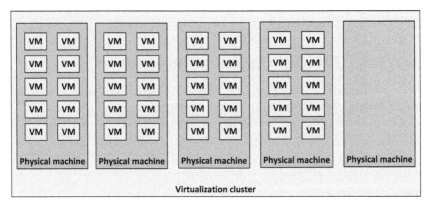

Figure 89: Using a spare physical machine

In Figure 89, one physical machine is running as a spare to take over the load of any failing physical machine. Under normal conditions the spare server is not doing any work.

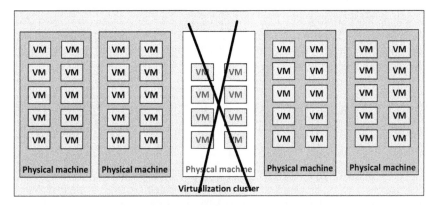

Figure 90: Failing physical machine

When one physical machine fails (Figure 90), the virtual machines running on it are automatically restarted on the spare physical machine.

An alternative is to have all physical machines running at lower capacity. For instance, when 5 machines are in a virtualization cluster, and each machine could host ten virtual machines, the total load of all servers should be 4×10 = 40 virtual machines. Instead of having one spare server running, the workload can also be spread over all machines, each hosting $\frac{40}{5}$ = 8 virtual machines.

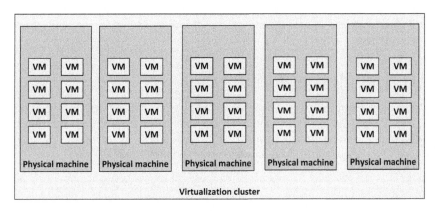

Figure 91: All machines used

This way all resources are used as much as possible since the hypervisor will provide extra resources like RAM and CPU to the virtual machines automatically, even though it is still possible to handle a failure of a physical machine. In that case the four remaining physical machines still have the capacity to run 8 extra virtual machines and the virtual machines that ran on the failed physical machine can automatically be restarted on the other physical machines (Figure 92).

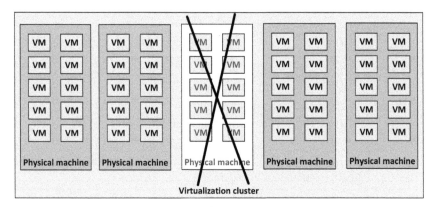

Figure 92: Failing machine when all machines were used

10.4 Compute performance

The performance of computers is dependent on the architecture of the server (which is described in earlier sections), the speed of the memory and CPU, and the bus speed.

10.4.1 Moore's law

Today, all computers use microprocessors as their Central Processing Unit (CPU). Before the invention of microprocessors, a single CPU was built using one or more circuit boards, containing large numbers of Integrated Circuits (ICs). Each IC contained from tens to a few hundred transistors.

In 1971, Intel released the world's first universal microprocessor, the 4004. A microprocessor is nothing more than a very complex IC, combining the functions of all the individual ICs and the circuitry needed to create a CPU, effectively creating a processor on a chip.

Picture 38: Intel 4004 microprocessor[76]

The 4004 chip itself was 3 mm wide by 4 mm long and consisted of 2,300 transistors. The chip was mounted in an DIP package with 16 connection pins (the DIP package was much larger that the chip itself of course). Coupled with one of Intel's other products, the RAM chip, the microprocessor allowed computers to be much smaller and faster than previous ones. The 4004 was capable of performing 60,000 instructions per second, which was about as much as the ENIAC computer that filled a complete room and weighed several tons.

Since the introduction of the first CPU in 1971, the power of CPUs has increased exponentially. This makes today's computers much more powerful than we could possibly have imagined forty years ago.

Moore's law states that the number of transistors that can be placed inexpensively on an integrated circuit doubles approximately every two years. This trend has continued for more than half a century now. The law is named after Intel's co-founder Gordon E. Moore, who described the trend in his 1965 paper "Cramming more components onto integrated circuits"[77], when he worked at Fairchild.

Over the years, the number of transistors on a CPU raised from 2,300 on the first CPU (the 4004 in 1971) to 7,200,000,000 on an Intel Broadwell-EP Xeon in 2017. This is an 3,100,000-fold increase in 45 years' time!

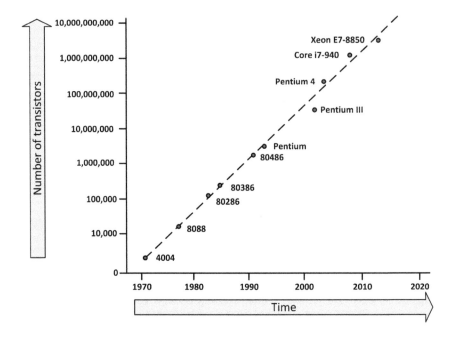

Figure 93: Moore's law

Figure 93 clearly shows the trend. Please note that the vertical scale is logarithmic instead of linear, showing a 10-fold increase of the number of transistors in each step.

Note that Moore's law only speaks of the number of transistors; not the performance of the CPU. The performance of a CPU is dependent on a number of variables, like the clock speed, the use of caches and pipelines, and the width of the data bus. When we look at the performance gain we see a doubling of CPU performance every 18 months; even faster than what Moore's law states.

Obviously, Moore's law cannot continue forever, as there are physical limits to the number of transistors a single chip can hold. In 2017, the connections used inside a high-end CPU had a physical width of 14 nm (nanometer). This is extremely small – the size of 140 atoms (the diameter of an atom is of the order of 0.1 nm[78])! It is expected that in 2020, 5 nm CPUs are produced, where the traces on the chip are a mere 50 atoms wide.

When designing an infrastructure, it sometimes makes sense to take Moore's law into account by not purchasing too much spare capacity in advance. By purchasing and implementing new servers "just in time", the purchased server will have twice the processing capacity of a server you could have purchased 18 months earlier, for the same price. Therefore, to get the full benefits of Moore's law, the infrastructure (management) must be designed to handle just in time upgrades.

10.4.2 Increasing CPU and memory performance

Various techniques have been invented to increase CPU performance. The most important ones are increasing the clock speed, caching, prefetching, branch prediction, pipelines, and use of multiple cores. These technologies are explained in the following sections.

While the inner working of a CPU cannot be changed, it is useful to understand some of it. Not only for choosing an optimal processor architecture for a certain situation, but also to be able to tune external parameters (like compiler options for application programmers) to have software running in an optimal way on a certain CPU, and to find root causes in case of performance problems.

10.4.2.1 Increasing clock speed

In the early years, CPU clock speed was the main performance indicator. A 33 MHz 80486 processor was clearly slower than a 66 MHz 80486 processor. While this is still true in some ways, today's processor clock speed is not the most important indicator of speed anymore.

CPU clock speed is measured in Hertz (Hz) – clock ticks or cycles per second. A MHz is a million cycles per second and a GHz is a billion clock cycles per second.

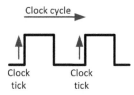

Figure 94: Clock ticks and clock cycles

The CPU processes instructions stored in memory. These instructions need to be fetched, decoded, executed (for which often data needs to be fetched from memory as well), and the result must often be written back to memory. In principle, each of these steps is executed sequentially. Each step in the sequence is executed when an external clock signal is changed from 0 to 1 (the cock tick). The clock signal is supplied to the CPU by an external oscillator.

Depending on the type of CPU instruction, one or more clock ticks are needed to execute the instruction. The used CPU architecture has a large influence on the number of clock ticks needed for an instruction. Because of the very complex technologies used in today's CPUs, it is not easy to determine in advance how many clock ticks a certain instruction will take to complete. Caching, pipelines, and out of order execution of instructions are used to optimize the CPU and get as much as possible done in as few clock ticks as possible.

Today's CPUs use clock speeds as high as 3 GHz, sometimes even higher. Because of physical limitations, oscillators cannot run at this speed. Therefore, an oscillator with a lower frequency is used (for instance 400 MHz) and this clock rate is multiplied on the CPU chip. An 8 times multiplication of 400 MHz leads to a CPU clock of 3200 MHz or 3.2 GHz. The oscillator speed is used for other parts of the system board as well (like the RAM). This speed is known as the Front Side Bus (FSB) speed.

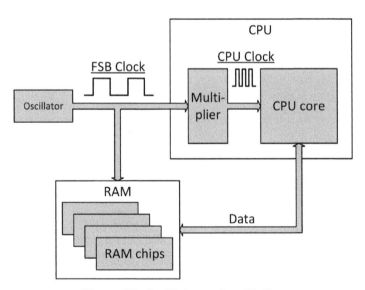

Figure 95: Oscillator and multiplier

Note that the speed of the FSB and CPU are linked; changing the oscillator speed will change both the FSB and the CPU speed. Changing the multiplier only changes the CPU speed.

10.4.2.2 CPU Caching

Dynamic RAM, typically used for the main memory, is about 5 times slower than static RAM. While static RAM is very fast, it is also expensive: it takes about 6 times as much circuitry compared to dynamic RAM.

All CPUs in use today contain on-chip caches. A cache is a relatively small piece of high speed static RAM on the CPU that temporarily stores data received from slower main memory. The purpose of cache memory is to speed up the fetching of instructions and data the CPU needs.

Main memory RAM runs at a considerably lower clock speed than cache memory. Cache memory runs at full CPU speed (say 3 GHz), whereas main memory runs at the CPU external clock speed (say 100 MHz, which is 30 times slower).

The memory path between RAM and CPU cache is typically 64 bits wide, while the data path between the caches and the CPU core is typically 256 bits wide. This allows for transfer of multiple words of data in one CPU clock tick.

Most CPUs contain two types of cache: level 1 and level 2 cache. Level 1 cache is smaller than level 2 cache, but also faster. Since it is very hard to create very fast static memory, able to run at CPU speed with close to zero latency, level 1 cache is placed closest to the core of the CPU.

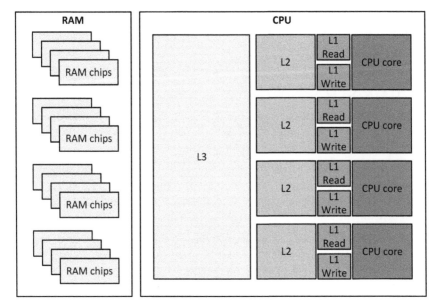

Figure 96: CPU Cache

The level 1 cache is fed by level 2 cache, which in turn gets its data from RAM. Level 1 cache is usually split between a read-only instruction cache and a read/write data cache, whereas level 2 cache is used for both reading and writing data and instructions.

Some multi-core CPUs also have a large level 3 cache; a cache shared by the cores. This optimizes the use of the limited amount of cache memory available on the CPU chip.

Some CPUs use an exclusive cache system, which means that the cached memory is in only one of the available caches.

10.4.2.3 Pipelines

The first CPUs handled one instruction at a time. Only when an instruction was fully finished, the next instruction would be handled. Handling instructions can be split up in multiple stages:

- Fetching the instruction from memory.

- Decoding the instruction.

- Executing the instruction.

- Writing the result of the instruction back to memory or a register.

Early processors first fetched an instruction, decoded it, then executed the fetched instruction, and wrote the result back before fetching the next instruction and starting the process over again.

Figure 97: Instruction phases

Later, CPUs started to use so-called pipelines. The width of the pipeline is the same as the number of instruction stages. The idea behind the pipeline is that while the first instruction is being executed, the second instruction can be fetched (since that circuitry is idling anyway), creating instruction overlap.

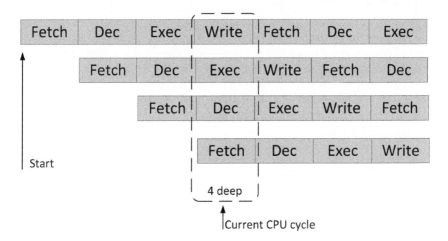

Figure 98: Instruction overlap in a 4 stages deep pipeline

Ideally this leads to one instruction being executed per available clock tick. But because some instructions need the output from the previous instruction as input, these instructions are held until the previous instruction has completed its current stage. To overcome delays associated with this pipeline design, most processors have broken down the execute and/or fetch cycle into a number of extra stages to optimize the pipelines to try and execute instructions each and every clock tick.

10.4.2.4 Prefetching and branch prediction

When a CPU needs data from memory, it first checks its level 1 cache (as this is the fastest memory available). When the data is not available in the level 1 cache, the CPU tries the level 2 cache. If the data is not available there as well (and there is no higher-level cache available), it fetches the data from RAM.

Let's assume all caches are empty and the CPU needs an instruction. Since the data could not be found in cache, it is fetched from RAM. After the instruction is executed by the CPU, it needs the next instruction. Usually this instruction is stored at the next address location in RAM. To speed up the CPU, prefetching is done by the cache memory system. Using prefetching, when an instruction is fetched from main memory, also the next instructions are fetched and stored in cache, so that when the CPU needs the next instruction it is already available in cache.

Unfortunately, most programs contain jumps (also known as branches), resulting in cache misses because the next instruction is not the next instruction in memory.

To prevent as much cache misses as possible; the cache system tries to predict the outcome of branch instructions before they are executed by the CPU (called branch prediction). The cache system recognizes JUMP instructions and checks where the next instruction after the JUMP is located. The cache then fills itself with these instructions from main memory. Of course, this system is not foolproof, but in practice more than 80% of the processor instructions are delivered to the CPU from cache memory using prefetching and branch prediction.

10.4.2.5 Superscalar CPUs

Essentially all general-purpose CPUs developed since about 1998 are superscalar. A superscalar CPU can process more than one instruction per clock tick. This is done by simultaneously dispatching multiple instructions to redundant functional units on the processor. Each functional unit is not a separate CPU core, but an execution resource within a single CPU such as an arithmetic logic unit (ALU), a bit shifter, or a multiplier. In a superscalar design, the processor actually has multiple data paths where multiple instructions can be executed simultaneously, one in each data path.

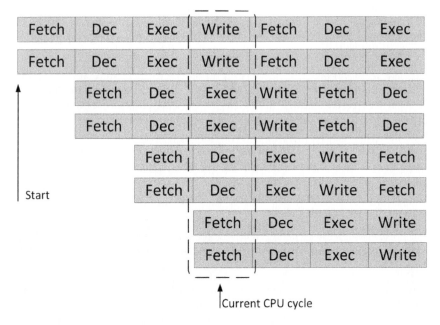

Current CPU cycle

Figure 99: Superscalar CPU

In order for superscalar CPUs to perform well, the CPU dynamically checks for data dependencies between instructions. In a superscalar CPU, a dispatcher circuit reads instructions from memory and decides which ones can be executed in parallel, dispatching them to the redundant functional units. This obviously makes the CPU logic very complex.

10.4.2.6 Multi-core CPUs

With CPU clock speeds accelerating past the 1 GHz mark around 2002, many predicted new CPUs would reach speeds of 10 GHz in the future. Instead, the fastest commercial CPUs have been between running between 3 GHz and 4 GHz for a number of years now. There are several reasons for this.

High clock speeds (way beyond radio frequencies) traveling over a circuit board make connections on the circuit board work as a radio antenna, creating interference with other connections in the circuit board. This could make the circuitry vulnerable to instability. Only a very rigid circuit board design makes this effect manageable.

A frequency of 3 GHz means a wavelength of 10 cm. This means that when signals travel for more than a few cm on a circuit board, the signal gets out of phase with the clock.

But the most problematic issue with using very high clock speeds is the temperature of the CPU. When a CPU runs at 3 GHz, transistors on that CPU change their current flow 3 billion times per second. Transistors in the CPU create heat whenever they switch current. At 3 billion switches per second and with the very high density of CPUs (containing billions of transistors on a very small surface), the CPU can heat up tremendously at certain spots. At a rate of more than 3 GHz some heat spots on the CPU cannot be cooled effectively anymore, resulting in a meltdown of the CPU. The majority of today's CPUs should not exceed temperatures of 95 degrees Celsius and most will run between 70-90 degrees Celsius.

For these reasons the clock speed at which a CPU can run reliably is limited to approximately 4 GHz. For a while this problem was seen as the end of Moore's law.

Multi-core CPUs are a solution for these problems. Until about 2005, most CPUs were single core processors. The CPU consisted of one central processing unit that fetched, decoded, and executed machine code instructions, called the core of the CPU. A multi-core processor is a CPU with multiple separate cores, each with their own cache. It is the equivalent of getting multiple processors in one package. If these cores were placed on a single chip without any modification, the chip would consume twice as much power and generate a large amount of heat. To solve this, the cores in a multi-core CPU run at a lower frequency to reduce power consumption.

All PCs and servers now have multi-core CPUs. It is likely to see a huge increase of the number of cores in a CPU in the future. The general trend in processor development has moved from dual-core chips to CPUs with tens or even hundreds of cores.

Moore's law leads to having more cores on a single CPU instead of having CPUs running on higher clock speeds. This has some side effects that might not be obvious.

I recently executed a performance test of a new VMware infrastructure, using the latest CPUs. To be able to check the performance increase, a copy of the virtual machines from the existing production environment was installed on the new infrastructure. That way, the performance of the new environment could be compared with the performance of the existing environment.

The amount of RAM and the number of CPU cores for each virtual machine were set to the same value as in the old production environment, to show how much faster the new CPUs performed.

We found, however, that the new hardware seemed not to be much faster than the five-year-old hardware currently in use in production.

The reason was that while the total performance of each CPU was much higher (because each physical CPU had much more cores), the individual CPU cores were not running much faster than the cores on the CPUs from five years ago.

10.4.2.7 Hyper-threading

Certain Intel CPUs (like the Core i3/i5/i7 and Xeon CPUs) contain a propriety technology called hyper-threading. Hyper-threading makes a single processor core virtually work as a multi-core processor.

Hyper-threading (recent versions of which are called simultaneous multithreading, or SMT) allows a single physical processor core to behave like two logical processors, essentially allowing two independent threads to run simultaneously. Unlike having twice as many processor cores — that can roughly double performance — hyper-threading can provide some increase in system performance by keeping the processor pipelines busier.

It is not enough that a processor supports hyper-threading — the BIOS must support it as well.

10.4.3 Virtualization performance

Consolidating multiple virtual machines on one physical machine increases CPU usage, and thus reduces CPU idle time. This is generally considered a good thing and is a primary driver for the use of virtualization. But it also means that the physical machine needs to handle the disk and network I/O of *all* running virtual machines (possibly dozens of them). This can easily lead to an I/O performance bottleneck.

So, when choosing a physical machine to host virtual machines, consider getting a machine with not only plenty of CPU and memory capacity, but also one capable of very high I/O throughput. Mainframes, midrange, and x86 systems with multiple PCI bridges are best suited to handle the high I/O load needed in a virtualized environment.

Compared to running operating systems directly on a physical machine, by definition, virtualization introduces performance penalties, both in resources required to run the hypervisor and in reduced performance on the virtual machines due to operation transformations. This makes the performance of virtualization solutions always a point of discussion.

But opinions about virtualization performance are mostly just that – they are rarely backed with hard numbers. Some performance degradation is evident, as an extra layer is added, but it is usually less than 10% of the total performance.

Databases should be carefully evaluated before migrating them to a virtual machine. Databases generally require a lot of network bandwidth and high disk I/O performance. This makes databases less suitable for a virtualized environment. However, the involvement of the hypervisor can be minimized by providing a virtual machine (running a database) with a Raw Device Mapping. RDMs allow a virtual machine unrestricted exclusive access to a physical storage medium. RDMs prevent almost all interference from the hypervisor, diminishing the performance overhead of the hypervisor on storage to almost zero.

Most large databases on physical machines utilize all available hardware capacity. This means that implementing such a database in a virtual machine only allows the physical machine to handle one virtual machine, reducing some of the benefits of virtualization. Virtualization, however, still ensures that the database server can easily be migrated (possible without downtime) to another physical server. Management of the servers is unified as well when all servers run hypervisors, even if they just run one virtual machine.

10.5 Compute security

10.5.1 Physical security

Servers can be physically secured using the following features:

- Disable external USB ports in the BIOS. USB ports enable connectivity of external devices, which is a security threat. USB devices can be storage devices (which can be used to spread viruses and worms or for creating illegal data copies), network devices like a Wi-Fi or Bluetooth device (which can be used to get uncontrolled access to the server), or other devices.

- BIOS settings in an x86 server should be protected using a password. Using the BIOS password is a good practice since via the BIOS external USB ports can be enabled, and other parameters can be set.

- Some servers allow the detection of the physical opening of the server housing. Such an event can be sent to a central management console using for instance SNMP traps. If possible, enable this to detect unusual activities.

10.5.2 Virtualization security

Virtual machines must be protected the same way as physical machines. They should run anti-virus software, be equipped with host based firewalls, and have all security patches applied. But the use of virtualization introduces new security vulnerabilities of its own.

If possible, firewalls and Intrusion Detection Systems (IDSs) in the hypervisor should be deployed. These firewalls, IDSs and also the virtual switches should be managed by the same systems managers that manage these devices in the physical world (i.e. the network systems managers), not the virtualization systems managers.

Don't forget that the virtualization platform itself needs patching too! Since a hypervisor is in fact a small operating system, they are also vulnerable to attacks. And when malicious software is installed in the hypervisor, it is impossible to detect it from within the virtual machines!

To minimize the risk of an attack on the hypervisor, the size and complexity of the hypervisor should be kept to a minimum, reducing the attack target area. VMware ESX, for example, uses a small (approximately 32 MB) hypervisor that directly runs on the hardware, while Hyper-V uses a complete Windows operating system.

10.5.2.1 DMZ

Consider using separate physical machines to increase security for servers inside the DMZ. These physical machines can run all the virtual machines needed in the DMZ, while still preserving physical separation from systems outside of the DMZ.

10.5.2.2 Systems management console

Virtual machines are managed using a systems management console. This systems management console connects to all hypervisors and virtual machines and provides functions like shutting down (clusters of) virtual machines, starting virtual machines, adding or removing resources of virtual machines (storage, memory, CPUs), and connecting to server consoles. The systems management console therefore poses a major security risk. When the security of the systems management console is breached, effectively all virtual machine's security is breached. The systems management console must therefore be thoroughly protected.

It is good practice to implement separation of duties in the systems management console. Not all systems managers should have access to all virtual machines. Special user accounts and passwords should be configured for high risk operations like shutting down physical machines or virtualized clusters. And all user activity in the systems management console should be logged to a physical machine in a locked room, not accessible for systems managers.

11

OPERATING SYSTEMS

11.1 Introduction

An operating system is the set of programs that, after being initially loaded into a computer by a boot program, controls all the other programs in a computer. It also manages a computer's internal workings – its memory, processors, internal and peripheral devices, the file system, etc. Operating systems are designed to make best use of a computer's resources. PCs, laptops, virtual machines, servers, and tablets all use an operating system. But most other devices containing a (small) computer use an operating system as well: a mobile phone, a network router, a storage array, a car, a television, or sometimes even a washing machine.

Operating systems provide an abstraction layer between (virtualized or physical) hardware and software applications. As a service to applications, low level hardware management like process management, memory management, interrupt management, multi user management, file locking, and file sharing are all handled by the operating system.

Operating systems also provide services to applications in the form of Application Programming Interfaces (APIs), for example for file management, I/O interfaces (like video and keyboard), hardware drivers (like printer drivers), and other hardware.

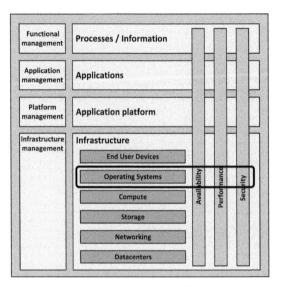

Figure 100: Operating systems in the infrastructure model

Early operating systems could execute only one program at a time. At any given time, one user had sole use of the computer. He would arrive at a scheduled time with program and data on punched cards or on tape. The program would be loaded into the machine, and the machine would be set to work until the program completed and another user could use the computer.

Through the 1950s, many major features were pioneered in the field of operating systems, including multitasking. Now it was possible to have multiple users' jobs run in parallel.

During the 1960s, IBM introduced the concept of a single operating system (OS/360) for all of its mainframes. IBM's current mainframe operating systems are still descendants of this original operating system: applications written for OS/360 can still run on today's machines.

Personal computers neither had the capacity, nor the need for the complex operating systems that had been developed for mainframes. Instead, minimalistic operating systems were developed, often loaded from ROM, known as Monitors. One of the early disk based operating systems for personal computers was CP/M. Parts of CP/M were imitated in MS-DOS, which became extremely popular when chosen as the default operating system for the IBM PC.

The most popular operating systems running on servers today are Microsoft Windows, Linux, and UNIX. On end user devices, Windows, Linux, Mac OS X, and mobile operating systems iOS and Android are popular.

Besides these popular operating systems, some other operating systems are in use, typically designed for special purposes, like real-time operating systems, or operating systems for embedded systems and consumer products, like cars or DVD players.

11.2 Operating System building blocks

An operating system basically performs two operations:

- It enables multiple users, multiple processes, and multiple applications to run together on a single piece of hardware.

- It hides the technical complexities of the underlying hardware from the applications running on top of the operating system.

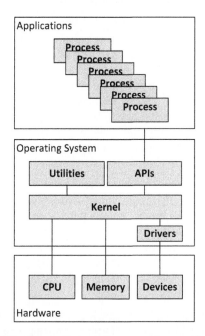

Figure 101: Operating system working environment

In Figure 101, the working environment of an operating system is shown.

The **kernel** is the heart of an operating system. It starts and stops programs, manages the file system, and performs other so called "low level" tasks that most programs need. And, perhaps most importantly, the kernel schedules access to hardware to avoid conflicts if two programs try to access the same resource or device simultaneously.

Drivers are small applications that connect specific hardware devices, like a printer of a network card, to the kernel.

Utilities are applications that are considered part of the operating system, like user interfaces (text-based shells and GUIs), installation and configuration tools, logging tools, editors, system update processes, and web browsers.

Applications consist of one or more **processes** that communicate with the operating system using system calls that are invoked through Application Programming Interfaces (**APIs**).

In the next sections the most important functions of an operating system are explained in more detail.

11.2.1 Process scheduling

In most computer systems, a large number of multiple processes are running simultaneously, while each CPU core is physically only capable of running one process at a certain time. Operating systems create the illusion of multiple running processes in parallel by scheduling each process to run only during a short time frame. This principle is also known as preemptive multitasking. Periodically, the operating system decides if a running process is to be suspended in favor of another process, or if the running process can keep on running for a while. Processes that wait for something (usually for I/O) are suspended until the I/O request is finished, freeing the CPU for other processes.

Process scheduling is fairly complex, as switching processes introduces some overhead. The dilemma is that too frequent switching of processes generates a lot of overhead, while on the other hand having each process run for too long would make the system seem to perform slow for processes that are waiting for a free CPU core. A good scheduling algorithm guarantees each process gets its fair share of CPU time. It ensures that the CPU is used efficiently, minimizes response times for interactive users, while still providing enough resources for batch processes.

The most basic process scheduler uses a round robin schedule, where each process gets the same amount of CPU time. This assumes, however, that all processes are equally important at all times. This is often not the case, so round robin scheduling is enhanced with priority scheduling. Priority scheduling assigns processes a priority compared to the other processes. Prioritizing algorithms can become very complex, because they must take into account many contradictory rules in a dynamically changing environment. But because operating systems have evolved over decades, the scheduling algorithms have become very sophisticated. Therefore, it is usually a bad practice to try to outsmart the scheduling algorithm by manually changing process priorities.

11.2.2 File systems

The operating system virtualizes the complexities of handling individual disk blocks or communication with a SAN or NAS by providing a file system to applications. File systems usually consist of directories (also known as folders) with files or other directories in them.

The operating system hides the complexity of managing the files and the directory structure. It also manages the security of the files: who has permission to read, write, create, and delete files and directories.

Various types of file systems exist. Most operating systems can handle multiple types of file systems on multiple disks at the same time, and the user or application is typically unaware of the file system in use. Some popular file systems are:

- **FAT** (File Allocation Table), vFAT, and FAT32, used in MS-DOS, older versions of Windows, and removable storage devices like USB memory sticks.
- **NTFS** (New Technology File System) used in Windows.
- **UFS** (Universal File System) and **VxFS** (Veritas File System) used in most UNIX flavors.
- **Ext** (and Ext2, Ext3, Ext4) - used in Linux.

NTFS, VxFS and Ext4 are examples of journaling file systems. They keep track of changes made to files in a journal log before committing them to the main file system. This allows for greater availability and fast recovery in case of a malfunction like a power failure, because the journal can be used by the operating system to guarantee that a change to the storage medium is either made entirely successfully or not made at all (this principle is often referred to as atomicity).

File systems must be mounted before they can be used by the operating system. Mounting means that a disk and the file system on it are recognized by the operating system. After mounting, the file system is typically given a drive letter (Windows), a drive name (OpenVMS), or a mount point in the global directory tree (UNIX and Linux).

Most operating systems provide file sharing functionality. File sharing enables files on one system to be accessed by (users on) other systems. This access can be limited to a combination of read, write, visibility, and delete access rights. Protocols like NFS (which originates from UNIX), and SMB/CIFS (originating from Windows), are used for file sharing. An operating system that shares files provides similar functionality as a NAS (see 9.2.6).

Some file systems provide disk and/or file encryption functionality to secure the stored data.

11.2.3 APIs and system calls

System calls are programming functions which provide a hardware-independent interface to tasks the operating system can perform for applications.

For instance, in an application, the function call

```
int read(int handle, void *buffer, int nbyte);
```

in the C programming language, or

```
int readfile (string $filename, bool $use_include_path =
false, resource $context)
```

in the PHP programming language, both use the system call

```
READ(FILEHANDLE, DESTINATION DATA POINTER,
NUMBER_OF_BYTES)
```

in the operating system to read a number of bytes from a file and to copy the read bytes to memory.

When an application process reads a file using the system call READ, the operating system takes care of:

- Looking-up the file in a file allocation table

- Looking up the disk blocks associated with the file on disk

- Instructing the disk controller to fetch the needed disk blocks

- Copy the disk blocks to memory

- Providing a pointer to the disk blocks in memory

The application has no knowledge of all of this complexity; it just receives the contents of the file in a buffer.

System calls are grouped and presented to application processes as Application Programming Interfaces (APIs). APIs describe the available system calls in an operating system and how they can be used by programmers in their applications.

11.2.4 Device drivers

One of the main functions of an operating system is to manage all hardware. The operating system provides a single interface for multiple related devices, like all printers and all video cards, and it manages the use of these devices for multiple users and processes.

I/O devices are controlled using device drivers. Device drivers are pieces of software that interact with the device's hardware (like an Ethernet network adapter or a SCSI disk adapter), and that provide an Application Programming Interface (API) to the operating system.

In Figure 102 this is illustrated.

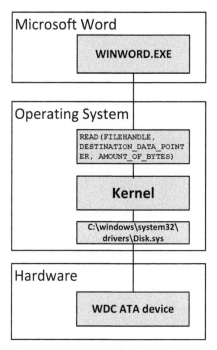

Figure 102: Example of the use of operating system components

In this example, Microsoft Word is started by the user and the user opens a document. Microsoft Word is run as a process called WINWORD.EXE in the operating system. WINWORD.EXE uses an API system call the operating system provides. The system call is understood by the kernel, that uses a driver (Disk.sys) to open a file on the hard disk (WDC ATA device), containing the document the user needs.

11.2.5 Memory management

It is the operating system's task to manage the available memory in a system. The operating system allocates and de-allocates memory on behalf of applications and manages what happens when the amount of requested memory exceeds the physical amount of memory.

Memory management in today's operating systems is very complex; it includes cache management, paging, high volume data transfers, multi-core processors, memory management units (MMUs), thin memory provisioning (memory overcommitting), and Direct Memory Access (DMA).

Fortunately, the operating system takes care of all of this and just provides chunks of memory to applications. Applications simply allocate the memory they need and de-allocate it when it is not needed anymore. The rest is done by the operating system.

While memory capacity has grown tremendously over the last decades, programs still tend to use all available memory and often degrade systems' performance by using every byte available.

Or, as Parkinson's law[79] states: "Data tends to expand to fill the space available for storage".

11.2.6 Shells, CLIs and GUIs

A shell provides a user interface to the operating system. The primary purpose of shells is to launch another program by end users. The name shell originates from shells being an outer layer of interface between the user and the kernel of the operating system.

There are two types of shells: Command-Line Interfaces (CLIs) and Graphical User Interfaces (GUIs).

In a CLI, the user types commands on a keyboard on an operating system provided command-prompt (a sequence of characters to indicate readiness to accept commands, like C:\ or $). The best known CLI based shells are the

UNIX shells (bash, sh, csh) and Windows' cmd.exe (also known as a DOS box).

In a GUI, the user uses a mouse to click on icons or buttons the operating system provides. The best-known GUI based shells are Microsoft Windows and X Window (UNIX and Linux).

11.2.7 Operating system configuration

The configuration of an operating system is stored in an operating system specific database or in text files.

An example of a configuration database is the Windows registry. It stores the configuration of the Windows environment and of the applications running on Windows. Windows provides tools (in the so-called Control Panel) to setup its configuration. These tools use the registry for storage.

UNIX and Linux use text based configuration files, typically stored in the `/etc` directory. In this directory, each operating system functionality uses a separate file (like `resolv.conf` for DNS or `host.conf` that contains the computer name). These text files can be edited manually, but for most used configuration parameters, user-friendly tools are provided. These tools still edit the text files, but that is hidden from the user.

Not all UNIX systems use text files, however. IBM's AIX, for example, uses an Object Data Manager (ODM) database to store system settings.

Other operating systems use similar configuration tools and storage for their configuration parameters.

11.2.8 Popular operating systems

11.2.8.1 z/OS

One of the first operating systems was IBM's OS/360, introduced in 1964. It was a batch processing system, created for the IBM system/360 mainframe computer. Later, OS/360 MFT (Multitasking with a Fixed number of Tasks) and OS/360 MVT (Multitasking with a Variable number of Tasks) provided multitasking to mainframes. The successor of OS/360 was OS/370, which introduced the concept of virtual memory in 1972 (see section 10.2.5.4 for more information on virtual memory).

MVS, released in 1974, was the primary operating system on the System/370 and System/390. The 64-bit version of MVS for the zSeries was named z/OS and was introduced in 2000. IBM's z/OS is now the most used mainframe operating system. It runs on IBM mainframes only.

Extreme backward compatibility is one of z/OS's main design philosophies: programs written for MVS in 1974 can still run on today's z/OS without modification.

Reading and writing a tremendous amount of data and performing relatively simple calculations on it (for example, "read in these 400,000 records of data, do 6 calculations on each, and then output 400,000 separate reports") is a typical use of mainframes running z/OS.

While z/OS is still most used for this type of batch processing, it can be used interactively as well. A system running z/OS can support thousands of interactive users simultaneously.

z/OS doesn't always have the default settings that we take for granted on other systems. Most of the settings are to be set by systems managers. Many settings and details are site-specific, so a new user on a particular z/OS system needs to find his way around the system first in order to work with it.

11.2.8.2 IBM i (OS/400)

IBM i is an operating system only used on IBM's Power Systems (previously called iSeries and AS/400 systems) midrange systems.

In 1969, eight years after DEC introduced the PDP-1, IBM introduced its first minicomputer: The System/3. Because the system was relatively expensive and was less advanced than the DEC systems, the System/3 was never very popular. The IBM System/32, introduced in 1975, and its successor, the System/34, were also not very popular, but the System/38 (in 1978) and the System/36 (in 1983) were.

Users found the System/36 and its operating system easy to use. IBM kept this in mind when designing the OS/400 operating system for the new series of AS/400 midrange systems. Over the years, the name of the operating system has changed from OS/400 to i5/OS to IBM i[80].

One of the biggest advantages of IBM i is its completeness. Communications, transaction processing, and system security were implemented as intrinsic parts of the operating system from the start. IBM i also has a relational database manager built in as an integral part of the operating system. Features for the implementation and maintenance of data security are implemented natively as part of the operating system.

The latest version is known officially as "IBM i 7.2" and was released to general availability in 2014[81].

11.2.8.3 OpenVMS

OpenVMS is an operating system developed by DEC. VMS means Virtual Memory System.

The first version of VMS (introduced in 1977) ran on a 32-bit DEC VAX system. VMS was rewritten in 1992 for DEC's 64-bit Alpha processor. From that moment on the name was changed in OpenVMS. OpenVMS is not open source software (as the name suggests), but the source listings are available for purchase.

DEC was taken over by Compaq in 1998, and in 2001 OpenVMS was ported to Intel's Itanium (IA-64) processor. Compaq was taken over by HP in 2002. OpenVMS is now maintained by VMS Software, Inc. that licensed it from HP. In June 2015 OpenVMS for HP Integrity servers based on Intel Itanium 9500 series processors was released[82].

OpenVMS is known as a robust and stable operating system. Sometimes people joke that the uptime of Windows is measured in days, of UNIX in months, but of OpenVMS systems in years.

> *At the hacking conference DEFCON9, held in 2001, none of the 4300 hackers present was able to break-in into an OpenVMS system, running an HP Secure Web server. As a result, the system was declared "cool and unhackable" by the hackers.*

OpenVMS is a multi-user operating system designed for use in time sharing, batch processing, real-time processing, and transaction processing.

Organizations typically use OpenVMS for various purposes, including mail servers, network services, manufacturing, or transportation control and monitoring, critical applications, and databases. OpenVMS is typically used in environments where system uptime and data access is critical.

11.2.8.4 UNIX

UNIX is a multitasking, multi-user operating system, originally created by AT&T.

In 1969, at Bell Labs, Ken Thompson, Dennis Ritchie, and others got hold of a little-used PDP-7 system. They used the machine to create a new time sharing multi-user multitasking operating system, based on earlier work on a system called MULTICS.

The first UNIX version was written entirely in PDP assembler, which made it highly dependent on the hardware. In 1973, UNIX was rewritten in the new C programming language (C was also created by Dennis Ritchie, together with Brian Kernighan). This made UNIX portable to multiple types of computer hardware.

In 1975, version 6 was the first to be widely available outside of Bell Labs (later AT&T). In 1982, UNIX was licensed to a number of computer manufacturers, including Sun Microsystems and Hewlett-Packard. Most of these vendors started to market their own UNIX versions based on the original UNIX source code. They adapted the code to meet their own hardware and software requirements.

In early 1993, AT&T sold its UNIX System Laboratories to Novell. In 1994 Novell transferred the rights to the UNIX trademark and the specification to The Open Group. Subsequently, it sold the source code and the product implementation (UNIXWARE) to SCO.

Because UNIX is written almost entirely in the C programming language, and because the source code is published, it has been ported to a wider variety of machine architectures than any other operating system.

Originally, AT&T registered "UNIX" as a trademark, so although anyone could create their own version of UNIX and market it, they were not allowed to call it UNIX. As a result, vendors came up with different names for their UNIX flavors:

Vendor	UNIX flavor
IBM	AIX
Oracle/Sun	Solaris
HP	HP-UX
Apple	Mac OS X (built on FreeBSD, discussed in the next section)

Table 25: UNIX flavors

These versions are 90% the same, but have some minor differences, like the wording of error messages, the order of commands used to startup the machine, or the location of certain files.

Each of these flavors needs specific hardware. HP-UX only runs on HP Integrity systems, and these systems cannot run for example AIX.

Applications running on a particular flavor of UNIX cannot run on another flavor without (at least) recompiling. This means that software vendors must provide separate versions of their applications for each flavor of UNIX.

UNIX popularized the hierarchical file system with nested subdirectories, a feature now implemented in most other operating systems as well. All files and directories appear under the so-called root directory "/", even if they are stored on different physical disks. UNIX has no concept of drive letters; drives are mounted on a branch in the directory tree, providing disk space for that particular branch.

UNIX typically uses a large set of small tools that do only one thing, and do it very well. To perform complicated tasks, commands can be combined using a system called pipes. Pipes feed the output of one command to the input of another command, without storing the intermediate result. For instance, the UNIX command:

```
ls | sort
```

prints a sorted list of files on the screen. The pipe sign "|" ensures that the output of the "ls" command is routed (as input) to the "sort" command. Since after the sort command there is no further pipe specified the final output is send to the standard output system: the screen.

Of course, this is a very simple example. In practice these chains of piped commands can get very long and complex.

In UNIX, everything is treated as a file, even printers, modems, the keyboard and the screen. This allows piped commands, for instance, to use typed input from the keyboard, process them using some application, and have the output send automatically to a printer.

11.2.8.5 Linux

Linux is a UNIX-like operating system, but is not derived from the UNIX source code. Instead, it was developed independently by a group of developers in an informal alliance on the internet as a free operating system for the x86 platform.

In 1987, Andrew Tanenbaum, who was a professor of computer science at the Vrije Universiteit, Amsterdam in the Netherlands, wrote a clone of UNIX, called MINIX (MIni uNIX), for the IBM PC. He wrote MINIX especially for his students to teach them how an operating system worked. Tanenbaum wrote a book[83] that not only listed the 12,000 lines of MINIX source code, but also described each important part of the source code in detail, including the theory about why it was programmed the way it was.

Linus Torvalds, at the time a student at the University of Helsinki, studied MINIX in an operating system course and bought a PC to try it. In 1991, Torvalds wanted to explore the multitasking possibilities of the new Intel 80386 CPU in his PC and decided to create a small multitasking, multi-user operating system himself with the help of the internet community. On USENET, he asked developers on the internet to help him with the development[84]. Because of the open source nature of Linux many developers contributed with kernel patches, device drivers, and additions like multilingual keyboards, floppy disk drivers, support for video card devices, and much more.

It is important to understand that Linux is actually only an operating system *kernel*. Today's Linux distributions consist of the Linux kernel and its drivers, and the GNU project's applications, libraries, compilers, and tools.

The GNU project (GNU is a recursive acronym for "GNU's Not UNIX!") was launched in 1984 by Richard Stallman, to develop a free UNIX-like operating system. By 1990, the GNU project had recreated all the major components of the UNIX-like system except one – the kernel. Combining Linux with the almost-complete GNU system resulted in a complete operating system: the GNU/Linux system.

Linux and the GNU tools are licensed under the GNU General Public License, ensuring that the all source code will be free for all to copy, study, and to change.

Soon, commercial vendors showed interest. Linux itself was, and still is, free. What the vendors did was compiling the source code, adding some tools and configurations of their own, and releasing it in a distributable format. Red Hat, SuSe, Ubuntu and Debian are some of the best-known Linux distributions. Extended with Graphical User Interfaces (like X-window System, KDE, or GNOME), user-friendly Linux distributions became very popular.

Today Linux is a very mature operating system. Companies like Red Hat and Novell (who purchased SuSe and Caldera) sell professional Linux distributions including support contracts. Linux is used in servers, workstations, mobile devices, all Android smartphones, and appliances like set-top boxes, firewalls and NAS devices. Ninety-five per cent of the supercomputers listed in the top 500 list of the fastest computers in the world[85] are running Linux.

Since Linux runs on many hardware platforms it is very attractive for software vendors to create applications for it. Many business software today is released on Linux before being released on the various flavors of UNIX.

Since Linux's design is derived from UNIX's design, Linux commands and scripts are to a large degree similar to those of UNIX. Linux not only uses the same (well-known) commands, but also the same file structure, scripting language, pipes, etc. This allows experienced UNIX systems managers to use Linux without the need for much extra knowledge. Porting systems from UNIX to Linux is therefore generally much easier than porting them to for instance Windows.

11.2.8.5.1 Linux support

Linux is created as an open source project. This means that the source code of Linux is published and freely available. While this allows users to change the source code to their needs, this is hardly ever done, due to the complexity of the Linux source code and the limited benefits of changing the code.

Most organizations demand professional support for their software. And although Linux can be downloaded from the internet for free, professional support is certainly not free. Most Linux distribution vendors, like Red Hat and SuSe, and some independent vendors, offer support contracts for Linux.

11.2.8.5.2 Linux on mainframes

While Linux typically runs on x86 servers, some Linux distributions can be used on IBM mainframes, running in virtual machines.

Linux does not use 3270 (virtual) display terminals typically used on mainframes, but uses X-Windows emulators on PCs instead. The emulated LAN on the mainframe can be used to connect multiple Linux virtual machines and to provide an external LAN route for them.

Linux on mainframes operates with the ASCII character set, while mainframes typically use the EBCDIC character set. With Linux, EBCDIC is only used when writing to character based devices like displays and printers. Specialized Linux drivers handle the character translation between ASCII and EBCDIC.

11.2.8.6 BSD

Berkeley Software Distribution (BSD), sometimes called Berkeley UNIX, is a UNIX operating system derivative developed and distributed by the University of California, Berkeley. BSD was the basis for three open source development projects that continue to this day.

11.2.8.6.1 FreeBSD

FreeBSD is the most widely used BSD-derived operating system. FreeBSD is a complete operating system; the kernel, device drivers, and all of the utilities, such as the shell, are held in the same source code tree. (This in contrast to Linux distributions, for which the kernel, utilities, and applications are developed separately, and then packaged together in various ways, called distributions.)

11.2.8.6.2 NetBSD

NetBSD has been ported to 57 hardware platforms across 15 different processor architectures. Due to its convenient license and portability, NetBSD is often used in embedded systems.

11.2.8.6.3 OpenBSD

OpenBSD includes a number of security features absent, or optional in other operating systems, and has a tradition in which developers audit the source code for software bugs and security problems.

In the 10+ years of its existence, only three security bugs have been found in OpenBSD. OpenBSD is widely known for the developers' insistence on open source code, high quality documentation, and focus on security and code correctness. The OpenBSD project maintains ports for 17 different hardware platforms.

11.2.8.7 Windows

The most popular operating system ever is without a doubt Microsoft Windows. The first version of Microsoft Windows was released in 1985, but was not used much. Windows 1.0 was actually not an operating system, but rather a graphical "operating environment" that ran as an application op top of the MS-DOS operating system. Microsoft Windows version 2 was released in 1987, and was hardly more popular than its predecessor. But Windows 2.0 *could* run Microsoft's new graphical applications: Excel and Word for Windows. In 1990, Microsoft Windows 3.0 was the first successful Windows version. Its user interface was seen as a serious competitor to the user interface of Apple's Macintosh.

Windows NT arrived in 1992 and turned out to be a huge success. It was the first version of Windows designed to run on servers. Windows NT was no longer a layer built on MS-DOS, but instead it was a real operating system with its own kernel, memory management, and device drivers. Deployed in many datacenters as an easy to use application, file, and print server, Windows NT was strong competition for Novell's NetWare operating system.

In late 1995, Microsoft released Windows 95, positioned as the new operating system for desktops. Windows 95 provided a new Graphical User Interface (GUI) that made other Windows versions look old fashioned. Windows 95 introduced the "start" button, from where all applications could be started. This feature greatly increased the usability for first time users of Windows.

Windows NT 4 included the Windows 95 style GUI. By this time most companies were starting to switch from Novell servers to Windows NT 4. Even some UNIX systems were being replaced by Windows NT 4 systems. This was largely due to the huge amount of commercial power Microsoft had put in making Windows 95 successful. The vast adoption of Microsoft software by home users accelerated Microsoft's absorption in the business market.

With Windows 2000, Microsoft introduced an implementation of LDAP directory services, called Active Directory. With this development, the last hurdle for a number of systems managers to adopt Windows as a server operating system was taken away, as their Novell Directory Service (NDS), Netscape Directory Service, or Banyan Vines could easily be migrated to Microsoft's Active Directory.

Some versions of Windows were targeted at workstations, including Windows XP, Windows Vista, Windows 7, 8 and 10. The server operating systems were named after the year of release: Windows server 2003, 2008 and 2012.

For a long time, Windows suffered from two great weaknesses: stability and security.

The stability of Windows was not as good as competing products like Novell NetWare and UNIX systems. While NetWare and UNIX would run for at least a year without crashing, it was not uncommon that a Windows server crashed once a day. The infamous "Blue Screen Of Death" was the screen showing that a Windows server had crashed.

Picture 39: A crashed Windows system

The main cause of this instability was the need for backwards compatibility of Windows. While technology allowed for more and more enhanced features to be built in operating systems, Microsoft decided that every version of Windows needed to be able to run all already developed software without recompilation. This meant that all sorts of tweaks were built into Windows to be able to handle old applications.

Another issue was caused by the fact that Windows runs on all kinds of hardware (as opposed to UNIX or Apple systems, which are designed for specific hardware). All sorts of new, old, and obscure video cards, modems, printers, CPUs, disk drives, etc. that were supposed to work in Windows, mostly interfaced with device drivers created by third parties. The quality of these third-party drivers was not always guaranteed and was a cause of many problems.

Another weakness was the security of Windows. The main reason for this was that Windows was based on MS-DOS – a single user / single tasking operating system. Multi-user features and concurrently running multiple applications was built in later, leading to all kinds of issues. Because of the need for backward compatibility, and because most applications were not designed with multi user usage in mind, these applications had to run with the highest possible user permissions (administrator rights). This elevated security level led to applications being able to bring down other applications or even Windows itself. It also provided hackers the possibility to change or delete files on Windows computers that were not part of a user application (like the Windows kernel files). This led to the rise of viruses and worms attacking Windows. And because Windows was so popular, a hacker that could exploit a vulnerability in Windows could use it to attack almost all PC based systems in the world.

In 2002, Microsoft recognized the security and stability issues, and spent several months' full-time effort of all developers to update the Windows code base to make it more stable (the Trustworthy Computing initiative). As a result, today's Windows versions are pretty stable and secure.

Because of Window's popularity, a large collection of software is available that runs on it. Microsoft provides a fairly complete stack of business solutions like SharePoint, BizTalk and Exchange. They also provide a development environment (Visual Studio and the .Net framework). Many organizations therefore have a "Microsoft unless" strategy – software is purchased from Microsoft or built using Microsoft tools, unless there is no solution from Microsoft available.

11.2.8.7.1 Support

Windows is closed source software. Only one company (Microsoft) has access to the source code and knows how Windows works internally. This means that users are very dependent on Microsoft for support and updates, and they must follow updates and software upgrades to be able to keep that support. This leads to frequent (and usually costly) upgrade projects. Extended support is sometimes possible, but at a price.

11.2.8.8 End user operating systems

While most operating systems described earlier run on either servers or workstations, some operating systems are exclusively designed to be used on end user devices. Some examples are:

- **Windows** workstation versions (XP, Vista, Windows 7, Windows 8, and Windows 10) - Microsoft's PC operating system.

- **Mac OS** - Apple's operating system for laptops and desktops, based on BSD.

- **Ubuntu** - Linux distribution specially designed for laptops and desktops.

- **iOS** - Apple's operating system for mobile devices (iPhone, iPad, etc.), based on BSD.

- **Android** - Google's operating system for mobile devices, based on Linux.

11.2.8.9 Special purpose operating systems

Some operating systems are created for special purposes like the ones used in firewalls, intrusion detection and prevention systems, routers, phones, ATM machines, media centers, etc. These operating systems are typically based on existing operating systems (usually Linux or Windows), but stripped of all unneeded features.

An example of a special type of operating system is a real-time operating system (RTOS). Real-time operating systems guarantee to perform tasks in a predefined amount of time. For instance, initiating a process after a hardware based interrupt is guaranteed to be finished within 2 ms. Real-time operating systems are used where handling events within a predefined time is critical, for instance in factories, power plants and vehicles. An example of a real-time operating system is QNX.

11.3 Operating system availability

To enhance the availability of an operating system, failover clustering is often used.

11.3.1 Failover clustering

A failover cluster is a group of independent servers running identical operating systems (known as "nodes"), that are connected via a network, and that are controlled by cluster software running on the nodes. Examples of cluster software products are:

- **Parallel Sysplex** for IBM mainframes.

- **HACMP** for IBM AIX UNIX.

- **MC/Service Guard** for HP-UX UNIX.

- **Windows Cluster Service** for Microsoft Windows.

- **Heartbeat** and **Pacemaker** for Linux.

A failover cluster provides high availability to applications by managing each running application within a node as a package of application components, called a resource pool or an application package. A resource pool is the single unit of failover within a cluster. It typically contains:

- **Application name** and identifier.

- **Start script** for the application.

- **Stop script** for the application.

- **Monitor script** for the application – this script continuously checks the status of the application. If the application does not work as expected, a restart or failover is initiated.

- **Virtual IP address** the application can be addressed with.

- **Mount points** for storage – the disks that must be available to the application.

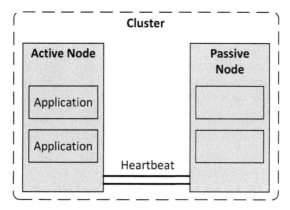

Figure 103: Cluster heartbeat

A cluster network typically consists of redundant physical Ethernet connections that carry heartbeats between all nodes in the cluster, as well as membership and state change information. A heartbeat allows nodes to detect the unavailability of nodes by regularly sending packets to each other's network interfaces.

Monitoring the health of the operating system and applications running on the node can be done by for instance checking the process table (are all processes still running?), or by connecting to the application and testing its ability to communicate (for instance by connecting to a database server, a web server, or a mail server and check if it responds as expected).

In most failover clusters all nodes are able to access data on shared storage, but every individual disk is mounted to one active application only at any given time. If an application is restarted on another node, the application can still use the data on the shared storage since the application package describes the needed mount points and the cluster software automatically remounts the configured storage to the new active application.

This usage of shared storage is also called 'shared nothing clustering', as opposed to for instance Distributed Lock Management (DLM) clustering. With DLM clustering each cluster node can access the same resource, for instance a disk, *at the same time*, and a lock management mechanism is responsible to manage the data in order to avoid corruption.

In a cluster, every active application has a standby counterpart available on a passive node that sits idle until a failover is needed. After a failover, this standby application becomes active and provides service to clients. The passive node should have enough capacity to run the failed-over application without performance degradation.

In case of for instance a server crash or a power outage, all applications running on that server node will not be brought down cleanly. When the applications are restarted on another node in the cluster, standard crash recovery should take place. The file system must take care of performing necessary file system checks before mounting, and the application must perform its standard recovery on startup.

It is essential to understand that application recovery in case of a failover is identical to an application startup following a server power failure.

A spare node could be added to a cluster to handle failovers. This is called a N+1 cluster, where N represents the number of nodes with active applications, and 1 indicates a single spare node. In a larger cluster, N+2 or N+3 can also be used to provide more redundancy.

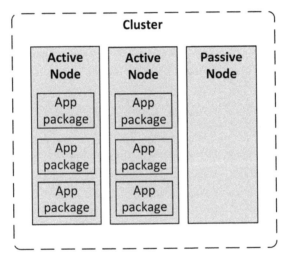

Figure 104: N+1 cluster

An alternative is an N to N cluster, where there is no spare idle node, but each node has some amount of spare capacity to host additional applications in case of a failover.

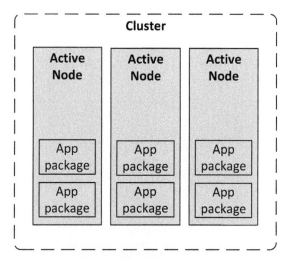

Figure 105: N+N cluster

The advantage of an N+N cluster is that the available hardware is always used. All memory and CPU cycles in the operating system can be used by all running applications. But when a failover occurs, less memory and CPU cycles are available to the applications, possibly leading to some performance degradation.

11.3.1.1 Voting and quorum disks

When in a cluster with an even number of nodes (most clusters contain two nodes) nodes are disconnected from each other, the status of the other nodes is unknown to each node. This means that one of two situations occurs:

- Each node decides that the other node must be down, so each node decides to be the new active node in the cluster (leading to a so-called split-brain situation)

- Each node decides that it has lost contact with the active cluster, so both nodes decide to stop (effectively bringing down the cluster)

To solve this problem, when a node in the cluster fails, a voting mechanism determines which part of the cluster is faulty and which part of the cluster is working properly.

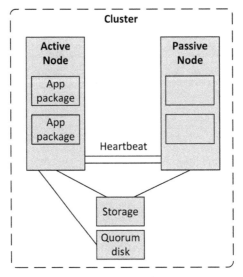

Figure 106: Cluster with quorum

Because in a two-node cluster there is no majority possible in a voting system, a virtual third node is used, usually in the form of a shared disk, called a quorum disk. The quorum disk acts as one vote in the voting system.

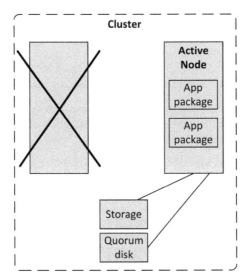

Figure 107: Cluster failover

Since the quorum disk is always assigned to one (and only one) node at any time, and because a faulty node releases it quorum disk automatically, the properly working node gets two votes: one from itself, the other from the quorum disk. The faulty node will stop working, because it has only one vote. This way no split-brain situation can occur.

11.3.1.2 Cluster-aware applications

Some cluster-aware applications, like Oracle RAC, Microsoft SQL Server, and Microsoft Exchange Server, may run active instances on multiple nodes. This enhances switch-over times in case of a failure, because the application does not need to be started on another node before it can service clients.

For these so-called cluster-aware applications, failover clusters provide scalability in addition to high availability. Client requests can be distributed among multiple cluster nodes, and systems managers can meet increased demand and traffic by adding additional nodes to the cluster.

11.4 Operating system performance

The performance of an operating system is highly dependent on the performance of the underlying hardware, the type of load generated by the applications running on the operating system, and, to a smaller extend, on the configuration of the operating system itself.

Some performance can be gained by increasing memory, and decreasing the kernel size.

11.4.1 Increasing memory

An operating system should have enough memory to run all applications needed at any time. When an application needs more than the available memory, memory is freed by either moving less used memory pages to disk (called paging), or, when memory is really low, by moving an entire application's allocated memory to disk (called swapping). While some paging is not bad, swapping totally ruins the performance of an operating system, because data stored on disk is at least three orders of magnitude slower than data stored in RAM memory. Swapping must therefore be avoided at all times by increasing memory or by running less (demanding) applications.

Another reason why increasing memory benefits the operating systems' performance is disk caching. In most operating systems, all memory not used by applications is used to cache disk blocks. This is the main reason why the performance of operating systems usually increases when memory is added. Operating systems use highly sophisticated algorithms to optimize disk caching. For instance, when an application doesn't use a block of memory for some time, it is paged to disk, freeing the memory block to be used for disk cache instead.

In general, tweaking the memory management system of an operating system provides little benefits.

11.4.2 Decreasing kernel size

Some operating systems (like UNIX and Linux) allow tuning kernel parameters of the operating system. Unused features (like support for IPv6 or floppy disk drives) can be switched off when they are not used, leading to a smaller kernel size.

A smaller kernel has the following benefits:

- It simplifies the kernel, leading to a lower risk of crashes and a smaller security attack surface.

- Since the kernel must be in memory at all times (it cannot be paged or swapped-out), a smaller kernel will free up memory for applications and disk caching.

- Switched-off features don't need patching to keep them up-to-date.

- The operating system starts faster when the kernel is small.

To create a smaller kernel, the kernel must be recompiled or re-linked. This is a highly automated, low risk operation on most UNIX and Linux systems. A restart of the operating system is of course needed after a kernel rebuild.

Not all operating systems allow rebuilding the kernel. For instance, the Windows kernel cannot be rebuilt.

11.5 Operating system security

The security of an operating system can be enhanced by:

- Patching
- Hardening

- Virus scanning

- Host-based firewalls

- Log analysis

- Limitations of user accounts

11.5.1 Patching

All operating system vendors (semi-)automatically provide small software updates called patches for their operating systems when bugs or design flaws are fixed, security holes are closed or small improvements are made. In general, patches come in three categories:

- **Regular patches** are meant to fix low priority software bugs. Some regular patches fix multiple bugs at once.

- **Hot-fixes** repair a bug or flaw in the operating system that needs to be fixed fast. Typically, hot-fixes are used to close a security hole or to fix an error introduced by another patch or service pack. In most cases, hot-fixes should be installed as soon as possible.

- **Service packs** (also known as support packs or patch packs) are a collection of patches and hot-fixes that are packed together and can be installed in one deployment. Sometimes service packs also introduce new functionality to the operating system.

While it is good practice to install all patches, hot-fixes, and service packs as soon as possible, they should be tested before deploying them in production, since they could introduce unwanted effects in the infrastructure.

Patches hot-fixes, and service packs are usually provided with release notes describing what changes they make to the operating system. It is good practice to read these release notes before installing the patch. When a patch or hot fix does not have impact on a specific deployment it can be discarded, knowing that the next service pack will include the patch anyway.

11.5.2 Hardening

Hardening is a step by step process of configuring an operating system to protect it against security threats. In a hardening process the operating system is stripped down to support only essential services and processes. Unnecessary protocols and subsystems are switched off, and unused user accounts are removed or disabled. All new and relevant hot-fixes, patches, and service packs are applied.

It is good practice to harden all operating systems in the infrastructure using a hardened operating system configuration template. This template is then used to instantiate new operating systems ensuring security is optimal and is consistent in all deployments.

11.5.3 Virus scanning

When installing server operating systems that are vulnerable to viruses (typically Windows, Linux and end user operating systems), it is good practice to install a virus scanner as well.

Virus scanners can have an impact on the performance of the operating system, so the virus scanner must be configured to only scan high risk files and directories based on a risk analysis. For instance, it makes no sense to protect a database table file with a virus scanner.

For more information on viruses and malware see section 6.2.4.

11.5.4 Host-based firewalls

Most operating systems, including Windows, Linux, and UNIX, provide a built-in host-based firewall.

A host-based firewall is a software firewall that is installed as part of a running operating system in the infrastructure, protecting an individual host from unwanted network traffic. Host-based firewalls provide an extra security layer, in addition to network firewalls (as explained in section 8.6.1), and other security measures.

Much like network firewalls, host-based firewalls typically block all incoming network traffic. Rule sets define which type of traffic is allowed to communicate with the operating system, based on the source and destination IP address, the TCP or UDP port and the running process sending and/or receiving the network traffic.

It is good practice to enable host-based firewalls on all machines; on servers, but especially on end user devices.

11.5.5 Limiting user accounts

Most operating systems by default include local user accounts that can login to the operating system. These default users sometimes have default passwords that of course should be changed as soon as possible. It is even better to remove the default usernames altogether.

In addition, most operating systems have a special super user account called *"root"*, *"supervisor"*, *"admin"*, or *"administrator"*. These accounts have almost unlimited power on the operating system and should be used only to provide permissions to user accounts bound to a physical person. The password of the super user account should be very secure (long and complex), should be stored in a safe place and changed regularly. Under normal circumstances, these accounts should never be needed, as it should be possible to do all work using a user-bound account with sufficient rights.

Operating systems only store encrypted passwords (although it is sometimes configurable not to, which is a bad idea). When a user logs in, his password is encrypted and compared to the stored encrypted password. If the two are equal the login succeeds. There is no way to calculate or extract the original password from the encrypted one; therefore, in early UNIX systems, everyone could read the password file with all encrypted passwords. When weak passwords are used however, brute force of dictionary attacks can be used to find the passwords. The encrypted passwords should therefore never be disclosed.

12

END USER DEVICES

12.1 Introduction

Humans interact with applications using end user devices. Typical end user devices are desktop PCs, laptops, virtual desktops, mobile devices like phones and tablets, and printers.

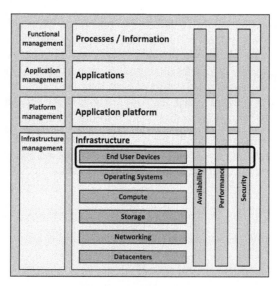

Figure 108: End user devices in the infrastructure model

The first end user devices were teletypes. Teletypes were electromechanical typewriters that provided a user interface to early mainframes, sending typed data to the computer and printing the response.

Picture 40: Teletype[86]

Later, electronic terminals replaced the teletypes. Terminals provided a monitor screen instead of printed paper, allowing full screen editing and instant output. Terminals were "dumb", as they did not have their own processing power. They relayed typed-in commands to the mainframe computer and the mainframe computer sent data back to the terminal to be displayed. Terminals were used for decades to interact with mainframe and midrange computers.

In 1981, IBM introduced the Personal Computer (PC). The IBM PC became the de facto end user device in many office environments, allowing office workers to have full control over their own computer for the first time.

Picture 41: The original IBM PC-XT[87]

IBM developed the PC in about a year. To achieve this, they decided to build the machine with "off-the-shelf" parts from a variety of manufacturers. They also decided on an open architecture, enabling other manufacturers to produce and sell peripheral components and compatible software without having to purchase licenses. IBM even sold an IBM PC Technical Reference Manual which included complete circuit diagrams and a listing of the ROM BIOS source code.

The result was that many parties copied the PC – the so-called PC clones. These clones (or IBM-compatible PCs) used the same architecture, used the same chipset as the IBM PC, and used reversed-engineered BIOS software (because even though the source code was published, it was still copyrighted). This allowed clones to run unmodified IBM software. One of the first and most successful companies building clones was Compaq, which would later become part of HP.

All of the IBM PC software was developed by third parties. The most influential one being Microsoft that provided the DOS operating system and office tools like Word and Excel.

While IBM was already a large manufacturer of computers before the introduction of the PC, in contrast, Apple was founded by two hobbyists. In 1984, Apple introduced the Apple Macintosh. It was the first commercially successful personal computer to feature a mouse and a GUI rather than a command line interface. It was designed to be used by consumers, and not as an office tool.

Both the Mac and the PC evolved over time to become much faster. Color video screens and sound boards became the norm, and laptops became the most used form factor.

The introduction of tablets and smartphones made the end user experience truly mobile.

12.2 End user device building blocks

End user devices can be categorized as:

- Desktop PCs
- Laptops
- Virtual desktops
- Mobile devices
- Printers

All of these categories are discussed in the following sections.

12.2.1 Desktop PCs and laptops

The most used end user devices today are desktop and laptop computers based on Intel's x86 architecture, mostly referred to as PCs. While Apple iMacs also run on the x86 platform, according to Gartner[88], in 2014 more than 90% of the x86 based PCs run the Microsoft Windows operating system.

Over the years, PCs have become very powerful. This enables them to run complex software and to store relatively large amounts of data. But because of the sheer complexity of the PC itself, the very advanced operating systems, the amount of locally installed software, and the performance, availability, and security issues related to all of these aspects, many organizations are searching for more cost-effective and simple solutions.

But people are attached to their PCs. The term personal computer is still correct – most users feel their PC is their personal tool that systems managers should not tamper with. This is one of the main reasons why the adoption of alternatives like thin clients (see 12.3.4) has never been as successful as it could have been.

Nowadays, most laptops are as powerful as desktop PCs. And because users can take them home or use them on the road, they are even more "personal" than desktops. Laptops, however, have some disadvantages compared to desktop PCs, like:

- Laptops frequently get lost or stolen. On average, 10% of the laptops are lost or stolen during their life cycle[89]. These laptops must be replaced, the user cannot work in the meantime, and data on the laptop that was not backed-up is lost.

- Laptops break more easily than desktops, because they are more vulnerable to drops, bumps, coffee spills, etc.

- Since most laptops are taken home every night, the chance of illegal or malicious software being installed on the laptop is much higher than on a desktop PC in the office.

12.2.2 Mobile devices

The use of mobile devices has grown tremendously over the last few years and their use will most likely increase much more in the years to come.

Mobile devices in the context of this book are devices that connect to the IT infrastructure using wireless public or off-site Wi-Fi networks. Typical mobile devices are smartphones and tablets, but modern computerized networked devices like cars, smart watches, music players or digital cameras are also considered mobile devices.

While the computing power of some mobile devices is getting comparable to desktop and laptop computers, mobile devices have some specific properties that infrastructure architects must be aware of.

Mobile devices typically connect to the IT infrastructure using public networks based on for example UMTS or LTE technology (these technologies are explained in chapter 8). The bandwidth of these connections is lower than that of Wi-Fi and wired Ethernet connections. Also, connection speed can heavily fluctuate as the users move around, and it sometimes can fluctuate quite fast when the mobile device is used inside a car or train. The reliability of the connections is therefore worse than that of Wi-Fi or wired Ethernet connections. When moving around, connections sometimes drop for short periods of time or drop altogether. Signal noise can force resending large numbers of network packets. Applications using mobile devices must cope with these network limitations.

Another limitation of mobile devices is the small form factor forcing limited keyboard and screen sizes. Applications' user interfaces must be re-engineered to handle these smaller sizes.

12.2.3 Bring Your Own Device (BYOD)

Ten years ago, PCs used in the office were superior to those people had at home. This situation has changed. While most organizations use standard PCs or laptops with a limited set of business software, users at home have access to fast, sexy laptops of the brand they like, tablets and smart phones that allow them to run thousands of highly attractive apps and they have fast broadband internet connections at home that are often faster than the shared network in the office.

To attract new employers and because people will take their personal device to the office anyway, most organizations are now confronted with a concept called Bring Your Own Device (BYOD).

BYOD allows people to bring personally owned – typically mobile – devices to the office, to use them to access the organization's applications and data, as well as their personal applications and data.

The BYOD concept creates a conflict of interests. To optimize stability of the organization's infrastructure and security, systems managers need to fully control the end user device, while the owners of the devices want full freedom. And since the user paid for the device (they brought their *own* device), it will not be acceptable for users to have systems managers erase the device (including all family photos or purchased music) in case of an incident, or to have personal data visible to the systems managers.

Virtualization techniques can be used to create isolated environments on these devices. Some solutions implement a hypervisor on the device that runs two virtual machines:

- One virtual machine with has access to the organization's data and applications and is fully managed by the organization's systems managers. This virtual machine is managed using Mobile Device Management (MDM) software that can be used to monitor, maintain and secure virtual machines on mobile devices. When needed, the virtual machine can be remotely wiped to remove all sensitive data.

- One virtual machine that is owned and managed by the end user. This machine runs whatever applications the user wants (browsers, social network clients, games, music players, video players, etc.).

Both virtual machines use the same underlying hardware like network connectivity, touch screen, GPS, compass, and the sound system. But since both virtual machines are run on top of a hypervisor, no sensitive data will be available from the user's managed virtual machine.

12.2.4 Printers

Printers are used in almost all organizations to provide paper output. Most used printer types are:

- Line printers

- Laser printers

- Inkjet printers

- Multi-Functional Printers

- Specialized printers like dot matrix printers, line printers, plotters, and thermal printers

12.2.4.1 Laser printers

The original laser printer called EARS was developed at the Xerox Palo Alto Research Center in 1971, based on Xerox copier technology. In 1992, Hewlett-Packard released the popular LaserJet 4, with a Canon based engine, a 600 by 600 dot per inch resolution laser printer used in many office environments for many years.

A laser printer rapidly produces high quality text and graphics on plain sheets of paper. In laser printers, the image is produced using a so-called drum. This photoreceptive drum is electrically charged using high voltages. After lighting it with a laser beam (which eliminates the electrostatic charge on all places, except the image), the electrostatic charge left on the drum attracts toner (ink powder) that transfers the image on paper. A fuser then heats the toner to burn it on paper.

Picture 42: HP's LaserJet 4 printer

Both monochrome and color laser printers are in use. In color printers four toners are used, one for each basic color (cyan, magenta and yellow), and one for black. Each color is put on paper separately. This makes color printing more expensive and sometimes slower than monochrome printing.

12.2.4.2 Inkjet printers

In 1976, the inkjet printer was invented. But it took until 1988 for the inkjet to become a home consumer item with Hewlett-Packard's release of the Deskjet inkjet printer. Inkjet printers are relatively cheap and produce high quality printouts, usually in color.

Inkjet printers create text and graphics by propelling droplets of ink onto paper through high print head resolution, making them ideal for office environments. Inkjet printers don't need to warm up and use much less energy than a laser printer.

Some professional inkjet printers provide wide format printing, with a print width ranging from 75 cm to 5 m. They can be used for instance to create advertising billboards.

12.2.4.3 Multi-Functional Printers (MFPs)

A Multi-Function Printer (MFP) is an office device which not only acts as a printer, but also as a scanner, a photocopier, and a fax machine. It typically provides centralized document management and production in an office setting. Multi-functional printers are available from most printer manufacturers; they are quickly replacing separate printers in office environments.

Picture 43: Multi-Function Printer (MFP)

In most situations, one MFP is placed on each floor in an office building, so everyone on that floor can use it. Therefore, most MFPs use Active Directory or another authentication functionality to start the actual printing only when a user is authenticated to the printer (typically with the same pass used to enter the building). This "printing on demand" enhances security as no printed paper with possibly sensitive text is left on the MFP waiting to be collected. And because a single printer is used, people are forced to walk to the printer which is not only good exercise, but also is a psychological barrier to avoid unneeded printing. For those people that don't want to stand in line waiting for their printout, some MFPs have separate locked mail bins where one can collect printouts.

MFPs are essentially a type of computer themselves. They contain memory, one or more processors, often some kind of storage, such as a hard disk drive or flash memory, and an operating system. An MFP should therefore be handled like a computer – patches must be installed, and the hard drive should be erased before repair.

Because the MFP is a computer connected to the network, monitoring of print quotas, toner/ink levels, etc. can be done remotely.

12.2.4.4 Specialized printers

12.2.4.4.1 Dot Matrix printers

In dot matrix printers, characters are drawn out of a matrix of dots, where each dot is produced by a tiny metal rod driven forward by a tiny electromagnet. The moving portion of the printer is called the print head.

The printer typically prints one line of text at a time, character-by-character. Dot matrix printers are noisy during operation as a result of the hammer-like mechanism in the print head.

Figure 109: Output of a dot matrix printer

From the 1970s until the 1990s, dot matrix printers were by far the most common type of printer used with personal computers, the Epson MX-80 being one of the most popular dot matrix printers of all times.

Picture 44: The Epson MX-80 dot matrix printer[90]

Dot matrix printers can print on multi-part stationery or make carbon-copies, used for instance for printing invoices. Dot matrix printers have one of the lowest printing costs per page. They use continuous paper rather than individual sheets, making them useful for printing continuous data logs. Dot matrix printers are very reliable work horses and are therefore still in use in many places.

12.2.4.4.2 Line printers

Line printers are high speed printers that print one complete line of text at once. Line printers were mostly used in the early days of computing, but the technology is still in use for specific tasks. Line printers print at a speed of 600 to 1200 lines per minute. Line printers use paper of continuous fanfold paper rather than cut-sheets.

Picture 45: IBM 1403 line printer[91]

Multiple technologies can be used in line printers, using spinning drums, chains, or bands that contain the character set. Small hammers are used to push the paper to the passing characters at exactly the right moment, putting the characters on paper.

Modern line matrix printers are significantly more sophisticated than their predecessors, offering high resolution print quality and often laser-printer emulation, including the ability to print PostScript fonts[92].

Line printers are especially well-suited to shop floors and industrial environments, where dust, humidity, temperature extremes, and other factors can quickly bring laser printers to a standstill. Line printers are physically more durable than laser printers, and their consumables are both less costly and less harmful to the environment.

12.2.4.4.3 Plotters

A plotter is a specialized printer that draws vector graphics using a pen. They are mainly used in computer-aided design, for creating blueprints.

In large plotters, a roll of paper is placed over a roller that moves the paper back and forth for Y-axis motion, while the pen moves left and right on a track for X-axis motion. Small (A4, A3 or Letter paper) plotters do not move the paper at all; instead the pen moves over the paper.

Plotters can draw high quality complex line art, including text, but are slow because of the mechanical movement of the pen and paper.

Pen plotters have essentially become obsolete in most places, and have been replaced by large-format inkjet printers.

12.2.4.4.4 Thermal printers

A thermal printer produces a printed image by selectively heating thermal paper when the paper passes over the thermal print head. Thermal paper is impregnated with a chemical that changes color when exposed to heat. Thermal printers print quietly and fast. Since they are also small, light, and don't consume much power, they are ideal for portable and retail applications like point of sale terminals and voucher printers.

A major drawback of thermal printing is that the image will disappear when a print is exposed to sunlight or heat for a certain period of time.

12.3 Desktop virtualization

A number of virtualization technologies can be deployed for end user devices. Application virtualization can be used to run applications on an underlying virtualized operating system. And instead of running applications on end user devices themselves, using a thin client, applications can also be run on virtualized PCs based on Server Based Computing (SBC) or Virtual Desktop

Infrastructure (VDI). All of these technologies are explained in the next sections.

12.3.1 Application virtualization

The term application virtualization is a bit misleading, as the application itself is not virtualized, but the operating system resources the application uses are virtualized. Application virtualization isolates applications from some resources of the underlying operating system and from other applications, to increase compatibility and manageability.

The application is fooled into believing that it is directly interfacing with the operating system and all the resources managed by it. But in reality, the application virtualization layer provides the application with virtualized parts of the runtime environment normally provided by the operating system.

Application virtualization is typically implemented in a Windows-based environment

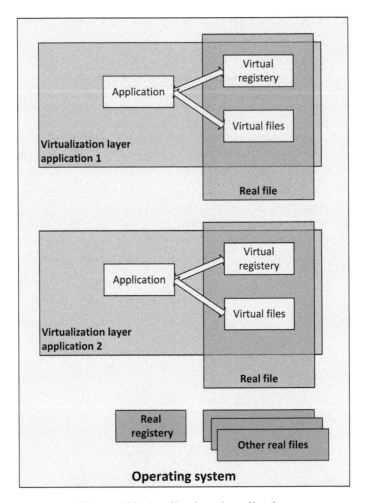

Figure 110: Application virtualization

The application virtualization layer proxies all requests to the operating system, but intercepts all file and registry operations. These operations are transparently redirected to a virtualized location, often a single real file.

Since the application is now working with one file instead of many files and registry entries spread throughout the system, it becomes easy to run the application on a different computer, and previously incompatible applications or application versions can be run side-by-side.

Examples of application virtualization products are Microsoft App-V and VMware ThinApp.

12.3.2 Server Based Computing

Server Based Computing (SBC) is a concept where applications and/or desktops running on remote servers relay their virtual display to the user's device. The user's device runs a relatively lightweight application (a thin client agent) that displays the video output, and that fetches the keyboard strokes and mouse movements, sending them back to the application on the remote server. The keyboard and mouse information is processed by the application on the server, and the resulting display changes are sent back to the user device.

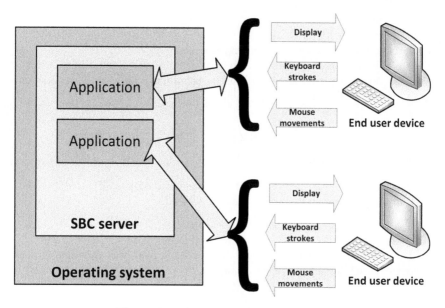

Figure 111: Server Based Computing

SBC requires a limited amount of network bandwidth because only changed display information is sent to the end user device and only keyboard strokes and mouse movements are sent to the server.

SBC is typically implemented in a Windows based environment, where the SBC server is either Windows Remote Desktop Service (RDS, formerly known as Windows Terminal Services) or Citrix XenApp (formerly known as MetaFrame Presentation Server). XenApp provides more functionality than RDS, but is a separate product, whereas RDS is part of the Windows operating system.

A big advantage of using SBC is that maintenance (like applying patches and upgrades) can be done at the server level. The changes are available instantly to all users – freeing systems managers of managing a large set of PC deployments.

With SBC, server-side CPU and RAM capacity is shared with applications from all users. Extensive use of CPU and/or RAM in one user's session can influence the performance of sessions of other users on the same server.

Application configurations are the same for all users and use the graphical properties of the SBC server instead of that of the client end user device.

Limitations on the desktop experience (slow response or keyboard lag) are mostly due to network latency or the configuration of the remote desktop. In most cases security and stability settings (protecting changes to shared resources) could also influence the experience. With a good configuration of the roaming user profile, folder redirection for network storage of user data, and the latest application virtualization techniques, limitations in desktop usage can be minimal.

12.3.3 Virtual Desktop Infrastructure (VDI)

Virtual Desktop Infrastructure (VDI) is a similar concept as SBC, only in VDI user applications run in their own virtual machine.

VDI utilizes a virtual desktop running on top of a hypervisor, typically VMware View, Citrix XenDesktop, or Microsoft MED-V. The hypervisor's primary task is to distribute available hardware resources between virtual machines hosted on a physical machine.

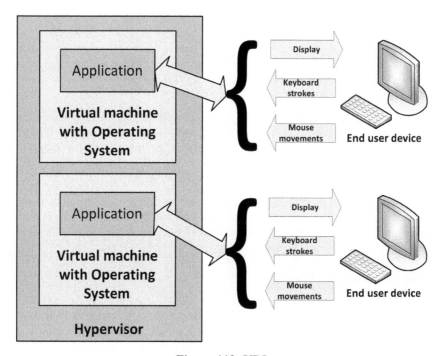

Figure 112: VDI

Just like with a physical PC, with VDI, each user has exclusive use of the operating system, CPU, and RAM, whereas SBC users share these resources. VDI enables applications and operating systems to run next to each other in complete isolation without interference.

Protocols supported to exchange video, keyboard, and mouse from client to virtual machine are the ICA (Independent Computing Architecture) protocol of Citrix, Microsoft's RDP (Remote Desktop Protocol), or the VMware PCoIP protocol.

VDI tends not to scale well in terms of CPU resources and storage IOPS, because each client uses an entire virtual machine. Booting a system leads to much I/O to the server. A so-called 'Logon storm' occurs when many virtualized systems boot up at the same time. These logon storms can partly be prevented by pre-starting a predefined number of virtual machines at configured time slots.

12.3.4 Thin clients

VDI and SBC both enable the hosting of desktops on central server farms and use the same protocols to deliver the output of application screens to users. Thin clients communicate with the SBC or VDI server. They come in two flavors: hardware and software based thin clients.

Hardware based thin clients are lightweight computers that are relatively inexpensive and have no moving parts or local disk drives. The devices have no configuration and can be used directly after plugging them into the network, making it easy to replace when one fails. They eliminate the requirement for upgrading PCs or laptops on a regular basis.

Software based thin clients are applications running in a normal client operating system like Windows, Linux, or Mac OS X. They can also run on mobile devices like tablets and smartphones.

12.3.4.1 PXE boot

The Preboot eXecution Environment (PXE) allows desktop PCs or thin clients to boot from an operating system disk image stored on the network instead of from a local hard disk. This allows for diskless thin clients (where no data is stored locally), leading to lower cost and less systems management effort. Since no operating system is stored on a local disk, no updates or patches are necessary; these are installed on the central PXE server. For PXE to work, the PC always needs a network connection. PXE is therefore not suitable for mobile devices like laptops.

PXE uses a combination of the DHCP and TFTP protocols. On PXE enabled PCs the BIOS tries to locate a PXE boot server on the network using DHCP (see section 8.2.8.1). The BIOS will ask the PXE boot server for the file path of the image to load (usually a Windows image), download it into the PC's RAM using TFTP, possibly verify it, and finally execute it.

The startup time of a PC using PXE is highly dependent on how fast a PXE image can be downloaded from the TFTP server. And because in most organizations each morning all PCs are started up around the same time, implementing a high performing TFTP server is crucial for fast startup times.

12.4 End user device availability

12.4.1 Reliability

Compared to a few years ago, today's hardware is much more reliable. End user devices now run mature, stable operating systems and applications. But to keep the cost of end user devices low, their hardware is still much less reliable than hardware installed in the datacenter. End user devices are designed to last only 3 to 5 years before they are replaced by new equipment, so the chance of a failing end user system is relatively high. And mobile devices like laptops or tablets can get physically damaged quite easily leading to hardware failures. Typical failures are hard disk crashes in laptops or screen cracks in tablets. A failing end user device immediately leads to downtime for a user and therefore loss of availability of business functions to the end user.

Systems management should therefore be ready to cope with failing systems. When an end user device fails, it should be easy to replace the device with a new one or to wipe the hard disk and install a fresh copy of the standard software set.

12.4.2 Backup of end user devices

Backup of local disks is very important, as still most of the work worldwide is first saved to a local disk on an end user device. Automated synchronization of local data to a server can be implemented to solve this problem. In these solutions, as soon as the device is connected to the network, local data is copied from the device to a server in the datacenter, where it is properly back-upped. For end users, it should be impossible to disable this synchronization function.

And of course, end users should be trained to save their work early and often. In practice, I have seen several occasions of people working on a document for a full day without hitting the Save button once! When close to the end of the day their text editor crashed, a full day work was gone.

Never trust technology – it will break, and typically at the most inconvenient moment!

12.4.3 Software stack

The availability of end user devices is also threatened by the instability of the application stack as a result of installing all kinds of software. End user devices should be protected from random installs of potential bad software by end users.

12.4.4 Printers and other equipment

Don't forget printers and other equipment. Make sure service contracts are in place to repair failing devices. And remember: a printer without enough supply of paper and toner/ink is just as unavailable as a defective printer!

12.5 End user device performance

The performance of end user devices is in most cases not a big issue. With today's hardware, when properly installed and managed, end user devices have few performance issues.

12.5.1 RAM

It is good practice to install enough RAM to run most needed applications simultaneously. In general, adding more RAM increases the performance of the end user device more than choosing a faster CPU.

12.5.2 Hard disk

The local disk drive's speed is also important for the performance of end user devices. The local disk drive is used to start the operating system and the applications, and to store temporary files and swap files. A faster disk – preferably an SSD disk – can positively affect the performance of the whole end user device in a big way.

12.5.3 Network connectivity

Also, the network connection can be crucial to get proper performance. Most data processed on a PC of laptop is transferred using the network. Make sure enough bandwidth is available for each end user device, both on a wired LAN and on a Wi-Fi network.

Using public wireless networks can dramatically slow down performance, as the bandwidth can be low and/or fluctuating. When end user devices are used with public wireless networks (like public Wi-Fi, or 3G) ensure the used software is capable of handling low bandwidth and unreliable connectivity. Technologies like Server Based Computing can help to make mitigate the effect of these issues.

12.6 End user device security

Securing end user devices is quite a challenge, as these devices are not located in a locked down datacenter, but are spread around offices, homes and client locations.

12.6.1 Physical security

When laptop computers are used, provide users with laptop cable locks to physically lock the laptop to an unmovable object to prevent theft.

If end user devices are at the end-of-life, or when they need repair, fully erase the hard disk first!

12.6.2 Malware protection

Malware protection software like a virus scanner needs to be installed on each device. They should check for all known viruses, spyware, rootkits, and other malware. As soon as a virus is located, files containing the virus must be quarantined immediately to prevent further propagation. Most virus scanners are capable of this sort of quarantining. When malware is detected, it should be reported automatically to a central systems management tool, to allow systems managers to take appropriate action. Of course, users should not be allowed to disable the functionality of the malware protection software.

As soon as new virus signatures are published by the virus scanner's supplier, they should be installed as soon as possible on all end user devices automatically. A regular full scan of each end user device should be scheduled as well; in case any infected file was missed.

12.6.3 Hard disk encryption

Because PCs and laptops usually have large hard disks installed, they can contain a large amount of (business critical) data. When a PC or laptop is stolen, lost, or replaced, chances are that sensitive data gets in the wrong hands. Therefore, every PC (and especially every laptop!) should have their full hard disk encrypted.

12.6.4 Mobile device management

Mobile devices are very attractive to thieves and must therefore be secured.

Mobile device management (MDM) can be used to monitor, maintain and secure devices that are not regularly connected to the organization's network. A good example is a mobile phone or tablet. Over the air distribution of software releases and updates of virus scanner signatures can be done using MDM.

When a mobile device is stolen, MDM enables systems management to remotely erase the device's content. Many tools are available for this, but keep in mind that the market for this software is young and most tools are not very mature at this point.

Software to locate the stolen device can be installed to help law enforcement locating the device and arresting the thief. It is sometimes even possible to remotely switch on the installed camera on stolen mobile devices to see the face and surroundings of the thief.

12.6.5 End user authorizations and awareness

End users should not be able to remove important software or alter system files or log files. Therefore, they should not have (access to) the administrator password of their device. When users need to install software (which is a frequent requirement in practice), they could be given the right to do so, without giving them the administrator password of their device

BIOS passwords can be used on laptops and desktops to further increase security. BIOS setting should be applied to prevent booting from USB sticks or DVD players.

But the security issue with end user devices is not so much a matter of the device as it is a matter of the end user. Users need to be aware of common security guidelines including the possibility of social engineering, using strong passwords and knowing how to handle sensitive data.

PART IV

–

INFRASTRUCTURE MANAGEMENT

13

INFRASTRUCTURE
LIFECYCLE

Where the chapters in Part III were about technological infrastructure building blocks, this part IV is about the systems management processes based on the infrastructure lifecycle.

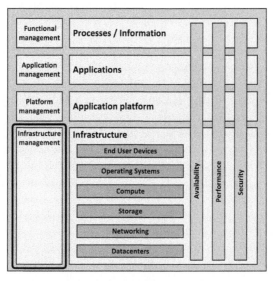

Figure 113: Infrastructure management

The infrastructure lifecycle encompasses the following steps:

- Determine the best deployment option for the infrastructure
- Purchasing infrastructure and services
- Build-up, testing and go-live
- Maintaining the infrastructure
- Deploying applications
- Decommissioning the infrastructure

All of these steps are described in the following chapters.

14

INFRASTRUCTURE DEPLOYMENT OPTIONS

14.1 Introduction

This chapter discusses how to select the best deployment option for infrastructure, based on requirements. Hosting options define *where* infrastructure is hosted, and deployment models define *how* infrastructure is deployed.

14.2 Hosting options

Infrastructure can be hosted on-premises, in a colocation, or the infrastructure can be outsourced.

With **on-premises hosting**, infrastructure components run on the premises of the organization using the infrastructure. This can be in the datacenter of an existing building, or in a dedicated, specially designed datacenter building.

As the datacenter is implemented in an organization owned building, the building must have enough space, an uninterruptable power supply (UPS), options to install sufficient cooling, fire prevention and detection, external redundant network capabilities with enough bandwidth, and sufficient floor loading capacity (see section 7.2.3.1 for more details on datacenter requirements).

Two major drawbacks of on-premises hosting are:

- Typically, on-premises datacenters don't scale well, as they are embedded in existing (office) buildings.

- As the organization owns and runs their own datacenter, it must have enough knowledge and staff available to manage the datacenter.

In contrast, a **colocation** is a third party dedicated datacenter where racks, floor space, and network bandwidth can be rented. A colocation provides power, cooling, and physical security, and hosts and connects customer owned infrastructure components. Colocation racks are empty – all infrastructure components must be provided and managed by the organization renting the colocation racks.

An organization can also decide to **outsource their entire infrastructure**. Full infrastructure outsourcing is a subcontracting service in which some third-party purchases, deploys, hosts, and manages the infrastructure, and performs its lifecycle management. The outsourcing is managed using Service Level Agreements and typically has a very rigid change management process. Outsourcing frees the organization from investing in hardware – only leaving operational cost. The outsourcing organization must have a demand organization and process in place in order to manage the outsourcing party, but it can be freed from internal infrastructure systems managers.

14.3 Enterprise infrastructure deployment

In a traditional enterprise infrastructure deployment, as shown in Figure 114, enterprise grade hardware delivers three infrastructure resources: compute, storage and network. These resources are implemented such that they provide high availability (using for instance redundant components, data replication, and RAID technology), high performance (using for instance caching, disk tiering, and large servers), and some security controls (like firewalls, network zoning, and IDS systems).

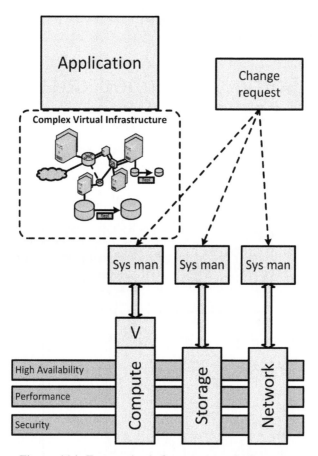

Figure 114: Enterprise infrastructure deployment

Most enterprise infrastructure deployments today implement compute virtualization to provide virtual machines.

Typically, each resource (compute, storage, and networking) is managed by a team of dedicated systems managers and changes are managed by a workflow based change process, where each systems manager is responsible to manually perform his part of the change.

Enterprise infrastructures can deliver complex virtual infrastructures to applications. The virtual infrastructure includes in most cases a number of virtual machines running Linux or Windows, virtual disks, replicated storage, automatic backup of data and redundant network connections. The virtual infrastructure is designed to meet the requirements of applications, and applications depend on the high availability, performance and security controls delivered by the infrastructure.

14.4 Software-defined datacenter - SDDC

A software-defined datacenter (SDDC) is an architecture in which all infrastructure resources – compute, storage and networking – are virtualized, and can be configured using software APIs.

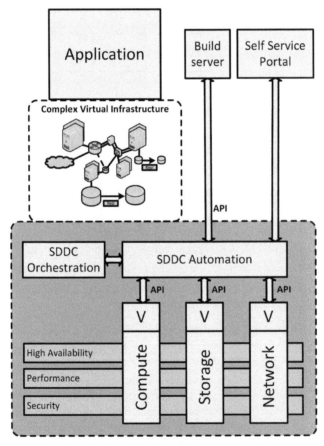

Figure 115: Software-defined datacenter

As shown in Figure 115, an SDDC is an extension on an enterprise infrastructure, where all resources are virtualized and managed by SDDC automation and orchestration software.

An SDDC is characterized by automation, orchestration, and abstraction of resources into software and code. By nature, code is more reliable than humans, which means that compared to a traditional datacenter, an SDDC is more secure and more agile. Changes are managed by an automated workflow, where an orchestrated change can lead to a number of automated changes in various resources.

An SDDC is the foundation for cloud computing. It enables developers, DevOps teams and systems managers to create and deploy new infrastructures using either a manual self-service portal, or a combination of a build server and APIs. It allows the user to request the desired infrastructure components, their sizing to meet performance demands, and their required availability; and automatically configures the SDDC components to deliver a secured infrastructure implementation. The SDDC software also provides tools for costing, logging, reporting, scaling (up and down), and decommissioning of the infrastructure resources.

Examples of SDDC automation and orchestration products are OpenStack's Horizon, IBM Cloud Orchestrator, and VMware vRealize.

An SDDC is not the solution for all problems – there are many applications that need a much more custom-designed infrastructure than the standard SDDC building blocks can deliver. Examples of these applications are SAP HANA, high performance databases, OLTP, high secure bank or stock trade transaction systems, and SCADA systems.

14.5 (Hyper) Converged Infrastructure

In a traditional infrastructure deployment, compute, storage and networking are deployed and managed independently, often based on components from multiple vendors. In a converged infrastructure, the compute, storage, and network components are designed, assembled, and delivered by one vendor and managed as one system, typically deployed in one or more racks. A converged infrastructure minimizes compatibility issues between servers, storage systems and network devices while reducing costs for cabling, cooling, power and floor space. Scaling up a converged infrastructure requires the deployment of additional racks.

Picture 46: Example of a converged system[93]

Where in a converged infrastructure the infrastructure is deployed as individual components in a rack, a hyperconverged infrastructure brings together the same components within a single server node.

A hyperconverged infrastructure comprises a large number of identical physical servers from one vendor with direct attached storage in the server and special software that manages all servers, storage, and networks as one cluster running virtual machines.

The technology is easy to expand on-demand, by adding nodes to the hyperconverged cluster.

Picture 47: Example of a hyperconverged system[94]

Hyperconverged systems are an ideal candidate for deploying VDI environments (see section 12.3.3), because storage is close to compute (as it is in the same box) and the solution scales well with the rise in the number of users.

A big advantage of converged and hyperconverged infrastructures is managing only one vendor, that provides hardware, firmware, and software. Vendors of hyperconverged infrastructures make all updates for compute, storage and networking available in one service pack and deploying these patches is typically much easier than deploying upgrades in all individual components in a traditional infrastructure deployment.

Drawbacks of converged and hyperconverged infrastructures are:

- Vendor lock-in – the solution is only beneficial if all infrastructure is from the same vendor.

- Scaling can only be done in fixed building blocks – if more storage is needed, compute must also be purchased. This can have a side effect: since some software licenses are based on the number of used CPUs or CPU cores, adding storage also means adding CPUs and hence leads to extra license costs.

14.6 Cloud computing

Cloud computing is one of the most important paradigm shifts in computing in recent years. Cloud computing is an outsourcing model, in which IT services are provided and paid based on actual on-demand use. Infrastructure as a Service (IaaS) is a specific service model of cloud computing.

14.6.1 Cloud definition

The most accepted definition of cloud computing is that of the National Institute of Standards and Technology (NIST)[95]:

Cloud computing is a model for enabling ubiquitous, convenient, on-demand network access to a shared pool of configurable computing resources that can be rapidly provisioned and released with minimal management effort or service provider interaction.

> *It is important to realize that cloud computing is not about technology; it is an outsourcing business model. It enables organizations to cut cost while at the same time focusing on their primary business – they should focus on running their business instead of running a mail server.*

Clouds are composed of five essential characteristics, four deployment models, and three service models.

14.6.2 Cloud characteristics

Essential cloud characteristics are:

- **On demand self-service** – As a result of optimal automation and orchestration, minimal systems management effort is needed to deploy systems or applications in a cloud environment. In most cases, end uses can configure, deploy, start and stop systems or applications on demand.

- **Rapid elasticity** – A cloud is able to quickly scale-up and scale-down resources. When temporarily more processing power or storage is needed, for instance as a result of a high-exposure business marketing campaign, a cloud can scale-up very quickly on demand. When demand decreases, cloud resources can rapidly scale down, leading to elasticity of resources.

- **Resource pooling** – Instead of providing each application with a fixed amount of processing power and storage, cloud computing provides applications with resources from a shared pool. This is typically implemented using virtualization technologies.

- **Measured service** – In a cloud environment the actual resource usage is measured and billed. There are no capital expenses, only operational expenses. This in contrast with the investments needed to build a traditional infrastructure.

- **Broad network access** – Capabilities are available over the network and accessed through standard mechanisms.

> *Be aware that when using off-premises cloud based solutions, the internet connection becomes a Single Point of Failure. Internet availability and internet performance becomes critical and redundant connectivity is therefore key.*

14.6.3 Cloud deployment models

A cloud can be implemented in one of four deployment models.

- A **public cloud** deployment is delivered by a cloud service provider, is accessible through the internet, and available to the general public. Because of their large customer base, public clouds largely benefit from economies of scale.

- A **private cloud** is operated solely for a single organization, whether managed internally or by a third-party, and hosted either on premises or external. It extensively uses virtualization and standardization to bring down systems management cost and staff.

- A **community cloud** is much like a private cloud, but shared with a community of organizations that have shared concerns (like compliance considerations). It may be owned, managed, and operated by one or more of the organizations in the community, a third party, or some combination, and it may exist on or off premises.

- In a **hybrid cloud** deployment, a service or application is provided by a combination of a public cloud, and a community cloud and/or a private cloud. This enables running generic services (like email servers) in the public cloud while hosting specialized services (like a business specific application) in the private or community cloud.

14.6.4 Cloud service models

Clouds can be delivered in one of three service models:

- **Software-as-a-Service (SaaS)** delivers full applications that can be used by business users, and need little or no configuration. Examples are Microsoft Office365, LinkedIn, Facebook, Twitter, and Salesforce.com.

- **Platform-as-a-Service (PaaS)** delivers a scalable, high available, open programming platform that can be used by developers to build bespoke applications that run on the PaaS platform. Examples are Microsoft Azure Cloud Service and Google App Engine.

- **Infrastructure-as-a-Service (IaaS)** delivers (virtual) machines, networking, and storage. The user needs to install and maintain the operating systems and the layers above that. Examples are Amazon Elastic Cloud (EC2 and S3) and Microsoft Azure IaaS.

The following figure shows the responsibility of the cloud provider for each service model.

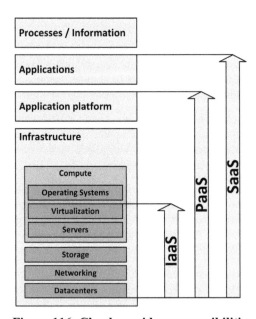

Figure 116: Cloud provider responsibilities

In the context of this book, IaaS is the most relevant service model.

14.6.5 Infrastructure as a Service (IaaS)

Infrastructure as a Service provides virtual machines, virtualized storage, virtualized networking and the systems management tools to manage them (see Figure 117).

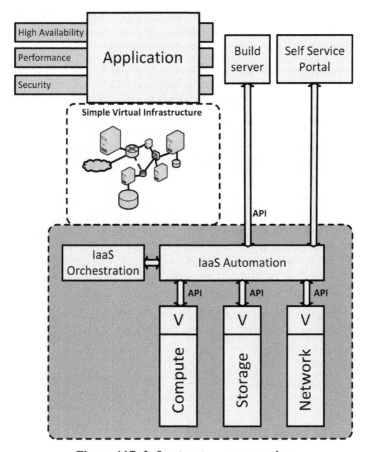

Figure 117: Infrastructure as a service

IaaS is typically based on cheap commodity white label hardware. The philosophy is to keep the cost down by allowing the hardware to fail every now and then. Failed components are either replaced or simply removed from the pool of available resources.

IaaS provides simple, highly standardized building blocks to applications. It does not provide high availability, guaranteed performance or extensive security controls. Consequently, applications running on IaaS should be robust to allow for failing hardware and should be horizontally scalable to increase performance.

In order to use IaaS, users must create and start a new server, and then install an operating system and their applications. Since the cloud provider only provides basic services, like billing and monitoring, the user is responsible for patching and maintaining the operating systems and application software.

Not all operating systems and applications can be used in an IaaS cloud; many software licenses prohibit the use of a fully scalable, virtual environment like IaaS, where it is impossible to know in advance on which machines software will run.

14.7 Infrastructure as code

Until recently, most servers, storage, and networks were configured manually. Systems managers installed operating systems from an installation medium, added libraries and applications, patched the system to the latest software versions, and configured the software to this specific installation. This approach is, however, slow, error prone, not easily repeatable, introduces variances in server configurations that should be equal, and makes the infrastructure very hard to maintain.

As an alternative, servers, storage, and networks can be created and configured automatically, a concept known as infrastructure as code.

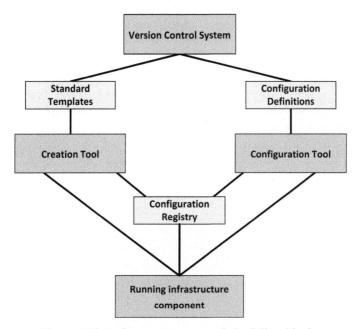

Figure 118: Infrastructure as code building blocks

Figure 118 shows the infrastructure as code building blocks. Tools to implement infrastructure as code include Puppet, Chef, Ansible, SaltStack, and Terraform. The process to create a new infrastructure component is as follows:

- Standard templates are defined that describe the basic setup of infrastructure components.

- Configurations of infrastructure components are defined in configuration definitions.

- New instances of infrastructure components can be created automatically by a creation tool, using the standard templates. This leads to a running, unconfigured infrastructure component.

- After an infrastructure component is created, the configuration tool automatically configures it, based on the configuration definitions, leading to a running, configured infrastructure component.

- When the new infrastructure component is created and configured, its properties, like DNS name and if a server is part of a load balancer pool, are automatically stored in the configuration registry.

- The configuration registry allows running instances of infrastructure to recognize and find each other and ensures all needed components are running.

- Configuration definition files and standard templates are kept in a version control system, which enables roll backs and rolling upgrades. This way, infrastructure is defined and managed the same way as software code.

The point of using configuration definition files and standard templates is not only that an infrastructure deployment can easily be implemented and rebuilt, but also that the configuration is easy to understand, test, and modify. Infrastructure as code ensures all infrastructure components that should be equal, are equal.

15

PURCHASING INFRASTRUCTURE AND SERVICES

Most large-scale IT projects require procurement of hardware, software, or services. The purchase process entails determining what is needed, getting an offer, ordering, delivery, warranty and renewal. Each of these topics is described in the following sections.

15.1 Determine what is needed

Before any purchase can be made, it must be crystal clear what is actually needed. In most cases, a Bill of Materials (BoM) is made that includes part numbers of all items. If allowed by the purchasing rules, I recommend working with suppliers to get the BoM right the first time. The supplier can verify that all needed items are on the BoM, including small items, like cables, connectors, and mounting brackets.

Apart from the bill of materials, typically a Statement of Work (SoW) is made. A SoW describes what the supplier will do, apart from delivering the goods. For example, should the supplier build up racks, place them in the datacenter, connect them to the power supply, label the cables, etc.? To mitigate the risk of misunderstanding, it must be clear from the start who does what.

The supplier can also have specific requirements. For instance, is a loading dock available to deliver goods to the datacenter, or is the elevator large enough to lift the equipment to the final destination? Do not forget to ask for these supplier requirements!

15.2 Getting an offer

In a large organization, the lead time for the internal procurement process can be several weeks, or even longer. This lead time is due to the time it takes to find a supplier, to handle contract issues and/or to get signatures from management to formally place the order. Often, after getting an offer from a supplier, procurement will try to get discounts, which could further delay the process. So, check as soon as possible how long this process will take, to adjust the project planning accordingly.

It must be noted that apart from the lead time to get an offer, it typically takes four to eight weeks for the supplier to deliver the goods.

15.3 Choice of suppliers

Most organizations use preferred suppliers for standard purchases. Having a small number of preferred suppliers makes the purchase process easier – contracts are already in place, and discounts can be negotiated because of large volume purchases.

In practice, organizations often choose for a predefined purchase policy for their software stack: when possible all software is either purchased from these suppliers, or built based on technology from these suppliers. An example is a *Microsoft and SAP unless* strategy. Using a standard product line from one supplier eases integration of components. The alternative is using a best of breed landscape, where each component is chosen based on the best quality or the most comprehensive feature set. Sometimes an organization chooses a standard software stack for commodity components (like office tools, file and web servers, CRM systems and email servers), and best of breed products for highly specific tasks, that are close to the core business processes.

With hardware, predefined choices are typically made as well. For instance, a policy could be to buy all network equipment from Cisco and all servers from HP. One reason for this is easier management of support contracts – when a hardware component fails, one telephone number to the supplier's support desk is all it takes to start the repair process. Another reason to limit the number of hardware vendors is to limit the knowledge needed in the organization to manage the components.

Having preferred suppliers can lead to a vendor lock-in; after some time, for practical reasons, it becomes unfeasible to change suppliers. If all hardware is from Dell, for instance, then changing to another supplier – like IBM – is often not good economics. The resulting lack of competition can lead to a higher price level in the long run and to a decrease in service levels.

15.4 Bidding and tendering

Getting an offer may involve a formal bidding process, also known as tendering. For instance, a company policy could state that any purchase over $250,000 requires a bidding process. If the cost of a product or service is over this threshold, a rigid purchase process must be followed. The reason for a bidding process can also be a regulation requirement; for instance, many public-sector organizations require a bidding process for large purchases.

In general, a bidding process comprises the following steps:

- **RFI – Request for Information**. In this step a relatively large group of suppliers is asked to inform the purchase department if they are capable of providing the required goods or service. This step involves writing an RFI document and giving the suppliers time to respond. An RFI process typically takes two to four weeks.

- **Short list**. In this step, based on the RFI responses, the purchase department creates a short list of suppliers that are most likely to be able to deliver the goods for a good price and with good service. A short list comprises typically three to five suppliers.

- **RFP – Request for Proposal**. In this step the suppliers in the short list are requested to make a proposal for the delivery. A full list of requirements is provided to them, including a draft statement of work. The suppliers typically get two to eight weeks to respond with an offer and a description of how they propose to provide the goods and/or services. There are often strict rules about the time table and the format in which the response must be given (for instance, all responses must be delivered in three-fold, before a certain date and time, in person to the head of purchasing).

- **Questions and clarification**. In this step, which is planned between the publication of the RFP and the supplier's responses, the suppliers are given the opportunity to ask questions about the RFP (in writing), in case something is unclear or in case there are multiple options to fulfill a requirement. Usually, these questions and the answers are communicated to all suppliers on the short list. Often, suppliers are hesitant to answer questions, because it reveals parts of their offer to other suppliers. Sometimes, the suppliers are requested to present their proposed solution in a face-to-face meeting before the offer is finalized.

- **Offer**. Typically, at the latest possible moment the suppliers provide the answers to the RFP, including an initial offer. The purchase department checks the offers on completeness (are all questions answered, is the prescribed procedure followed) and price.

- **Terms and conditions negotiations**. Next, the purchase department starts negotiations with the suppliers that provided the best response to the RFP. These are typically the top two suppliers. The terms and conditions of the delivery, including payment terms, warranty conditions, and discounts are discussed with them.

- **BAFO - Best and final offer**. In this step the preferred suppliers make a final price and SoW, which is their last chance to change the offer.

- **Award**. Based on the BAFO, the purchase department awards the supplier with the deal and the supplier can start the delivery.

As this list implies, this process can take a long time.

> *I have been in such a process several times, and it is very time and energy consuming, both for the supplier and the purchase department. As an example, at one occasion I was in a complex RFI/RFP process that took two years to complete!*

15.5 Ordering

Ordering is typically done by the purchasing department. They place the order and monitor the delivery time. When the order includes multiple delivery dates, a choice can be made to deliver the goods in partial deliveries or to deliver the goods in one delivery, but at a later date.

Because the delivery time is often weeks after the purchase order is placed, it makes sense to start ordering the goods as early as possible in the project.

15.6 Delivery

When the order is placed, after some time, the goods are delivered. For hardware, it is good practice to inform the department or person that has to physically receive the goods well in advance. Beware that the person that physically receives the goods, is not always the one formally accepting the delivery.

The formal acceptance must be done by someone who is entitled to do so, often someone from the project that asked for the goods, or someone from the purchasing department. Before signing for delivery, check the boxes for any damage and check for completeness of the delivery!

15.7 Warranty

Typically, a warranty period is one year for hardware and two months for projects. During the warranty period, defects will be fixed without additional cost. For projects, most of the time the project team will be dismantled after warranty period as well.

15.8 Renewal

When purchased goods are used for some time, they might need renewal. Hardware is often used for three to five years before it is replaced, and software typically has releases every few years. Service contracts are also often agreed upon for a fixed number of years.

Sometimes a renewal of the hardware, software licenses, or service contracts leads to a new purchase process.

Systems management should have a Life Cycle Management (LCM) process implemented to handle the renewal, as each piece of hardware and software has its own life cycle. Renewal of service contracts is often managed by the purchase department.

16

DEPLOYING THE INFRASTRUCTURE

After the infrastructure is purchased and delivered, it needs to be assembled and tested before it can be put into production.

16.1 Assembling the infrastructure

The first step in deploying a new infrastructure is assembling the infrastructure. After the datacenter is set-up to host hardware, the compute, operating system, networking, and storage must be set up. Finally, systems management tools should be installed.

Infrastructure can be assembled using the following checklist:

- **Build up the physical datacenter room**, including raised floors, uninterruptable power supply, cooling facilities, fire prevention and detection, and physical security.

- **Install redundant power cabling** using separate cables and fuses for every rack.

- **Install racks**. Ensure enough room is available to walk around the racks and to open all doors. Typically, separate racks are installed for network, storage, and compute components. Check if the computer floor can still be opened (no racks placed on multiple tiles).

- **Test the facilities.** Test alarms that should respond to a power failure or heating, ventilating and air conditioning (HVAC) failure. Perform a visual check of the facilities. Ensure cables are properly fixed in the racks and labelled. Measure the airflow, temperature, and humidity and test the physical security controls.

- **Install the server, networking, and storage hardware** in the racks. Ensure not too much equipment is placed in one rack to prevent racks from falling over, using too much power, or obstructing cooling air flow. Ensure cabling is properly installed and labelled. Ensure equipment can be sled out of the racks without damaging cabling. Check if maintenance on a component can be done without interfering with the other components.

- **Allow for a burn-in period** to ensure the equipment is not "dead on arrival" (DOA) or fails within the first day. Switch the equipment off and on several times to see if it doesn't break.

- **Check the power and cooling usage** of the equipment. Are they within the designed and specified range?

- **Configure the infrastructure components.** Configure routers, switches, and storage LUNs and install virtualization and operating systems, based on technical designs. Configure DNS, NTP and security configurations like network zoning and firewalls. Perform a basic test to check network connectivity and storage availability.

- **Install systems management tools** like backup and recovery, monitoring, logging, and IDS/IPS.

- **Test systems management processes.** Create incidents, create and handle changes, etc.

- **Provide as-built documentation** to the systems managers. Populate the Configuration Management Database (CMDB).

16.2 Testing the infrastructure

After assembling the infrastructure, it should be tested. Testing is done based on a test scope, and is performed in various test stages.

16.2.1 Test scope

Each test type has a predefined scope:

- **Functional tests** ensure the infrastructure delivers the required functionality. Is it possible to run applications on the implemented infrastructure? Can applications use compute resources and do they have access to storage? Can applications communicate with each other, to external parties, and with the end users?

- **Performance tests**, like load, stress, and endurance tests prove the infrastructure has enough resources to run applications with the required performance.

- **Security tests**, like penetration tests and vulnerability scans prove security controls are in place and are functioning as designed.

- **Availability** of the infrastructure can be tested by physical actions, like pulling cables from infrastructure components, or unexpectedly rebooting machines. A failover test, a fallback test and a disaster recovery test should be performed, and backup and recovery processes and disaster recovery plans should be tested.

16.2.2 Test stages

Testing the infrastructure is often done in a number of stages.

A **unit test** checks if individual infrastructure components, like servers, networking components, storage, and shared services meet the requirements, both on a functional and a non-functional level. Part of this test is for instance a redundancy test, where dual power supplies are tested by removing one of them from a running component.

In a **system integration test** the combination of components is tested including their interfaces. A system integration test checks both functional and non-functional requirements.

During a **fallback test** the fallback from the main datacenter to the secondary datacenter is checked on a technical level.

Migration test activities start when an application along with its database and other middleware components are installed and configured on the infrastructure. Migration testing ensures applications are installed without errors and data from previous systems can be migrated to the new system as designed.

An **acceptance test** is the final check of the delivered infrastructure and consists mainly of verifying that all tests are performed and that defects found in previous tests are either solved or accepted. The acceptance test leads to a discharge of the project for the delivery of the infrastructure.

16.3 Go live scenarios

There are a number of scenarios that can be used to put the new infrastructure in production as the replacement for an existing system – to "Go Live":

- **Big Bang** – In the big bang scenario, at a set time, the existing system is switched off and the new system is immediately put in production, possibly after a short data migration run. This is the riskiest scenario because it may be impossible to roll back to the old system after the system is live for some time, and because downtime can occur when something goes wrong during the switchover.

- **Parallel changeover** – In this scenario, both the new and the existing system run simultaneously for some time (typically weeks). This allows for testing the new system on both functionality and non-functional attributes, and ensuring it works with live production data before switching off the existing system. As both systems are running and processing data, switching back is possible at any time, minimizing risk. A big disadvantage of this scenario is the cost of maintaining both systems and the possible extra work to keep both systems in sync. Also, many system designs don't allow running two systems in parallel, for instance, if the system has many data interfaces with other systems.

- **Phased changeover** – In a phased scenario, individual components or functionalities of the existing system are taken over by the new system, one by one. This reduces risk, as the changeover can be done gradually and controlled. This scenario can be quite costly, since typically many interfaces between the existing and the new system must be created and maintained. These new interfaces introduce new risk to the scenario, as they must be tested extensively and could fail in production. Also, the existing system must be kept online until the last component or functionality is moved to the new system, which can lead to high cost.

While a big bang scenario has the highest risk, in practice, it is most often used, as the scenario is the least complex to execute, and because the risk is limited to the changeover moment, when the project team is at full strength and ready to jump in if anything fails.

The go-live should be very well prepared. After the go-live scenario is determined, a step-by-step plan must be created describing each step in the scenario in detail. This plan must be reviewed, tested and improved multiple times, well in advance of the go-live date to eliminate possible surprises and to minimize risk. The scenario should include intermediate tests and multiple "go/no go" milestones, where the go-live can be aborted if anything unexpected happens. The plan should also have a defined point of no return – a go decision at this point means there is no way back to the old system. Either because there is no time left to move back to the original situation, or because an irreversible step is taken (like an update of a critical data model).

At the go-live date, high alert is needed from the project team and from the systems managers, service desk and senior management to be able to fix any issues that might arise.

After the new system is live, on-site support should be available for some predefined time to fix any issues that may arise after the system is live; issues the service desk cannot be responsible for yet.

17

MAINTAINING THE INFRASTRUCTURE

While a typical infrastructure project takes a couple of months to complete, the infrastructure is often used in operation for many years, sometimes even decades. During its lifecycle, the infrastructure needs to be maintained to ensure reliable and secure operations.

17.1 Systems management processes

Systems management processes, like incident management, change management and configuration management can be implemented using one of the well-known and published frameworks and methods. While the full description of these frameworks is out of scope of this book, we briefly present the three most used ones: COBIT, ITIL and DevOps. Many books exist on these and other methods and frameworks. Some suggested reading is given in the appendix.

17.1.1 COBIT

Control Objectives for Information and Related Technology (COBIT) provides a structure for setting up IT Governance, an IT organization, and IT architecture. COBIT describes thirty-four IT processes. Within these processes, management objectives and associated measures, performance indicators, and maturity levels are described.

COBIT is focused on management issues and less on the detailed design of IT processes, such as in ITIL.

COBIT is a framework created by ISACA. The most recent version is COBIT 5, published in 2012.

17.1.2 ITIL

The IT Infrastructure Library (ITIL) is the most used approach to implementing systems management processes. ITIL entails the full life cycle of IT management, covering the entire IT organization and all supporting processes needed to deliver services to the end user. It describes processes like incident management, change management, problem management, release management, and capacity management.

ITIL is a registered trademark of the United Kingdom's Office of Government Commerce (OGC) – now part of the Cabinet Office. The current version is ITILv3, published in 2011.

17.1.3 DevOps for infrastructure

DevOps is a contraction of the terms "developer" and "system operator". DevOps teams consist of developers, testers and application systems managers, and each team is responsible for developing and running one or more business applications or services.

The whole team is responsible for developing, testing, and running their application(s). In case of incidents with the applications under their responsibility, every team member of the DevOps team is responsible to help fix the problem. The DevOps philosophy is *"If you built it, you run it"*.

While DevOps is typically used for teams developing and running functional software, the same philosophy can be used to develop and run an infrastructure platform that functional DevOps teams can use. In an infrastructure DevOps team, infrastructure developers design, test, and build the infrastructure platforms and manage their lifecycle; infrastructure operators keep the platform running smoothly, fix incidents, and apply small changes.

17.2 Monitoring

Monitoring continuously inspects IT components for events like error conditions or signs of (upcoming) failures, like a disk with only little free space left, unusually high CPU utilization, or extreme network bandwidth usage.

Monitoring systems like Nagios, Zabbix, HP Operations Manager, and BMC Patrol provide dashboards with overviews of an entire infrastructure landscape.

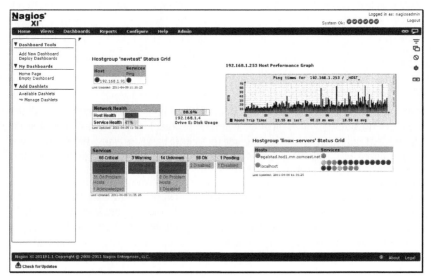

Figure 119: Example of a Nagios dashboard[96]

Monitoring systems can have alarms configured that trigger if a certain threshold is reached. The monitoring system can forward these alarms to systems managers, who can take action to fix the event that led to the alarm, preferably before the end users notice anything unusual.

17.3 Management using SNMP

The Simple Network Management Protocol (SNMP) can be used to remotely change or update configurations and collect statistics and performance information of infrastructure components. Devices that support SNMP include routers, switches, servers, workstations, printers, and even some racks and power strips.

SNMP uses a management/agent model. The agent on the monitored device communicates with the management server (the Network Management System

– NMS) that collects information from all attached devices. An agent has local knowledge of the system it resides on, and translates that information to the SNMP protocol. The NMS monitors and controls managed devices via the agents.

The SNMP protocol allows reading counters and statistics over the network to an NMS, which in turn show them to systems managers using values or graphs. This reading of values is done in regular polling intervals (like every 30 seconds).

SNMP also supports so-called *traps*. A trap is an alarm that is sent to the NMS when a certain value in a device exceeds its configured default (for instance when the network load exceeds 80%). Systems managers can immediately take action when a SNMP trap occurs.

Security in SNMP is implemented using a shared secret string (called the community name) which provides access to agent functionality. By default, the SNMP community strings are set to 'public' and 'private' for reading and writing configurations respectively. This should be changed immediately after a new installation.

Since SNMP version 1 and 2 do not implement encryption, they are considered insecure. Unfortunately, these versions are still used in many devices. SNMP version 3 provides strong security features by implementing encryption, strong authentication, and integrity measures.

17.4 Logging

Most infrastructure components generate log data. Examples are network routers and switches, operating systems, applications, databases, firewalls, and intrusion detection systems.

Log data from these sources can be used to correlate events and identify sources of application issues. Log data can also be used to identify trends to predict or even prevent unavailability, or to find security vulnerabilities or security breaches.

Logging usually provides a wealth of information about what happened on infrastructure components.

```
Sep  8 20:42:52 ubuntu-light rtkit-daemon[1698]: Supervising 3 threads of 1 processes of 1 u
Sep  8 20:42:52 ubuntu-light pulseaudio[1695]: [alsa-sink-Intel ICH] alsa-sink.c: ALSA woke
ally nothing to write!
Sep  8 20:42:52 ubuntu-light pulseaudio[1695]: [alsa-sink-Intel ICH] alsa-sink.c: Most likel
report this issue to the ALSA developers.
Sep  8 20:42:52 ubuntu-light pulseaudio[1695]: [alsa-sink-Intel ICH] alsa-sink.c: We were wo
vail() returned 0 or another value < min_avail.
Sep  8 20:42:52 ubuntu-light rtkit-daemon[1698]: Successfully made thread 1781 of process 17
Sep  8 20:42:52 ubuntu-light rtkit-daemon[1698]: Supervising 4 threads of 2 processes of 1 u
Sep  8 20:42:52 ubuntu-light pulseaudio[1781]: [pulseaudio] pid.c: Daemon already running.
Sep  8 20:42:53 ubuntu-light ntpdate[1138]: adjust time server 91.189.89.198 offset -0.45736
Sep  8 20:42:55 ubuntu-light dbus[404]: [system] Activating service name='org.freedesktop.UD
Sep  8 20:42:55 ubuntu-light udisksd[1848]: udisks daemon version 2.1.3 starting
Sep  8 20:42:55 ubuntu-light dbus[404]: [system] Successfully activated service 'org.freedes
Sep  8 20:42:55 ubuntu-light udisksd[1848]: Acquired the name org.freedesktop.UDisks2 on the
Sep  8 20:42:57 ubuntu-light dbus[404]: [system] Activating service name='org.blueman.Mechan
Sep  8 20:42:58 ubuntu-light blueman-mechanism: Starting blueman-mechanism
Sep  8 20:42:58 ubuntu-light dbus[404]: [system] Successfully activated service 'org.blueman
Sep  8 20:42:58 ubuntu-light blueman-mechanism: loading Ppp
Sep  8 20:42:58 ubuntu-light blueman-mechanism: loading RfKill
Sep  8 20:42:58 ubuntu-light blueman-mechanism: loading Network
Sep  8 20:42:58 ubuntu-light blueman-mechanism: loading Config
Sep  8 20:43:01 ubuntu-light NetworkManager[754]: <info> (eth0): IP6 addrconf timed out or f
Sep  8 20:43:01 ubuntu-light NetworkManager[754]: <info> Activation (eth0) Stage 4 of 5 (IPv
Sep  8 20:43:01 ubuntu-light NetworkManager[754]: <info> Activation (eth0) Stage 4 of 5 (IPv
```

Figure 120: Part of a log file from a Linux operating system

Logging often generates large amounts of data every day. The level of logging (to what detail logging is generated and hence the size of the logs) is usually configurable.

Logs may be directed to files and stored on disk, or directed as a network stream to a log collector system. Various commercial and open source tools can be used to analyze log data, like Splunk and Logstash.

In most cases, log analysis is performed for the following reasons:

- Compliance with security policies, law, or regulation
- System troubleshooting
- Forensics
- Security incident response

To be able to correlate logs from various sources, timestamps of log entries must match exactly. Therefore, it is important to have a time synchronization system like NTP (see 8.2.8.4) in place on all devices.

Since the amount of log data is typically very large, and datacenters are becoming denser, log analysis is increasingly moving into the Big Data realm. Big data reporting tools can be used to create overviews and to find anomalies.

Analyzing log files is something fundamentally different than monitoring. Both have different goals. Monitoring systems, like SNMP based systems, are real-time systems. As soon as something happens an alarm goes off. Log files are meant for analyzing situations afterwards.

Examining log files can also reveal performance issues, especially clues about bad behaving applications.

I once worked in a team helping a customer improve the performance of a web server. We found in the log files that the web application tried to open a non-existing file every time the home page was presented – in our case many thousand times a day.

Removing that specific call to the non-existing file from the HTML source improved the web server's performance immediately!

17.5 Capacity management

Capacity Management ensures the timely availability of sufficient infrastructural capacity to process, transport, and store data now and in the future. Capacity Management tries to avoid unexpected hardware purchases through the better use of available resources and providing sufficient lead time to extend the infrastructure. In order to perform capacity management, the following input is needed:

- **Monitoring of resources** to detect trends – for instance, reduced free disk capacity provides insight in when to purchase or free-up disk capacity.

- **Business plans** to anticipate on business changes that might have impact on the infrastructure – for instance a marketing campaign during the summer time could justify temporary adding server capacity.

- **Developments in technology**, for instance the possibility of upgrading servers when a higher capacity server blade becomes available.

18

DEPLOYING
APPLICATIONS

18.1 DTAP environments

In most organizations, the infrastructure not only hosts the production systems, but also development, test and acceptance systems. These DTAP (Development, Test, Acceptance, Production) environments are used in the software development process. In the development environment, new software is developed or existing software is modified. In the test environment, the software is tested by independent testers and in the acceptance environment the software is accepted by a delegation of the user population. When all tests are successful, the software is deployed in the production environment.

While the term DTAP suggests using four environments (or stages), in practice, often more environments are used. A real-world DTAP environment could contain a:

- **Sandbox** environment - The sandbox environment is setup as a pre-development environment, where preliminary tests can be performed on new technology or solutions. No service level agreements are made for this environment, as the availability, performance, and security cannot be guaranteed. The environment is not part of the backup process, as the usage of the environment is temporarily by default. After testing new technology or a new solution, the sandbox environment will be erased to allow for new tests.

- **Development** environment - The development environment is used to develop new software and configurations. Development leads to a new software release.

- **Test** environment - The test environment is used to functionally test new releases.

- **User Acceptance test** environment - This environment is used to allow end users to functionally test new releases.

- **Non-Functional acceptance** environment – This environment is setup to be identical to the production environment to enable reliable performance, availability, and security testing.

- **Hot Fix** environment - The Hot Fix environment contains a functional copy of the production environment and is used to find fixes for production problems and to test these fixes before they are deployed to the production environment.

- **Production** environment - The production environment runs the actual software for end users. Since the system is live and serves many users, both internally and externally, changes in the production environment are only allowed as a result of a strict and formal change process through the DTAP stages. The production environment does not contain any unnecessary tools like compilers, editors, and other utilities.

Apart from these DTAP environments, a **Systems Management environment** is often used to manage the other environments.

18.2 Blue-Green deployment

A hot fix environment can be used in conjunction with the production environment in a so-called blue-green deployment, where both environments switch roles when new software is deployed. Let's call the production environment the blue environment and the hot fix environment the green environment.

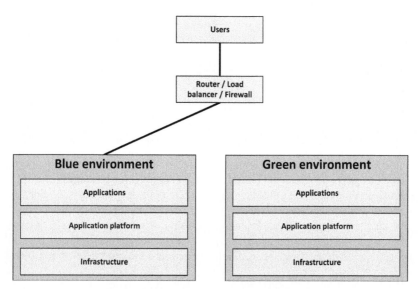

Figure 121: Blue-Green deployment

At any time one of the two environments, let's say the blue environment, is live and a new software release is tested in the green environment. Once the software is working in the green environment, the routing is switched so that all incoming requests go to the green environment; it is now the production environment – the blue one is now idle and can be considered the new hot fix environment. If anything goes wrong, routing can be switched back to the blue environment.

Once the green environment is live and stable, the blue environment can be used as the staging environment for the final testing step for the next deployment. When deploying the following release, a switch is made from green to blue in the same way it was done from blue to green in the previous cycle. That way, both green and blue environments are regularly cycling between live, previous version (for rollback) and staging for the next version.

18.3 Continuous Delivery

Continuous delivery speeds up the time and effort it takes to deploy changed and new applications in production. The primary goal of continuous delivery is to make software deployments painless, predictable, low-risk, routine events that can be performed at any time, on demand.

The traditional way of developing software led to large implementations that had to be scheduled long in advance. Continuous delivery, on the other hand, allows performing multiple software deployments per day with one mouse click – from a long-term release planning and maintenance weekends to a deployment button that can be touched any time a software change is made.

To enable continuous delivery, automation is key. Tooling is needed and pushing software from development via a testing stage to production must be fully automated. A deployment pipeline is a key part of continuous delivery.

In the deployment pipeline, every change in the software version control system triggers a process which creates deployable packages and runs automated unit tests and other validations such as static code analysis. Because the outcome of the tests is known in a few minutes, developers get feedback they can use to fix any deficiencies quickly. After the unit tests, a more comprehensive automated acceptance test is run. Once all packages pass all the automated tests, they are available for on-demand release by the business owner of the software.

19

DECOMMISSIONING INFRASTRUCTURES

At the end of its lifecycle, infrastructure must be decommissioned. The decommissioning process can be broken down into preparation, execution and cleanup activities.

19.1 Preparation

Preparation for the decommissioning process comprises the following steps:

- Prepare a plan (interview specialists, plan a date)

- Communicate that the system will go down well in advance

- Check for interdependencies with other systems and remove any dependency

- Determine if and how long backup or archived data must be retained. Remember, data retention for compliance purposes is mandatory!

- Check if the system is really not used anymore (firewall logs can be helpful here, as they show any network communications with the system)

- Ask for vendor assistance if needed

- Inform the floor manager of the datacenter

19.2 Execution

The decommissioning process is executed by the following steps:

- Create a final backup
- Remove the system from the monitoring and alerting system
- Remove the system from the backup schedule
- Close the network communications, for instance by disabling firewall rules related to the system, or by manually removing network cables
- Switch off the system and stand by to redeploy it immediately if any dependency pops up
- Physically remove hardware
- Remove cabling and patching related to the system

19.3 Cleanup

After the decommissioning, the following steps are performed to cleanup:

- Check if no SLAs and licenses are active and paid for decommissioned systems
- Remove firewall rules that are no longer needed
- Remove unneeded installation software from the software vault
- Update documentation and remove redundant documentation
- Wipe all data and/or destroy data media like disks and tapes that were part of the decommissioned infrastructure
- Remove databases, database schemes, or database tables used by the decommissioned system
- Remove DNS records and administered IP addresses
- Remove all user credentials and system roles from the Identity and Access Management system
- Inform the finance department that the system is decommissioned (because of bookkeeping)
- Remove all decommissioned components from the CMDB database

PART V - APPENDICES

Abbreviations

Abbreviation	Meaning
ADSL	Asymmetric Digital Subscriber Line
AES	Advanced Encryption Standard
ALU	Arithmetic Logic Unit
AMD	Advanced Micro Devices
API	Application Programming Interface
ARM	Advanced RISC Machine
ASHRAE	American Society of Heating, Refrigerating and Air-conditioning Engineers
ASIC	Application-specific Integrated Circuit
ATA	Advanced Technology Attachment
ATM	Asynchronous Transfer Mode
b	Bit
B	Byte (8 bits)
BAFO	Best and Final Offer
BCM	Business Continuity Management
BCP	Business Continuity Management
BGP	Border Gateway Protocol
BI	Business Intelligence
BIND	Berkeley Internet Name Domain
BIOS	Basic Input/Output system
BOOTP	Bootstrap Protocol
BSD	Berkeley Software Distribution
BSOD	Blue Screen Of Death
BTU	British Thermal Unit
BYOD	Bring Your Own Device
CCITT	Comité Consultatif International Télégraphique et

Abbreviation	Meaning
	Téléphonique
ccNUMA	Cache-coherent Non Uniform Memory Access
CCTV	Closed-circuit television
ccUMA	Cache-coherent Uniform Memory Access
CDN	Content Distribution Network
CDP	Continuous Data Protection
CERT	Computer Emergency Response Team
CFCC	Coupling Facility Control Code
CIA	Confidentiality, Integrity and Availability
CICS	Customer Information Control System
CIDR	Classless Inter-Domain Routing
CIFS	Common Internet File System
CLI	Command-Line Interface
CMDB	Configuration Management Database
CNA	Converged Network Adapters
COBIT	Control Objectives for Information and Related Technology
COP	Coefficient Of Performance
CP	Central processors
CPC	Central Processor Complex
CPU	Central Processing Unit
CRAC	Computer Room Air Conditioner
CRAH	Computer Room Air Handler
CRM	Customer Relationship Management
CSMA/CD	Carrier Sense Multiple Access with Collision Detection
DAS	Direct Attached Storage
DASD	Direct Attached Storage Device
DAT	Digital Audio Tape
DBMS	Database Management System
DDoS	Distributed Denial of Service
DDS	Digital Data Storage
DES	Data Encryption Standard
DHCP	Dynamic Host Configuration Protocol
DLM	Distributed Lock Management
DLT	Digital Linear Tape
DMA	Direct Memory Access
DMI	Direct Media Interface
DMZ	De-Militarized Zone
DNS	Domain Name System

Abbreviation	Meaning
DNSSEC	DNS Security Extensions
DOA	Dead on arrival
DoS	Denial of Service
DRAM	Dynamic Random-Access Memory
DRP	Disaster Recovery Planning
DSL	Digital Subscriber Line
DTAP	Development, Test, Acceptance, Production
EBCDIC	Extended Binary Coded Decimal Interchange Code
EDGE	Enhanced Data rates for GSM Evolution
EEPROM	Electrically erasable programmable read-only memory
EER	Energy Efficiency Ratio
ENIAC	Electronic Numerical Integrator And Computer
EPROM	Erasable Programmable Read Only Memory
ERP	Enterprise Resource Planning
ESCON	Enterprise Systems CONnection
ESD	Electro Static Discharge
ETL	Extraction, Transformation and Load
FAT	File Allocation Table
FC	Fibre Channel
FCoE	Fibre Channel over Ethernet
FICON	Fiber Connection
FLOPS	Floating Point Operations Per Second
FSB	Front Side Bus
FTP	File Transfer Protocol
Gb	Giga bit
GB	Giga Byte
GB/s	Gigabyte per second
Gbit/s	Gigabit per second
GFS	Grandfather-Father-Son
GHZ	Giga Hertz
GNU	GNU's Not Unix
GPRS	General packet radio service
GPU	Graphics Processing Unit
GSM	Global System for Mobile Communications
GUI	Graphical User Interface
HBA	Host Bus Adapter
HCI	Hyperconverged infrastructure
HIDS	Host-based Intrusion Detection System

Abbreviation	Meaning
HSDPA	High Speed Downlink Packet Access
HSM	Hierarchical Storage Management
HVAC	Heating, Ventilation, and Air Conditioning
Hz	Hertz
I/O	Input/Output
IaaS	Infrastructure as a Service
IAM	Identity and Access Management
IC	Integrated Circuit
ICA	Independent Computing Architecture
ICMP	Internet Control Message Protocol
IDE	Integrated Drive Electronics
IDS	Intruder Detection System
IDSN	Integrated Services Digital Network
IFL	Integrated Facility for Linux
IGRP	Interior Gateway Routing Protocol
ILM	Information Lifecycle Management
IMP	Interface Message Processors
IOPS	Input-Output Per Second
IP	Internet Protocol
IRQ	Interrupt ReQuest
ISA	Industry Standard Architecture
ISDN	Integrated Services Digital Network
ISP	Internet Service Provider
ISPF	Interactive System Productivity Facility
IT	Information Technology
ITIL	IT Infrastructure Library
JCL	Job Control language
kb	Kilobit (1024 bits)
kB	Kilobyte (1024 bytes)
kHz	Kilo Hertz
KVM	Keyboard, Video, Mouse
kW	Kilowatt
LAN	Local Area Network
LCM	Life Cycle Management
LDAP	Lightweight Directory Access Protocol
LDOM	Logical Domain
LED	Light-Emitting Diode
LPAR	Logical Partition

Abbreviation	Meaning
LTE	Long Term Evolution
LTO	Linear Tape-Open
LUN	Logical Unit Number
LXC	Linux Containers
MAC	Media Access Control
Mb	Megabit
MB	Megabyte
MB/s	Megabyte per second
Mbit/s	Megabit per second
MDM	Mobile Device Management
MER	Main Equipment Room
MFP	Multi-Functional Printer
MHZ	Mega Hertz
MIB	Management Information Base
MIPS	Million Instructions Per Second
MLC	Multi-Level Cell
MMF	Multi-Mode Fiber
MMU	Memory Management Unit
MPLS	Multi-Protocol Label Switching
ms	Milli-seconds
MTBF	Mean Time Between Failures
MTTR	Mean Time To Repair
MTU	Maximum Transmission Unit
MVS	Multiple Virtual Storage
MW	Megawatt
NAC	Network Access Control
NAS	Network Attached Storage
NAT	Network Address Translation
NCP	Network Control Protocol
NFR	Non-functional Requirement
NFS	Network File System
NFS	Network Interface Controller
NFV	Network Function Virtualization
NIDS	Network-based Intrusion Detection System
NL-SAS	Near-Line Serial Attached SCSI
nm	Nanometer
NTFS	New Technology File System
NTP	Network Time Protocol

Abbreviation	Meaning
NUMA	Non Uniform Memory Access
OC	Optical Carrier
ODS	Operational Data Store
OEM	Original Equipment Manufacturer
OS	Operating System
OSD	On Screen Display
OSI	Open Systems Interconnection
OSPF	Open Shortest Path First
PaaS	Platform as a Service
PB	Petabyte
PC	Personal Computer
PCH	Platform Controller Hub
PCI	Peripheral Component Interconnect
PCIe	Peripheral Component Interconnect Express
PHP	PHP: Hypertext Preprocessor
PIN	Personal Identification Number
PKI	Public Key Infrastructure
POF	Plastic Optical Fiber
POP	Point-Of-Presence
PPP	Point-to-point Protocol
PPTP	Point-to-point Tunneling Protocol
PROM	Programmable read-only memory
PSTN	Public Switched Telephone Network
PSU	Power Supply Unit
PU	Processing Unit
PUE	Power Usage Effectiveness
PXE	Preboot Execution Environment
PXE	Quarter-inch cartridge
QoS	Quality of Service
RADIUS	Remote Authentication Dial In User Service
RAID	Redundant Arrays of Independent Disks
RBAC	Role Based Access Control
RDP	Remote Desktop Protocol
RDS	Remote Desktop Service
RFI	Request For Information
RFID	Radio-frequency identification
RFP	Request For Proposal
RIP	Routing Information Protocol

Abbreviation	Meaning
RISC	Reduced instruction set computer
ROM	Read Only Memory
RPM	Revolutions Per Minute
RPO	Recovery Point Objective
RS-232	Recommended Standard 232
RSTP	Rapid Spanning Tree Protocol
RTO	Recovery Time Objective
RTOS	Real-time Operating System
SaaS	Software as a Service
SAN	Storage Area Network
SAP	System Assisted Processor
SAS	Serial Attached SCSI
SATA	Serial ATA
SBC	Server Based Computing
SCADA	Supervisory Control And Data Acquisition
SCSI	Small Computer System Interface
SDC	Software Defined Compute
SDDC	Software Defined Datacenter
SDH	Synchronous Digital Hierarchy
SDLT	Super Digital Linear Tape
SDN	Software Defined Networking
SDS	Software Defined Storage
SDSL	Symmetric Digital Subscriber Line
SEER	Seasonal Energy Efficiency Ratio
SER	Sub Equipment Room
SFTP	Secure File Transfer Protocol
SIMM	Single In-line Memory Module
SLC	Single Level Cell
SMB	Server Message Block
SMF	Single Mode Fiber
SMP	Symmetric Multi-Processor
SMS	Short Message Service
SNMP	Simple Network Management Protocol
SoC	System on a Chip
SONET	Synchronous Optical Networking
SoW	Statement of Work
SPARC	Scalable Processor ARChitecture
SPEC	Standard Performance Evaluation Corporation

Abbreviation	Meaning
SPOF	Single Point of Failure
SRAM	Static random-access memory
SSD	Solid State Disk
SSH	Secure Shell
SSL	Secure Sockets Layer
SSO	Single Sign-On
STP	Spanning Tree Protocol / Shielded Twisted Pair
TB	Terabyte
TCB	Trusted Computing Base
TCP	Transmission Control Protocol
TFTP	Trivial File Transfer Protocol
TIA	Telecommunications Industry Association
TKIP	Temporal Key Integrity Protocol
TLS	Transport Layer Security
TMR	Triple Modular Redundancy
TPC	Transaction Processing Performance Council
TSO	Time Sharing Option
TTL	Time to Live
TTY	Teletype
UDP	User Datagram Protocol
UFS	Union File System
UMA	Uniform Memory Access
UMTS	Universal Mobile Telecommunications System
UPS	Uninterruptable Power Supply
USB	Universal Serial Bus
UTP	Unshielded Twisted Pair
VDI	Virtual Desktop Infrastructure
VDSL	Very High Digital Subscriber Line
VGA	Video Graphics Array
VLAN	Virtual LAN
VLSM	Variable-Length Subnet Masking
VM	Virtual Machine
VMDK	Virtual Machine Disk
VMM	Virtual Machine Monitor
VMS	Virtual Memory System
VoIP	Voice over IP
VoLTE	Voice over LTE
VPAR	Virtual Partition

Abbreviation	Meaning
VPN	Virtual Private Network
VTL	Virtual Tape Library
VxFS	Veritas File System
VXLAN	Virtual Extensible LAN
WAN	Wide Area Network
WDM	Wavelength-division multiplexing
WLAN	Wireless Local Area Network
WLAN	Wi-Fi Protected Access
WPAR	Working Partitions
WWN	World Wide Name
WWW	World Wide Web

IS 2010.4 Curriculum reference matrix

IS 2010.4 based courses offer an introduction to IT infrastructure issues for students majoring in Information Systems. It gives the students the knowledge and skills that they need for communicating effectively with professionals whose special focus is on hardware and systems software technology and for designing organizational processes and software solutions that require in-depth understanding of the IT infrastructure capabilities and limitations.

This book covers all topics that are part of the IS 2010.4 curriculum. Many universities worldwide already use this book in their IS 2010.4 based courses.

In the matrix provided in this appendix, the relation between the IS 2010.4 curriculum topics and sections in this book is specified.

Topic	Section in this book
Core computing system architecture concepts	2 2.1
Core computing system organizing structures	2.2 2.3 2.4 2.5
Core technical components of computer-based systems	10.2
Role of IT infrastructure in a modern organization	1
Operating systems	11
Core operating systems functionality	11.2
Internal organization of an operating system	11.2
Types of devices that require and use operating systems	11.1

Topic	Section in this book
Multitasking and multithreading	10.4.2.5 10.4.2.7 11.2.1
File systems and storage	11.2.2
User interfaces	11.2.6
Operating system configuration	11.2.8
Securing an operating system	11.5
Virtualization of computing services	10.2.5
Networking	8
Types of networks	8.1 8.2
Core network components	8.2.1
TCP/IP model	8.2.4.1 8.2.5.1
Physical layer: wired and wireless connectivity	8.2.2
Data link layer: Ethernet	8.2.3
Network layer: IP, IP addressing and routing	8.2.4
Transport layer: TCP	8.2.5
Application layer: core internet application protocols	8.2.8
Network security and security devices	8.6
The internet as a key networking platform	8.1
Network device configuration	8.2.3.3 8.2.4.5
Organizing storage on organizational networks	9
Datacenters	7
Securing IT infrastructure	6
Principles of encryption and authentication	6.3.4
Component level security: clients, servers, storage network devices, data transport, applications	7.5 8.6 9.5 10.5 11.5 12.6
Perimeter security: firewalls	8.6.1
Using public networks for secure data transport: VPNs	8.2.6.1
The role of IT control and service management frameworks (COBIT, ITIL, etc.) in managing the organizational IT infrastructure	17

Topic	Section in this book
Ensuring business continuity	4.4.4
Grid computing	5.5.10
Cloud computing, computing as a service	14.6
System performance analysis and management	5.3 5.4 5.5 16.2
Purchasing of IT infrastructure technologies and services	15

Further reading

More information about the subjects described in this book can be found in the following sources. I have used these sources when performing research for this book.

Apart from these sources, I have used Wikipedia extensively, especially for checking historic facts and dates, and for checking technical details. Please join me in donating a small amount of money to Wikipedia:

http://wikimediafoundation.org/wiki/Ways_to_Give

Books

- Tom Gilb. **Principles of Software Engineering Management**. Addison- Wesley, 1988.

- Andrew S. Tanenbaum. **Operating Systems: Design and implementation.** Prentice-Hall, 1987

- Bruce Robertson, Valentin Sribar. **The Adaptive Enterprise.** Addison Wesley, 2002.

- L. Bass, P. Clements and R. Kazman. **Software Architecture in Practice (3rd Edition).** Addison-Wesley Professional, 2012.

- Adam Gordon, Javvad Malik, Steven Hernandez. **Official (ISC)^2 guide to the CISSP CBK Fourth Edition.** CRC Press, 2015.

- William J. Brown, Raphael C. Malveau, Hays W. "Skip" McCormick III, Thomas J. Mowbray. **Anti-patterns - Refactoring Software,**

Architectures, and Projects in Crisis. Wiley Computer Publishing, 1998.

- Paul Dyson, Andy Longshaw. **Architecting Enterprise Solutions.** Wiley, 2004.

- B. Elliott. **Designing a structured cabling system to ISO 11801: Cross-referenced to European CENELEC and American Standards (Second edition).** Woodhead Publishing Limited, 2002.

- Jennifer Acuna-Narvaez, Ashoka Reddy Linda Sandberg, Irene D. Sideris, Scott Vetter. **RS/6000 Systems Handbook.** IBM. 1999.

- Hewlett-Packard Company. **Architecture HP 9000 V-Class Server Second Edition.** Hewlett-Packard Company. March, 1998.

- IBM. **Mainframe concepts.** International Business Machines Corporation, 2008.

- A. Ranjbar, K. Hutton. **CCDP Self-Study: Designing Cisco Network Architectures.** Cisco Press, 2004.

- Tom Clark. **Designing Storage Area Networks.** Addison Wesley 2003.

- Peter H. Salus. **A Quarter Century of UNIX.** Addison Wesley, 1994.

- Paul Andrews. **Gates: How Microsoft's Mogul Reinvented an Industry-- and Made Himself the Richest Man in America.** Touchstone, 2002.

- Bob Ducharme. **The Operating Systems Handbook: UNIX, OpenVMS, OS/400, VM, and MVS.** McGraw-Hill Companies, 1994.

- Paul Goransson, Chuck Black. **Software Defined Networks: A Comprehensive Approach.** Morgan Kaufmann, 2014.

- ISACA. **CRISC Review Manual.** 2015.

- Kief Morris. **Infrastructure as Code – Managing Servers in the Cloud.** O'Reilly, 2016.

- Adrian Mouat. **Using Docker – Developing and Deploying Software with Containers.** O'Reilly, 2016.

Papers

- E. van der Wijngaard. **Using the Infrastructure Architecture Method.** 2001.

- R. Kazman, M. Klein and P. Clements. ATAM: **Method for Architecture Evaluation.** Report CMU/SEI-2000-TR-004, 2000.

- K. Trivedi, D. S. Kim, A. Roy, D. Medhi. **Dependability and Security Models.** Keynote paper Proceedings of 7th International Workshop on the Design of Reliable Communication Networks, October 2009.

- W. Greene, B. Lancaster. **Carrier Grade: Five Nines, the Myth and the Reality.** Pipeline Volume 3, Issue 1. 2006.

- Microsoft. **Microsoft High Availability Overview.** White Paper, 2008.

- Microsoft. **Overview of Failover Clustering with Windows Server 2008.** White Paper, 2007.

- Microsoft. **Windows Server 2008 Failover Clustering Architecture Overview - New Features and Capabilities.** White Paper, 2007.

- The Open Group. **The UNIX Operating System: A Robust, Standardized Foundation for Cluster Architectures.** Cluster White Paper.

- Eric Hennessey. **High Availability for Mission- Critical Applications - Protecting Applications with Veritas Cluster Server.** White paper, 2008.

- Hewlett-Packard. **Designing high availability solutions with HP Serviceguard and HP Integrity Virtual Machines**. Technical White paper, 2010.

- VMware. **VMware High Availability - Easily Deliver High Availability for All of Your Virtual Machines**. White paper, 2009.

- ADC. **TIA-952 Data Center Standards Overview.** White paper, 2006.

- Uptime Institute. **Data Center Site Infrastructure Tier Standard: Topology.** 2009.

- Liebert. **Evaluating the economic impact of UPS technology.** White paper, 2004.

- American Society of Heating, Refrigerating and Air Conditioning Engineers, Inc. **2008 ASHRAE Environmental Guidelines for Datacom Equipment.** 2008.

- Robert E Moncrief II. **RS/6000**. 2002.

- Per Stenstrom. **A Survey of Cache Coherence- Schemes for Multiprocessors.** Lund University, 1990.

- Yi Zhang. **Non-blocking Shared Data Structures for Shared Memory Multiprocessor Systems - Thesis for the Degree of Licentiate of Philosophy.** Department of Computing Science Chalmers University of Technology and Göteborg University, 2001.

- Microsoft. **Hyper-V Cloud Fast Track Program - Reference Architecture Technical White Paper**. Microsoft White paper, 2011.

- Herco van Brug. **VDI & Storage: Deep Impact.** PQR White paper, 2010.

- Fujitsu Siemens. **Storage basics. An introduction to the fundamentals of storage technology**. Fujitsu Siemens White paper, 2009.

- Larry Freeman. **The NetApp Storage Efficiency Guide.** NetApp White paper, 2009.

- Peter Baer Galvin. **VMware vSphere Vs. Microsoft Hyper-V: A Technical Analysis**. CTI White paper, 2009.

- VMware. **VMware ESX server 2 Architecture and Performance Implications**. White paper, 2005.

- VMware. **VMware High Availability (VMware HA): Deployment Best Practices vSphere 4.1**. Technical white paper, 2010.

- VMware. **Using VMware Infrastructure for Backup and Restore**. Best Practice, 2006.

- Citrix. **The three levels of high availability - Balancing priorities and cost**. White paper, 2009.

- Citrix. **Technical guide: Using a comprehensive virtualization solution to maintain business continuity**. White paper, 2009.

- Citrix. **Technical and commercial comparison of Citrix XenServer and VMware**. White paper, 2010.

- Microsoft. **Windows Server 2008 Hyper-V Product Overview – An Early look**. White paper, 2007.

- Microsoft. **Performance Tuning Guidelines for Windows Server 2008**. White paper, 2009.

- VMware. **Understanding Full Virtualization, Paravirtualization, and Hardware Assist**. White paper, 2007.

- Microsoft. **Microsoft High Availability Overview.** White Paper, 2008.

- Eric Hennessey. **High Availability for Mission-Critical Applications, Protecting Applications with Veritas™ Cluster Server.** White paper, 2008.

- IBM. **Z/Architecture Principles of Operation**. White Paper, 2008.

- Cisco. **Cisco Application Centric Infrastructure (ACI) at a Glance.** White paper, 2013.

- SNIA: Mark Carlson, Alan Yoder, Leah Schoeb, Don Deel, Carlos Pratt, Chris Lionetti, Doug Voigt. **Software Defined Storage**. White paper, 2015

Index

Host-based firewall, 344
Hosting options, 373
Hot Fix environment, 406
Hot site, 65
Hot swappable components, 297
Hot-fixes, 343
HP Integrity systems, 286
HP-UX, 328
HSDPA, 163
Humidity, 131
Hybrid cloud, 381
Hyperconverged Infrastructure, 377
Hyper-threading, 313
Hypervisor, 274

I

IAM, 102
IBM i (OS/400), 326
IBM PC, 292, 348
ICMP protocol, 171
IDE, 209
Identification, 102
IDS, 198
IGRP, 172
Impact, 91
Incremental backup, 240
Infrastructure as a Service (IaaS), 383
Infrastructure as code, 384
Infrastructure lifecycle, 371
Infrastructure-as-a-Service (IaaS), 382
Inkjet printer, 354
In-memory databases, 82
Integrity, 94
Intel CPUs, 259
Internet Service Provider, 193
Intrusion Detection System (IDS), 198
Intrusion Prevention System (IPS), 198
IOPS, 244
IP protocol, 164
IPS, 198
IPsec, 177
IPv4, 164, 165
IPv6, 164, 170
iSCSI, 231
ISP, 193
Itanium processor, 260
ITIL, 400

J

Journaling file systems, 321

K

Kerberos, 103
Kernel, 320
Kernel size, 342
Kryder's law, 212
KVM switch, 137

L

L2TP, 177
Laptop, 350
Laser printer, 353
Latency, 196
Layered network topology, 188
Layered security, 104
LCM, 391
LDAP, 103
Leased lines, 155
Least privilege, 104
Life Cycle Management, 391
Line printer, 357
Link aggregation, 190
Link state protocol, 172
Linux, 329
Linux Containers (LXC), 279
Load balancing, 84
Load testing, 78
Lockstepping, 271, 299
Log data, 402
Logical Partition (LPAR), 273
Logical Unit Numbers (LUNs), 216
LPAR, 273, 286, 291
LTE, 164
LTO tapes, 214
LUN, 216
LXC, 279

M

MAC address, 158, 160
Mainframe, 281
Mainframe virtualization, 286
Malicious code, 98
Malware protection, 367
MC/Service Guard, 336
MD5, 109
MDM, 368

U

UDP protocol, 173
UFS filesystem, 321
UMA, 289
UMTS, 163
Uniform Memory Access (UMA), 289
Uninterruptable Power Supply, 123
Unit test, 395
UNIX, 327
Unshielded Twisted Pair, 150
UPS, 123
USB, 265
User Acceptance test environment, 406
User profiling, 75
UTP, 150

V

VDI, 362, 379
VDSL, 157
Vendor lock-in, 389
Vertical scaling, 83
Virtual Desktop Infrastructure (VDI), 362
Virtual LAN, 183
Virtual machine, 269
Virtual machine monitor (VMM), 274
Virtual machine sprawl, 271
Virtual memory management, 276
Virtual NIC, 184
Virtual Private Network (VPN), 176
Virtual switch, 185
Virtual tape library, 215
Virus, 99

Virus scanning, 344
VLAN, 183
VMS, 327
VPN, 176
VPN tunnel, 176
VTL, 215
Vulnerability, 91
VxFS filesystem, 321
VXLAN, 184

W

WAN, 162
WAN link compression, 197
Warm site, 65
Warranty, 391
Wavelength-Division Multiplexing, 152
Wide Area Network, 162
Wi-Fi, 159
Wi-Fi Protected Access (WPA), 160
Windows, 332
Windows Cluster Service, 336
WLAN, 159
Worm, 99
WPA, 160
WPAR, 292

X

x86 processor, 259
x86 servers, 292
x86-64 processor, 260

Z

z/OS, 325
Zones, 292

End notes

[1] Source: http://oldcomputers.net/zx81.html

[2] Copyright: Beareyes.com
Source: http://bj.beareyes.com.cn/2/lib/201211/27/20121127416_2.htm

[3] Box, G. E. P., and Draper, N. R., (1987), Empirical Model Building and Response Surfaces, John Wiley & Sons, New York, NY, p. 424

[4] Source: http://www.datacenterknowledge.com/archives/
2014/05/30/survey-enterprise-data-centers-fail-often-colos/
?utm_content=buffer2c086&utm_medium=social&utm_source=
linkedin.com&utm_campaign=buffer

[5] Source: http://www.energie-nederland.nl/wp-
content/uploads/2013/04/EnergieTrends2014.pdf

[6] "Understanding the Cost of Power Interruptions to U.S. Electricity Consumers", p38, University of California Berkeley, 2004.
https://emp.lbl.gov/sites/all/files/REPORT%20lbnl%20-%2055718.pdf

[7] Gartner RAS Core Research Note G00208328, Ronni Spaffort,
29 October 2010, RA6 05012011

[8] "When more Website visitors hurt your business: Are you ready for peak traffic?", Equation Research, 2010.
http://www.informationweek.com/whitepaper/Internet/
Traffic-Reporting-Monitoring/
when-more-website-visitors-hurt-your-business-ar-wp1273171222135

[9] Key findings from the "Consumer Response to Travel Site Performance" study conducted by PhoCusWright and Akamai.
http://www.phocuswright.com/Free-Travel-Research/
Consumer-Response-to-Travel-Site-Performance

[10] "Feeling good at the right time: Why people value predictability in goal attainment", Nadav Klein and Ayelet Fishbach, Journal of Experimental Social Psychology, Volume 55, November 2014, pp 21–30.
http://home.uchicago.edu/~nklein/RightTime.pdf

[11] Source: http://berriprocess.com/en/todas-las-categorias/item/
47-ley-del-cuello-de-botella

[12] http://www.seagate.com/www-content/product-content/enterprise-performance-savvio-fam/enterprise-performance-15k-hdd/ent-perf-15k-5/en-gb/docs/enterprise-performance-15k-hdd-ds1797-3-1406gb.pdf

[13] http://www.anandtech.com/show/6372/memory-performance-16gb-ddr31333-to-ddr32400-on-ivy-bridge-igp-with-gskill

[14] http://www.extremetech.com/extreme/188776-how-l1-and-l2-cpu-caches-work-and-why-theyre-an-essential-part-of-modern-chips/2

[15] Copyright: ddgenome
Source: http://www.flickr.com/photos/ddgenome/3730193968/sizes/z/in/set-72157603633991423/

[16] Copyright: ddgenome
Source: http://www.flickr.com/photos/ddgenome/3730196210/sizes/z/in/photostream/

[17] Copyright: Lgate74
Source: http://en.wikipedia.org/wiki/File:Ups_batteries.jpg

[18] https://www.ashrae.org/resources--publications/bookstore/datacom-series#thermalguidelines

[19] Copyright: Paul Morris
Source: http://www.flickr.com/photos/aa3sd/3709581232/

[20] Copyright: Chassis Plans (http://www.chassis-plans.com)
Source: http://en.wikipedia.org/wiki/File:Chassis-Plans-KVM.jpg

[21] "Report to Congress on Server and Data Center Energy Efficiency". U.S. Environmental Protection Agency ENERGY STAR Program. August 2, 2007.
http://www.energystar.gov/ia/partners/prod_development/downloads/EPA_Datacenter_Report_Congress_Final1.pdf

[22] Gartner Symposium/ITxpo 2007 Emerging Trends.
http://www.gartner.com/newsroom/id/503867

[23] Source: Federal Statistical Office, Data on energy price trends.
https://www.destatis.de/DE/Publikationen/Thematisch/Preise/Energiepreise/EnergyPriceTrendsPDF_5619002.pdf?__blob=publicationFile

[24] The Green Grid. Describing Datacenter Power Efficiency, 20 february 2007.
http://www.thegreengrid.org/~/media/WhitePapers/Green_Grid_Metrics_WP.ashx?lang=en

[25] Typical price in the US, according to http://shrinkthatfootprint.com/average-electricity-prices-kwh

[26] According to a survey by the Uptime Institute in 2014.
http://www.datacenterknowledge.com/archives/2014/06/02/survey-industry-average-data-center-pue-stays-nearly-flat-four-years/

[27] Measuring to improve: comprehensive, real-world data center efficiency numbers. Google official Blog, 26 March 2012.
http://googleblog.blogspot.nl/2012/03/measuring-to-improve-comprehensive-real.html

[28] The Prineville data center has had PUE measurements as low as 1.06. http://www.datacenterknowledge.com/archives/2013/04/18/ facebook- unveils-live-dashboard-on-pue-water-use/

[29] http://www.uptimeinstitute.com/

[30] Copyright: Leonard Kleinrock
Source: http://en.wikipedia.org/wiki/File:Leonard-Kleinrock-and-IMP1.png

[31] Based on the numbers on http://www.internetlivestats.com/ internet-users/

[32] Copyright: F. Dominec
Source: http://commons.wikimedia.org/wiki/File:Coaxial_cable_cut.jpg

[33] Copyright: Dmitry Barsky
Source: http://www.flickr.com/photos/dbarsky/2262194362/in/ photostream

[34] According to http://www.ieee802.org/3/bs/

[35] Copyright: Cisco
Source: http://www.flickr.com/photos/ciscosp360/5334068230/sizes/z/in/ photostream/

[36] Source: https://www.nro.net/news/ipv4-free-pool-depleted

[37] According to the publication "Software Defined Storage For Dummies®, IBM Platform Computing Edition, John Wiley & Sons, Inc."

[38] Copyright: IBM Archives.
Source: http://www.ed-thelen.org/RAMAC/RAMAC-EngProtoType-.jpeg

[39] Copyright Poil
Source: http://en.wikipedia.org/wiki/File:Largetape.jpg

[40] As stated in this article: http://www.lto.org/technology/lto-generation-7/

[41] Copyright: Austin Murphy
Source: http://en.wikipedia.org/wiki/File:LTO2-cart-purple.jpg

[42] http://www.oracle.com/us/products/servers-storage/storage/ tape-storage/t10000-data-cartridges/overview/index.html

[43] Copyright: Clive Darra.
Source: https://www.flickr.com/photos/osde-info/20943120629/

[44] As published in Scientific American, July 2005
http://www.scientificamerican.com/article/kryders-law/

[45] Picture by Daniel Sancho.
Source: https://www.flickr.com/photos/teclasorg/2852716477/

[46] Source: https://www.oracle.com/sun/index.html and
http://downloads.quantum.com/sdlt320/handbook.pdf

[47] http://www.tapeandmedia.com/lto-7-tape-media-tapes.asp

[48] Copyright: Aaron Kuhn from Hatfield, PA
Source: http://en.wikipedia.org/wiki/
File:ADIC_Scalar_100_tape_library.jpg

[49] Copyright: Compellent Technologies
Source: http://www.crn.com/slide-shows/channel-
programs/208403760/the-hottest-companies-in-the-midmarket-
right-now.htm/pgno/0/7

[50] Copyright: LeSimonPix
Source: http://www.flickr.com/photos/photobysimon/
3260876496/sizes/z/in/photostream/

[51] Copyright: LeSimonPix
Source: http://www.flickr.com/photos/photobysimon/
3260037977/sizes/z/in/photostream/

[52] Care and Handling of CDs and DVDs: A Guide for Librarians and Archivists,
Fred R. Byers, ISBN 1-932326-04-9, page 20.
http://www.clir.org/pubs/reports/reports/pub121/pub121.pdf

[53] Source: https://en.wikipedia.org/wiki/Hard_disk_drive_performance_
characteristics

[54] An interesting story about the Colossus computer can be found here:
http://www.colossus-computer.com/colossus1.html

[55] Public domain picture. Source: https://commons.wikimedia.org/
wiki/File:ENIAC-changing_a_tube.jpg

[56] Copyright: Robert van Jemimus
Source: https://flic.kr/p/6SZom

[57] Copyright: Robert van Jemimus
Source: https://flic.kr/p/7zAdj

[58] Definition by Wikipedia:
https://en.wikipedia.org/wiki/Central_processing_unit

[59] Source: http://www.hardwarezone.com.sg/
feature-intel-xeon-5130-and-5160-2-way-smp-performance-review

[60] According to Intel's website: http://ark.intel.com/search/advanced?
FamilyText=Intel%C2%AE%20Xeon%C2%AE%20Processor
%20E5%20v4%20Family

[61] According to AMD's website: http://www.amd.com/en-
us/products/server/opteron/6000/6300#

[62] According to ARM's website:
http://www.arm.com/files/event/
1_2014_Physical_IP_Workshop_ARM_Embedded_Market.pdf

[63] Source: https://www.siliconrepublic.com/companies/softbank-
arm-takeover-completed

[64] According to Pracle's website: http://www.oracle.com/us/products/servers-
storage/sparc-m7-processor-ds-2687041.pdf

[65] Source: https://openpowerfoundation.org/wp-content/uploads/2016/04/5_Brad-McCredie.IBM_.pdf

[66] Picture by H.J. Sommer III, Professor of Mechanical Engineering, Penn State University
Source: http://commons.wikimedia.org/wiki/File:Magnetic_core.jpg

[67] Source: http://www.corememoryshield.com/report.html

[68] Copyright: Jonathan
Source: https://commons.wikimedia.org/wiki/File:PCIExpress.jpg

[69] http://www-03.ibm.com/systems/z/hardware/z13_specs.html

[70] http://public.dhe.ibm.com/common/ssi/ecm/zs/en/zsd03035usen/ZSD03035USEN.PDF

[71] Source: Computermuseum der Fakultät Informatik
http://computermuseum.informatik.uni-stuttgart.de/dev_en/pdp8e/

[72] http://www.v3.co.uk/v3-uk/news/2324612/lenovo-buys-ibms-mid-range-server-business-for-usd23bn

[73] https://www.pugetsystems.com/labs/articles/Linpack-performance-Haswell-E-Core-i7-5960X-and-5930K-594/

[74] http://top500.org/system/177999

[75] Source: https://devblogs.nvidia.com/parallelforall/inside-pascal/

[76] Copyright: Luca Detomi
Source: http://en.wikipedia.org/wiki/File:Intel_4004.jpg

[77] Electronics, Volume 38, Number 8, April 19, 1965
http://www.cs.utexas.edu/~pingali/CS395T/2013fa/papers/moorespaper.pdf

[78] Henry F. Holtzclaw & William R. Robinson. General Chemistry. Lexington, MA: Heath, 1988: 98.

[79] It is actually a variation of the original Parkinson's law, as originally formulated by Prof. Cyril Northcote Parkinson in 1958. The text can be found here: http://www.heretical.com/miscella/parkinsl.html
Parkinson's law of data can be found here: http://dictionary.reference.com/browse/parkinson's+law+of+data

[80] According to http://wiki.midrange.com/index.php/OS/400_101

[81] http://wiki.midrange.com/index.php/History_of_OS/400#Current_releases

[82] As announced in this press release: https://vmssoftware.com/news/PR20150601/PR20150601_VSI_8.4-IHI.pdf

[83] Andrew S. Tanenbaum. Operating Systems: Design and Implementation. Prentice-Hall, 1987, ISBN 0-13-637406-9

[84] The original usenet post can be found here: https://groups.google.com/forum/#!topic/comp.os.minix/dlNtH7RRrGA[1-25]

[85] Top500.org

[86] Copyright: picture by ArnoldReinhold - Own work, CC BY-SA 3.0
Source: https://commons.wikimedia.org/w/index.php?curid=31105488

[87] Copyright: Ruben de Rijcke
Source: http://commons.wikimedia.org/wiki/File:Ibm_pc_5150.jpg

[88] http://www.gartner.com/newsroom/id/
2705117?utm_source=Triggermail&utm_medium=
email&utm_term=Tech%20Chart%20Of%20The%20Day&utm_campaign=
SAI_COTD_041014

[89] According to Samsung:
http://www.storagevisions.com/2013/Book/Michael%20Willett.pdf

[90] Copyright: Nakamura2828
Source: http://en.wikipedia.org/wiki/File:Epson_MX-80.jpg

[91] Copyright: Waelder
Source: http://en.wikipedia.org/wiki/File:IBM_line_printer_1403.JPG

[92] Quote from http://smallbusiness.chron.com/line-printer-56785.html

[93] Copyright NetApp. Source: http://community.netapp.com/t5/
Technology/FlexPod-Continues-Market-Momentum/ba-p/82131

[94] Copyright au@cs.stanford.edu. Source: http://www-
cs-students.stanford.edu/~au/

[95] http://csrc.nist.gov/publications/nistpubs/800-145/SP800-145.pdf

[96] Source: http://www.intuittech.my/nagios_xi_gallery.html